# MURDLE

## SOLVE 100 DEVILISHLY DEVIOUS MURDER MYSTERY LOGIC PUZZLES

. . . . . . . . . . . . . . . . . . . . . . . . . . . . . . . . . .

# G. T. KARBER

SOUVENIR
PRESS

*For Dan & Dani*

First published in Great Britain in 2023 by
Souvenir Press,
an imprint of Profile Books Ltd
29 Cloth Fair
London
EC1A 7JQ
*www.souvenirpress.co.uk*

First published in the United States of America in 2023 by
St. Martin's Griffin, an imprint of St. Martin's Publishing Group

Designed by Omar Chapa

10

Printed and bound in Great Britain by Clays Ltd, Elcograf S.p.A.

The moral right of the author has been asserted.

A CIP catalogue record for this book is available from the British Library.

ISBN 978 1 80081 802 6

FSC
www.fsc.org
MIX
Paper from
responsible sources
FSC® C018072

# CONTENTS

# HOW TO SOLVE

Welcome to *Murdle,* the official publication of the case files of the world's greatest mystery-solving mind, Deductive Logico.

Unlike other memoirs of the crime-fighting life, these murdles are not mere tales, but puzzles for you to solve. And all you need to crack these cases is a sharp pencil and an even sharper mind.

To prove it, let's review Deductive Logico's very first case, which he cracked as a junior at Deduction College. The student body president had been murdered, and Logico was certain one of three people had done it:

**MAYOR HONEY**

He knows where the bodies are buried, and he makes sure they always vote for him.

6'0" • LEFT-HANDED • HAZEL EYES • LIGHT BROWN HAIR

**DEAN GLAUCOUS**

The dean of some such-and-such department at Deduction College. What does he do? Well, he handles the money, for one . . .

5'6" • RIGHT-HANDED • LIGHT BROWN EYES • LIGHT BROWN HAIR

**CHANCELLOR TUSCANY**

As the head of Deduction College, she has deduced exactly how much rich parents are willing to pay to get their children a degree in logic.

5'5" • LEFT-HANDED • GREEN EYES • BLOND HAIR

Young Logico also knew that each of them was in one of these places and had one of these weapons.

**THE STADIUM**
OUTDOORS

The field features the absolute highest quality fake grass money can buy.

**THE BOOKSTORE**
INDOORS

The biggest money-maker on campus. A sign offers a 2-for-$500 deal on textbooks.

**OLD MAIN**
INDOORS

The first building on campus and the least maintained. Paint is peeling off the wall!

**A SHARP PENCIL**
LIGHT-WEIGHT

Back then, they used actual lead. One stab and you'd die from lead poisoning.

**A HEAVY BACKPACK**
HEAVY-WEIGHT

Finally, a practical use for all those logic textbooks (hitting people with them).

**A GRADUATION CORD**
LIGHT-WEIGHT

It would be a high academic honor to be strangled by one of these.

Now, Logico knew that he could not make assumptions just from reading these descriptions! Sometimes mayors wore heavy backpacks, and sometimes teachers went to the stadium. No, the way to figure out who had what where was by studying the clues and evidence.

These were the facts he knew to be absolutely, perfectly true:

- Whoever was in the stadium was right-handed.

- The suspect with the sharp pencil resented the person at Old Main.

- The suspect with a graduation cord had beautiful hazel eyes.

- Dean Glaucous seemed to carry a lot of logic textbooks around.

- **The body was found next to peeling paint.**

And finally, he pulled out his detective's notebook and meticulously drew a grid, labeling each column and row with a picture representing each of the suspects, weapons, and locations.

The locations were listed twice—once on top, and once on the side—so that every square represented a unique potential pairing.

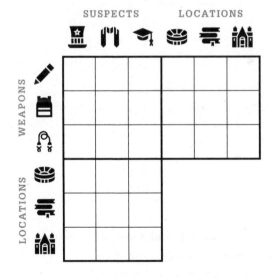

This tool—the deduction grid—was a powerful technology taught at Deduction College. It could help clarify your thoughts and identify the possible conclusions you could make.

But never before had it been used to solve a murder! In Deduction College, they apply logic only to the realm of the purely abstract. If all Xs are Ys and all Ys are Zs—that kind of thing. What Logico was doing here was new, exciting, and dangerous!

Once he drew his deduction grid, he had arrived at his favorite part:

the deducing! He went down the list of clues, and put each of them into his grid.

The first clue is: **Whoever was in the stadium was right-handed.**

According to Logico's notes on the suspects, only Dean Glaucous was right-handed. Therefore, Dean Glaucous was at the stadium.

Logico marked that down on his grid, as seen below. But that was not all Logico learned from that clue.

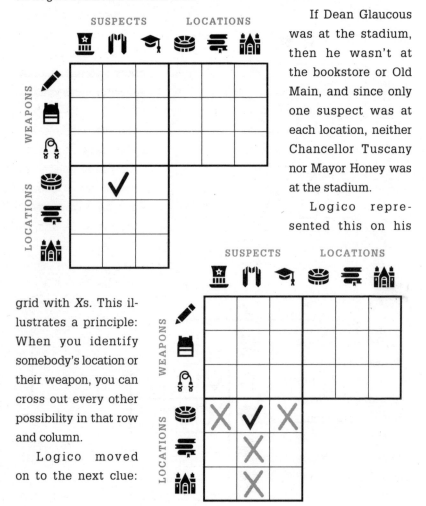

If Dean Glaucous was at the stadium, then he wasn't at the bookstore or Old Main, and since only one suspect was at each location, neither Chancellor Tuscany nor Mayor Honey was at the stadium.

Logico represented this on his grid with *Xs*. This illustrates a principle: When you identify somebody's location or their weapon, you can cross out every other possibility in that row and column.

Logico moved on to the next clue:

**The suspect with the sharp pencil resented the person at Old Main.**

It seems like this clue is telling us about personal relationships. But Logico was only concerned with facts. And the only fact this clue told him was that the suspect with the sharp pencil and the suspect at Old Main were two separate people. Therefore, *the sharp pencil was not at Old Main.*

And so, Logico marked that down in his deduction grid, too.

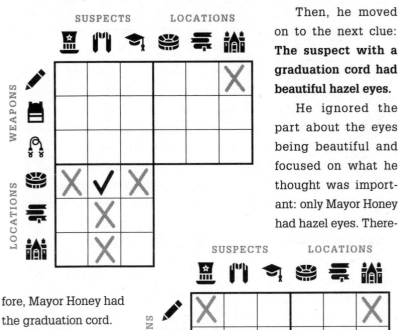

Then, he moved on to the next clue: **The suspect with a graduation cord had beautiful hazel eyes.**

He ignored the part about the eyes being beautiful and focused on what he thought was important: only Mayor Honey had hazel eyes. There-

fore, Mayor Honey had the graduation cord.

And again, Logico could cross out the entire row and column! After all, if Mayor Honey had the graduation cord, then neither Chancellor Tuscany nor Dean Glaucous

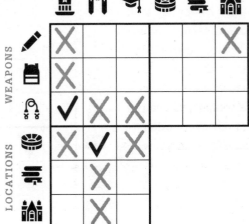

had it. And since each suspect had only one weapon, Mayor Honey couldn't have the heavy backpack or the sharp pencil.

Logico moved on to the next clue: **Dean Glaucous seemed to carry a lot of logic textbooks around.**

Now, what does that mean? Logic textbooks aren't one of the weapons! But, if

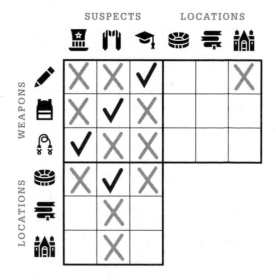

you read the descriptions of each weapon, you'll notice that the heavy backpack's says, "Finally, a practical use for all those logic textbooks (hitting people with them)." If Dean Glaucous was carrying a lot of logic textbooks around, he was using the backpack to do it!

You don't have to make leaps of logic in these puzzles: everything you need to know clearly appears in the descriptions. Is it possible that Dean Glaucous was carrying logic books around without a heavy backpack? Not to Deductive Logico!

Logico marked down that Dean Glaucous had the heavy backpack, and he crossed off the other possibilities in that row and column. Once he did that, Logico smiled. If Mayor Honey had the graduation cord and Dean Glaucous had the heavy backpack, Chancellor Tuscany must have had the sharp pencil. He marked this down as well.

This next step is the key to solving all the murder mysteries that appear in this book: Chancellor Tuscany had the sharp pencil. The sharp pencil is not at Old Main. Therefore, *Chancellor Tuscany could not be at Old Main.*

Therefore, Chancellor Tuscany was at the bookstore, since it was the only remaining location. And since she had the sharp pencil, the sharp pencil must have been at the bookstore, too.

Logico marked this on his deduction grid and crossed off the other boxes in each row and column. And from there, he deduced that Mayor Honey was at Old Main, so he marked that down too.

Since Mayor Honey was at Old Main with the graduation cord, the graduation cord must have been at Old Main. And since Dean Glaucous had the heavy backpack and was at the stadium, the heavy backpack was at the stadium, too.

*So satisfying!* Logico thought, as he looked at his completed grid. Now, he was ready for the final clue: **The body was found next to peeling paint.**

This last clue is special. It doesn't tell you who has what weapon where—it

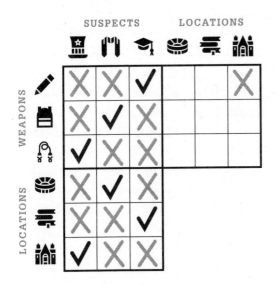

tells you about the murder itself!

By consulting his notes, Logico knew that this clue meant the murder had been committed in Old Main, because the description of Old Main mentions peeling paint. Therefore, since Mayor Honey was the suspect in Old Main, Mayor Honey must have committed the crime.

Confident in his deductions, Logico marched down to the chancellor's office where he confidently declared: **"It was Mayor Honey with the graduation cord at Old Main!"**

Chancellor Tuscany was impressed with his hard work, and she gave him an A-plus. Mayor Honey, however, was able to win reelection in a landslide, thanks to his populist tirades against the tyranny of logic. But that did not matter, because to Logico, it wasn't the consequences of his deductions that mattered: it was the deductive work itself.

And that is how young Logico became Deductive Logico, and how he first applied the theories of his college education to the problems of the real world. When he graduated, he moved to the city, and he began to offer his services as the only deductive detective in the business.

This book contains one hundred mysteries that Deductive Logico was able to solve using these techniques and others. There are ciphers to decode, witness statements to examine, and many other secrets to unlock. As you progress, and the mysteries become more challenging, you will find your reasoning skills being put to the test. Because logic is a many-splendored thing, there are always new techniques to learn and new deductions to make.

If you get stuck, do not despair! You can flip to the back of the book for a hint. And when you're ready to make your accusation, flip even farther back to the answers to see if you're right. With every mystery solved, a bigger story begins to emerge. So read carefully as you go, and remember: to a deductive detective, every case can be cracked using logic alone.

If you need more help, or want to solve more mysteries with others, then join the Detective Club at Murdle.com. Otherwise, you're on your own!

Good luck, gumshoe!

# DEGREE OF DIFFICULTY

Q — ELEMENTARY

QQ — OCCULT MEDIUM

QQQ — HARD BOILED

QQQQ — IMPOSSIBLE

# EXHIBIT A

## MEMBERSHIP CARD & PIN
This card and fedora pin confirm Logico's membership (#6KLM) in the Detective Club.

## SECRET DECODER RING
A mechanical device for reading and writing in Detective Code:

**DECODED**

A B C D E F G H I J K L M N O P Q R S T U V W X Y Z
Z Y X W V U T S R Q P O N M L K J I H G F E D C B A

**ENCODED**

## MAGNIFYING GLASS
Logico uses this to find clues and to read the fine print. Made with crystal from Emerald Industries.

## VHS TAPE AND BOOK
A mystery tape from Midnight Movies and a novel by Dame Obsidian. Plus a Detective Club bookmark.

## CUP OF COFFEE
The perfect fuel for solving armchair mysteries. The cup once belonged to General Coffee himself!

# THE CONTENTS OF DEDUCTIVE LOGICO'S DETECTIVE KIT

# ELEMENTARY

During the course of the following twenty-five mysteries, Deductive Logico's life was forever changed. He went from being a fresh-faced student, straight out of Deduction College, to the grizzled deductive he is today.

He learned things he had never suspected, and he saw things he would never forget.

Thankfully, he always carried with him his deductive wits and his Detective Kit (Exhibit A, seen to the left). So no matter how confusing his cases became, he could always figure them out.

Can you? Study the suspects, weapons, and locations. Read the clues carefully. Make your deductions. And finally, determine whodunit, with what, and where?

Some of you may find these first twenty-five mysteries *too* elementary (particularly those of you with degrees from a certified Deduction College).

If that's the case, then take the Detective Club's Elementary, My Dear Challenge: see *how fast* you can solve all twenty-five elementary murder mysteries *without getting a single one wrong.* Our current record, set by a member of the club prior to this book's publication, is thirty-six minutes.

Can you beat it?

# 1. MURDER IN HOLLYWOOD 🔍

When Deductive Logico was invited to a fancy dinner party at a mansion in the Hollywood Hills, he thought he had finally made it. Unfortunately, he was not the guest of honor: he was there to solve the murder of the guest of honor.

## SUSPECTS

**THE AMAZING AUREOLIN**

A magician who perfected the sawing-your-husband-in-two routine. Then, she made his body disappear.

**5'6" • LEFT-HANDED • GREEN EYES • BLOND HAIR**

**MIDNIGHT III**

The grandson of the founder of Midnight Movies and a self-described self-made man.

**5'8" • LEFT-HANDED • DARK BROWN EYES • DARK BROWN HAIR**

**DAME OBSIDIAN**

A mystery writer whose books have sold more copies than the Bible and Shakespeare combined.

**5'4" • LEFT-HANDED • GREEN EYES • BLACK HAIR**

## LOCATIONS

**THE ENORMOUS BATHROOM**
INDOORS

A bathroom that is bigger than Deductive Logico's house.

**THE BEDROOM**
INDOORS

A California king–sized bed, unmade, stands in a spotless white room.

**THE SCREENING ROOM**
INDOORS

Red velvet seats and a popcorn machine make this the ultimate screening experience.

## WEAPONS

**A FORK**
LIGHT-WEIGHT

Actually a lot more gruesome than a knife, if you think about it.

**AN ALUMINUM PIPE**
MEDIUM-WEIGHT

Safer than lead, unless it hits you in the head.

**A HEAVY CANDLE**
MEDIUM-WEIGHT

Heavy enough to kill, and yet it lightens the room.

## CLUES & EVIDENCE

- The Amazing Aureolin trusted the suspect who brought a fork.

- Midnight III was still brandishing an aluminum pipe when Logico arrived.

- A heavy candle was not found in the bedroom.

- Dame Obsidian was found hiding beneath red velvet seats.

- **The body was found inside a marble tub.**

SUSPECTS     LOCATIONS

WEAPONS

LOCATIONS

**WHO?**

**WHAT?**

**WHERE?**

# 2. AND THEN THERE WAS ANOTHER ONE 🔍

Deductive Logico was thrilled when he heard an old man had been killed on a secluded island. Of course, that was bad, but Logico had always wanted to solve one of those secluded island murders, and this was his big chance.

**SIGNOR EMERALD**

An Italian jeweler of great renown, Signor Emerald has traveled the world in search of rare, precious stones, which are always falling out of his pockets.

**5'8" • LEFT-HANDED • LIGHT BROWN EYES • BLACK HAIR**

**FATHER MANGO**

He has taken a vow of poverty, but he drives a BMW. He's taken a vow of obedience, but he has a staff of twenty-five. He's taken a vow of chastity, too, which is why he's on vacation.

**5'10" • LEFT-HANDED • DARK BROWN EYES • BALD**

**MISS SAFFRON**

Gorgeous and charming, but maybe not all there in the brains department. Or maybe that's what she wants you to think. Or maybe she wants you to think that's what she wants you to think.

**5'2" • LEFT-HANDED • HAZEL EYES • BLOND HAIR**

## LOCATIONS

### THE CLIFFS
OUTDOORS

A long drop, but maybe the jagged rocks would break your fall.

### THE ANCIENT RUINS
OUTDOORS

Some old standing stones with strange glyphs carved on them.

### THE DOCKS
OUTDOORS

Old, rotten docks that have certainly seen better days. Look out for sharks!

## WEAPONS

**A BEAR TRAP**
HEAVY-WEIGHT

If you think it's too gruesome to use on a person, just think how the bears feel!

**AN ORDINARY BRICK**
MEDIUM-WEIGHT

Just a regular, ordinary brick. Nothing special. Just a brick.

**A HARPOON**
HEAVY-WEIGHT

You could kill a fish with this. Or, honestly, you could kill anything with it.

## CLUES & EVIDENCE

- The suspect who brought an ordinary brick was a parishioner of Father Mango's.

- Miss Saffron had a bear trap in her purse.

- The suspect whose family's company produced Logico's magnifying glass was on the cliffs. (See Exhibit A.)

- The ancient ruins seemed to hypnotize the hazel eyes of the suspect standing beside them.

- **By the time Logico got there, the old man's body had been nibbled on by sharks.**

|  | SUSPECTS | | | LOCATIONS | | |
|---|---|---|---|---|---|---|
| WEAPONS | | | | | | |
| | | | | | | |
| | | | | | | |
| LOCATIONS | | | | | | |
| | | | | | | |
| | | | | | | |

**WHO?**

**WHAT?**

**WHERE?**

# 3. THE ART OF THE KILL 🔍

Deductive Logico visited an art museum, which was very confusing to him. No murder was as baffling as some of these paintings. So he was quite relieved when an experimental artist was killed in mysterious circumstances: finally, something he could understand.

## SUSPECTS

**CAPTAIN SLATE**

A real-life astronaut. The first woman to travel around the dark side of the moon, and also the first to be suspected of murdering her copilot.

5'5" • LEFT-HANDED • DARK BROWN EYES • DARK BROWN HAIR

**BISHOP AZURE**

A bishop in a local church, she has been known to pray for both her friends and her enemies. Of course, she asks for different things . . .

5'4" • RIGHT-HANDED • LIGHT BROWN EYES • DARK BROWN HAIR

**BLACKSTONE, ESQ.**

Incredibly talented at the most important skill for an attorney: getting paid.

6'0" • RIGHT-HANDED • BLACK EYES • BLACK HAIR

## LOCATIONS

**THE ROOFTOP GARDEN**
OUTDOORS

A rooftop garden! With pigeons! And you can feed the pigeons! Very cool.

**THE ENTRY HALL**
INDOORS

According to a plaque on the wall, even the architecture of the entry hall is art.

**AN ART STUDIO**
INDOORS

In the back of the museum, it's littered with flyers for art classes.

## WEAPONS

### A GLASS OF POISONED WINE
LIGHT-WEIGHT

This is your typical glass of poisoned wine. A mystery classic.

### AN ABSTRACT STATUE
HEAVY-WEIGHT

No matter how hard he looked at this, Logico did not understand.

### A RARE VASE
HEAVY-WEIGHT

Logico thought about how, technically, every vase someone makes by hand is rare, because there is only one of them.

## CLUES & EVIDENCE

- Blackstone, Esq., was suspicious of the person who brought an abstract statue.

- Captain Slate brought a glass of poisoned wine.

- An abstract statue was not in the art studio. (Sometimes the students' art seemed abstract, but that was just because it was bad.)

- Either Blackstone, Esq., was standing on top of flyers for art classes, or Captain Slate was in the rooftop garden.

- **The body of the experimental artist was found under a plaque on the wall.**

WHO? _____

WHAT? _____

WHERE? _____

# 4. THE LAST TRAIN TO MURDER

Once he got back to the mainland, Deductive Logico took a train. Unfortunately, somebody else took the life of the conductor. Now, the train was racing down the tracks, and nobody knew what to do except Logico: he knew he had to crack the case.

## SUSPECTS

**VICE PRESIDENT MAUVE**

A vice president of TekCo Futures. If she asks you to step into her metaverse, politely decline.

5'8" • RIGHT-HANDED • DARK BROWN EYES • BLACK HAIR

**CHEF AUBERGINE**

It is said that she once killed her husband, cooked him, and then served him at her restaurant. It's not true, but just the fact that it's said about her tells you something.

5'2" • RIGHT-HANDED • BLUE EYES • BLOND HAIR

**PHILOSOPHER BONE**

A dashing, dark philosopher who pioneered the ethical theory that he is not responsible for his actions, but he should be paid for them.

5'1" • RIGHT-HANDED • LIGHT BROWN EYES • BALD

## LOCATIONS

**THE LOCOMOTIVE**
INDOORS

The deafening sound of the steam engine prevents Deductive Logico from being able to think.

**THE CABOOSE**
INDOORS

The back of the train lets you see where you're leaving, and what you're leaving behind . . .

**THE ROOF**
OUTDOORS

What with the wind and the smoke from the smokestack, it's hard to get your bearings up here.

## WEAPONS

**AN IMPORTED ITALIAN KNIFE**
LIGHT-WEIGHT

It looks priceless, and that's technically true, because it's worthless.

**LEATHER LUGGAGE**
HEAVY-WEIGHT

This luggage is hideous. The leather looked way better on the cow.

**A ROLLED-UP NEWSPAPER (WITH A CROW-BAR INSIDE)**
MEDIUM-WEIGHT

You think, that's just a newspaper! But then . . . wham!

## CLUES & EVIDENCE

- A page from the classifieds was found near the heat of a steam engine.

- Chef Aubergine and the person who brought leather luggage had a history together.

- The tallest suspect never set foot in the caboose.

- Philosopher Bone was seen wandering around outdoors.

- **The conductor had been stabbed to death.**

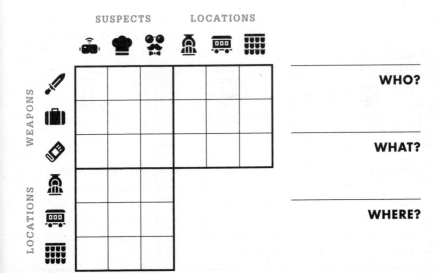

# 5. PHYSICIAN, HEAL MYSELF! 🔍

When Deductive Logico came to in a private hospital, his knew his injuries wouldn't hurt half as much as the bill. But his surgeon, Dr. Crimson, offered a trade: if he solved another patient's murder, they'd give him a two percent discount. He immediately agreed.

## SUSPECTS

**OFFICER COPPER**

The best part of being a policewoman criminal is that you can cut out the middleman and fail to investigate your own crimes.

**5'5" • RIGHT-HANDED • BLUE EYES • BLOND HAIR**

**DR. CRIMSON**

She's the smartest doctor she's ever met, according to her, and she's probably right. Yeah, she smokes, but if she gets cancer, she'll find a cure.

**5'9" • LEFT-HANDED • GREEN EYES • RED HAIR**

**SISTER LAPIS**

A nun who travels the world, doing God's work on His dime. Her habit is cashmere, and her habit is spending.

**5'2" • RIGHT-HANDED • LIGHT BROWN EYES • LIGHT BROWN HAIR**

## LOCATIONS

**THE PARKING LOT**
OUTDOORS

An enormous parking lot with uniformed valets parking luxury sedans.

**THE ROOF**
OUTDOORS

Huge AC units and other industrial equipment cover the roof, providing a number of excellent hiding spots.

**THE GIFT SHOP**
INDOORS

This hospital is so nice you can buy jewelry at the gift shop. But don't worry: there's a discount rack, too.

## WEAPONS

**A VIAL OF ACID**
LIGHT-WEIGHT

According to the label, you should not take a sip of this, no matter how tempting it seems.

**A HEAVY MICROSCOPE**
HEAVY-WEIGHT

The slides are so tiny, but the microscope's so heavy!

**A SURGICAL SCALPEL**
LIGHT-WEIGHT

Somehow, it being smaller makes it seem more dangerous.

## CLUES & EVIDENCE

- A vial of acid was certainly not on the roof. (They had acid-detecting sensors there.)

- The suspect who was in the gift shop had light brown eyes.

- Officer Copper had a weapon with a label on it reading DO NOT DRINK.

- Surprisingly, Dr. Crimson did not bring her surgical scalpel (or any surgical scalpel, for that matter).

- **The patient's body was found beneath a luxury sedan.**

SUSPECTS    LOCATIONS

|  | | | | | |
|---|---|---|---|---|---|
| | | | | | |
| | | | | | |
| | | | | | |

**WHO?**

**WHAT?**

**WHERE?**

# 6. MURDER IN THE ALLEY 🔍

While Deductive Logico was walking home, he was stopped in a dark alley by a dark figure who said that Dame Obsidian was guilty: she'd framed a semi-innocent magician (see Case 1: Murder in Hollywood). Before the dark figure could say more, he was murdered.

## SUSPECTS

### GENERAL COFFEE

An espresso connoisseur who once sent his men to die in the jungle to harvest a single bean.

6'0" • RIGHT-HANDED • DARK BROWN EYES • BALD

### COSMONAUT BLUSKI

An ex-Soviet spaceman whose blood flows red. Sure, that's normal, but for him it's patriotic.

6'2" • LEFT-HANDED • DARK BROWN EYES • BLACK HAIR

### MIDNIGHT III

He argues the studio should focus on murder mysteries again to regain their former glory.

5'8" • LEFT-HANDED • DARK BROWN EYES • DARK BROWN HAIR

## LOCATIONS

### THE METAL FENCE
OUTDOORS

Your typical chain-link fence. What more do you want?

### THE DUMPSTER
OUTDOORS

It does not smell good. No, it does not. It smells awful, actually.

### THE DISTRACTING GRAFFITI
OUTDOORS

The dragon-riding-a-motorcycle mural really ruins the noir vibes.

## WEAPONS

**PIANO WIRE**
LIGHT-WEIGHT

Somewhere out there, there's a piano missing a wire, and it's about to ruin a concert.

**A CROWBAR**
MEDIUM-WEIGHT

Honestly, they're used more often for crime than anything else.

**A POISONOUS DART**
LIGHT-WEIGHT

One stick of this dart and you're dead.

## CLUES & EVIDENCE

- Midnight III had that familiar chain-link pattern pressed into his face.

- Cosmonaut Bluski always packed for outer space: he had a light-weight weapon.

- The Detective Club sent Logico a message written in Detective Code: TVMVIZO XLUUVV WRW MLG SZEV GSV XILDYZI. (See Exhibit A.)

- Cosmonaut Bluski did not bring piano wire: he was tone-deaf.

- Either a crowbar or a poisonous dart was by the distracting graffiti.

- **There was an awful smell around the body—even for a body!**

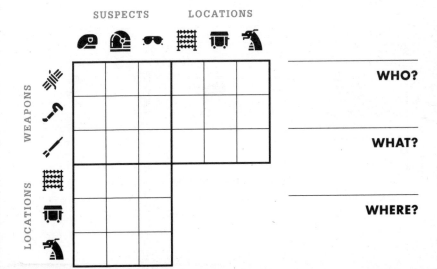

# 7. A QUAINT LITTLE VILLAGE SLAYING 🔍

Deductive Logico traveled to Dame Obsidian's quaint little village, and immediately, Logico learned a new word: "vicar." He didn't know what it meant, but he knew how to use it in a sentence, like, "The vicar has been murdered, and I'm going to find whodunit."

## SUSPECTS

**DAME OBSIDIAN**

One of her most famous books is about a mystery writer who frames an innocent magician. Suspicious!

5'4" • LEFT-HANDED • GREEN EYES • BLACK HAIR

**DEACON VERDIGRIS**

A deacon in the church. She handles the parishioners' donations and, sometimes, their secrets.

5'3" • LEFT-HANDED • BLUE EYES • GRAY HAIR

**EARL GREY**

He comes from a long line of Earl Greys. Yes, of the tea. No, he doesn't sign autographs. But he'll give you a free bag if you ask.

5'9" • RIGHT-HANDED • LIGHT BROWN EYES • WHITE HAIR

## LOCATIONS

**THE MANOR HOUSE**
INDOORS

The dame's. It's filled with giant portraits of many generations of dead rich white guys.

**THE CHAPEL**
INDOORS

A tiny church filled with stained-glass windows and secrets.

**THE ANCIENT RUINS**
OUTDOORS

These same standing stones again! Each of them has a strange labyrinth carved on its side.

## WEAPONS

**A BOTTLE OF CYANIDE**
LIGHT-WEIGHT

It's almond-scented poison, but it can also get rid of headaches (like your husband).

**A PAIR OF GARDENING SHEARS**
MEDIUM-WEIGHT

Gardening is a great hobby. But honestly, it's easier to get good tomatoes by killing for them.

**YARN**
LIGHT-WEIGHT

Sometimes, when you realize you've missed a stitch, you could just strangle somebody.

## CLUES & EVIDENCE

- Logico smelled almonds beneath a stained-glass window.

- Dame Obsidian was not in her manor house. Or any manor house, for that matter.

- Yes, he owned a tea empire, but Earl Grey never gardened, and he wouldn't be caught dead holding a pair of shears.

- Deacon Verdigris was visiting the ancient ruins to research an article he was writing about the local pagan practices prior to the arrival of the church.

- **The vicar was strangled—most embarrassingly—by a roll of yarn.**

WHO?

WHAT?

WHERE?

# 8. THE BUTLER DID IT (DIE) 🔍

Immediately after the last one, there was another murder in Dame Obsidian's house! That made her look even guiltier, Logico thought. Especially since it was her butler who was murdered. What kind of person kills somebody else's butler?

## SUSPECTS

**DAME OBSIDIAN**

As additional background: a week after Dame Obsidian's second husband disappeared, she paved over her garden. The papers had a field day with that. But her sales doubled.

5'4" • LEFT-HANDED • GREEN EYES • BLACK HAIR

**SIR RULEAN**

A sophisticated gentleman who was just recently knighted, if you believe the shoddy paperwork he carries with him.

5'8" • RIGHT-HANDED • BLUE EYES • RED HAIR

**MISS SAFFRON**

Gorgeous and stunning, but maybe not all there in the brains department. Or maybe that's what she wants you to think. Or maybe she wants you to think that's what she wants you to think.

5'2" • LEFT-HANDED • HAZEL EYES • BLOND HAIR

## LOCATIONS

**THE SPOOKY ATTIC**
INDOORS

Nothing but cobwebs, family heirlooms, and haunted paintings.

**THE MASTER BEDROOM**
INDOORS

The bed is so big that the bedroom had to be built around it.

**THE GROUNDS**
OUTDOORS

A meticulously maintained, solid green two-inch monoculture.

## WEAPONS

**A MAGNIFYING GLASS**
MEDIUM-WEIGHT

You could use this to find a clue, read the fine print, or start a small fire.

**AN ANTIQUE CLOCK**
HEAVY-WEIGHT

Tick, tock, tick, tock. Technically, time is killing us all slowly.

**AN AXE**
MEDIUM-WEIGHT

This axe could chop a tree down. Or a person down!

## CLUES & EVIDENCE

- Either Miss Saffron brought an axe or an axe was in the master bedroom.

- Sir Rulean had been hiding from the person who brought an axe.

- An antique clock was certainly not on the grounds: it was an inside clock.

- Miss Saffron was seen using a weapon to read the fine print in the ads of a gossip magazine.

- **Blood was splattered on a family heirloom.**

SUSPECTS      LOCATIONS

WEAPONS

WHO?

WHAT?

LOCATIONS

WHERE?

# 9. HEDGE YOUR BETS, THE CONSTABLE CRIED 🔍

While Logico was wondering if it were possible Dame Obsidian was actually innocent, he heard a scream from her hedge maze. He ran into it, got lost, figured it out, and then found Dame Obsidian, who he was now certain was innocent, on account of she was dead.

## SUSPECTS

**CONSTABLE COPPER**

The identical twin of Officer Copper. When their parents divorced, she moved across the ocean. But they have so much in common. Same height, same job, same propensity to violence.

5'5" • RIGHT-HANDED • BLUE EYES • BLOND HAIR

**LORD LAVENDER**

A politically conservative MP in the House of Lords, as well as the musical theater composer behind such hits as *Dogs* and *Mr. Moses Megastar*.

5'9" • RIGHT-HANDED • GREEN EYES • GRAY HAIR

**MISS SAFFRON**

Gorgeous and stunning, but maybe not all there in the brains department. Or maybe that's what she wants you to think. Or maybe she wants you to think that's what she wants you to think.

5'2" • LEFT-HANDED • HAZEL EYES • BLOND HAIR

## LOCATIONS

**THE FOUNTAIN**
OUTDOORS

A fountain at the center of the maze, if you can find it.

**THE LOOKOUT TOWER**
INDOORS

From above the garden, you can see everything. Plus, there's a map on the wall that reveals (some of) the maze's secrets.

**THE ANCIENT RUINS**
OUTDOORS

These same old ruins again! They were here long before the rest of the maze.

## WEAPONS

**A PAIR OF GAR-
DENING SHEARS**
MEDIUM-WEIGHT

They're getting a
little rusty, and they
might leave screws
behind.

**A FLOWERPOT**
MEDIUM-WEIGHT

If you use this to
murder, please re-
pot the flowers first.

**POISONED TEA**
LIGHT-WEIGHT

Enjoy a nice sip of
tea, followed by a
long, long nap.

## CLUES & EVIDENCE

- Poisoned tea was certainly not in the ancient ruins, nor was it in the fountain.

- The tallest suspect and the person who brought a pair of gardening shears had a history together.

- A flowerpot was not in the ancient ruins. Or was it? (It wasn't.)

- Miss Saffron was addicted to a product made by a friend of hers, Earl Grey, and she added just a little poison.

- **Dame Obsidian's body was found beside a blood-splattered map.**

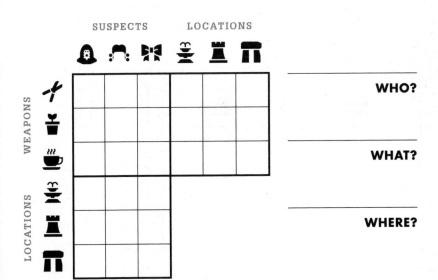

# 10. EAT, DRINK, AND BE MERRY, FOR A JERK JUST DIED 🔍

Because of a mistake he made with time zones (the hardest problem in all of deductive analysis), Logico missed his flight home. So he went to the village pub, where everyone was celebrating the death of a loud-mouthed jerk. They all wanted to know whodunit (so they could buy him drinks), and Logico was happy to oblige.

## SUSPECTS

**BROTHER BROWNSTONE**

A monk who has dedicated his life to the church, specifically to making money for it.

**5'4" • LEFT-HANDED • DARK BROWN EYES • DARK BROWN HAIR**

**COMRADE CHAMPAGNE**

A communist and a rich one. Comrade Champagne likes nothing more than to travel the world, sharing the message of communism with his fellow vacationers.

**5'11" • LEFT-HANDED • HAZEL EYES • BLOND HAIR**

**GRANDMASTER ROSE**

A chess grand master who is always plotting his next move. Like how to bump off his next opponent! (1. e4)

**5'7" • LEFT-HANDED • DARK BROWN EYES • DARK BROWN HAIR**

## LOCATIONS

**THE CENTER BAR**
INDOORS

They're giving out free drinks to celebrate the jerk being dead.

**THE CORNER BOOTH**
INDOORS

Shrouded in shadow, you sit at this booth if you don't want to be seen.

**THE CRAMPED BATHROOM**
INDOORS

So small it seems like it was designed for a discount airplane.

## WEAPONS

| **A CORKSCREW**<br>LIGHT-WEIGHT | **A BOTTLE OF WINE**<br>MEDIUM-WEIGHT | **A CRYSTAL BALL**<br>HEAVY-WEIGHT |
|---|---|---|
| Once Logico started looking, he saw weapons everywhere. | Watch out for stains, because the red doesn't come out. | If you look into it, it will tell you your future, so long as your future is a crystal ball. |

## CLUES & EVIDENCE

- A red stain was found in a teeny, tiny space.

- The chess player was suspicious of the person who brought a bottle of wine.

- A corkscrew was certainly not in the center bar.

- The suspect with the corkscrew had blond hair.

- **They were giving out free drinks right over the jerk's still-warm body!**

SUSPECTS      LOCATIONS

WEAPONS

LOCATIONS

WHO?

WHAT?

WHERE?

# 11. THE CASE OF THE COFFEE SHOP KILLER

Once Deductive Logico was back home, he went to his favorite coffee shop in order to ponder what had happened to Dame Obsidian. While he was lost in thought, a barista lost her life. He couldn't save her, but he could solve her murder.

**GENERAL COFFEE**

An espresso connoisseur who likes his coffee like he likes his war: always.

6'0" • RIGHT-HANDED • DARK BROWN EYES • BALD

**COACH RASPBERRY**

One of the best coaches this side of the Mississippi, regardless of which side you happen to be on. Some people say he has a gambling problem, but he just says he loves danger.

6'0" • LEFT-HANDED • BLUE EYES • BLOND HAIR

**BOOKIE-WINNER GAINSBORO**

He won the Bookington Award for his novel, which he will tell you within two minutes of meeting you. The book is six thousand pages long, and it's about dirt.

6'0" • LEFT-HANDED • HAZEL EYES • LIGHT BROWN HAIR

## LOCATIONS

**THE COURTYARD**
OUTDOORS

Sun-dappled tables and chairs sit beneath a magnificent oak. A great place for conversation . . . or murder.

**THE BEAN ROOM**
INDOORS

Full of bags and bags of beans. The smell is so strong and delicious that Logico wants to eat the beans.

**THE COUNTER**
INDOORS

There is a little bell that alerts the baristas you are here so they can start ignoring you.

## WEAPONS

### AN ORDINARY BRICK
**HEAVY-WEIGHT**

Just a regular, ordinary brick. Nothing special. Just a brick.

### A METAL STRAW
**HEAVY-WEIGHT**

Better for the planet than a plastic straw, but more deadly!

### A POISONED CUP OF COFFEE
**MEDIUM-WEIGHT**

It's poisoned with ricin, which is made from castor beans. So technically this is a two-bean soup.

## CLUES & EVIDENCE

- Bookie-Winner Gainsboro had never been in the courtyard, and he never wanted to go, if you asked him.

- Coach Raspberry used to run plays with the person who brought a poisoned cup of coffee.

- Logico found a regular brick chip buried beneath bags of beans.

- The person who was at the counter was the former owner of Deductive Logico's coffee cup. (See Exhibit A.)

- **A metal straw was used to commit the murder.**

SUSPECTS          LOCATIONS

WHO?

WHAT?

WHERE?

# 12. THE MYSTERIOUS MYSTERY BOOKSHOP MYSTERY 🔍

Deductive Logico decided to investigate the mystery of Dame Obsidian by investigating the mysteries of Dame Obsidian, so he went to a local mystery bookshop. But the first mystery he found was the death of the bookshop proprietor.

## SUSPECTS

**CAPTAIN SLATE**

A real-life astronaut. The first woman to travel around the dark side of the moon, and also the first to be suspected of murdering her copilot.

**5'5" • LEFT-HANDED • DARK BROWN EYES • DARK BROWN HAIR**

**COMRADE CHAMPAGNE**

A communist and a rich one. Comrade Champagne likes nothing more than to travel the world, sharing the message of communism with his fellow vacationers.

**5'11" • LEFT-HANDED • HAZEL EYES • BLOND HAIR**

**DIRECTOR DUSTY**

A true filmmaker. The only thing he cares about is getting his movie made. No matter what.

**5'10" • LEFT-HANDED • HAZEL EYES • BALD**

## LOCATIONS

**THE DISCOUNT RACK**
INDOORS

You can find a lot of great books here, and soon, a half-solved copy of *Murdle*.

**THE FRONT COUNTER**
INDOORS

Where you actually buy the books, or any of the little trinkets they have for sale.

**THE RARE BOOKS ROOM**
INDOORS

A single Dame Obsidian first edition costs more than Logico's father made in his lifetime.

## WEAPONS

**A TOTE BAG**
MEDIUM-WEIGHT

Bibliophile mafiosos use these canvas bags for hits. You can also carry books in them.

**A BONE FOLDER**
LIGHT-WEIGHT

Yeah, it's made from an animal bone, but just because you've killed before doesn't mean you'll kill again.

**A PAPERBACK**
MEDIUM-WEIGHT

Too light to hit someone over the head, but the ink is so cheap it's toxic.

## CLUES & EVIDENCE

- A tote bag was not found in the discount rack.

- A smudge of toxic ink was found by the front counter.

- An anti-shoplifting mirror caught the reflection of the eyes of the person in the rare books room: they were dark brown.

- There weren't any film books in the discount rack, so Director Dusty wasn't there.

- **A chip of animal bone was found inside the body of the proprietor.**

SUSPECTS      LOCATIONS

WEAPONS

WHO?

WHAT?

LOCATIONS

WHERE?

# 13. THE KILLING OF A COWBOY 🔍

Dame Obsidian had written mysteries in many different places and periods, and Logico was determined to read them all. The first was a Western, filled with red herrings, black hats, and a twist worthy of a lasso. A rancher had been killed, and it looked like the suspects were based on real people.

## SUSPECTS

**COWBOY RASPBERRY**

One of the best cowboys this side of the Mississippi, regardless of which side you happen to be on. Some people say he has a rustlin' problem, but he just says he loves danger.

6'0" • LEFT-HANDED • BLUE EYES • BLOND HAIR

**JUSTICE PINE**

Master of the rural courthouse and possessed of a firm belief in her own form of frontier justice.

5'6" • RIGHT-HANDED • DARK BROWN EYES • BLACK HAIR

**CORPORAL COFFEE**

Back in those days, if you liked coffee, you liked it black. And the corporal liked coffee.

6'0" • RIGHT-HANDED • BROWN EYES • BALD

## LOCATIONS

**THE SALOON**
INDOORS

The worst saloon that anybody who ever visited had ever visited.

**THE WATERING HOLE**
OUTDOORS

You can get the cleanest water in the West here. It's dark brown.

**THE "HOTEL"**
INDOORS

A "hotel" that provides certain "amenities" including "charging" by the "hour."

## WEAPONS

### A STABBIN' KNIFE
**MEDIUM-WEIGHT**

Just the kinda knife that's perfect for stabbin'.

### A CACTUS
**MEDIUM-WEIGHT**

Watch out for the needles—and also for someone hitting you with it.

### TAINTED MOONSHINE
**MEDIUM-WEIGHT**

This'll kill you, that's for sure. Even the smell is dangerous.

## CLUES & EVIDENCE

- Some needles were found soaking in dark brown water.

- Justice Pine was suspicious of the person who brought a stabbin' knife. (Reasonable.)

- Corporal Coffee had never been in the "hotel."

- Whoever had the cactus had blue eyes.

- **Tainted moonshine was used to murder the rancher.**

SUSPECTS     LOCATIONS

WEAPONS

LOCATIONS

**WHO?**

**WHAT?**

**WHERE?**

# 14. A VERY PROPER MURDER 🔍

Next, Logico read a book set in Victorian London—the capital of the whodunit! It was obviously based on heavy research, but the dame played all the hits: bloody letters, a shoe print in the snow, and the murder of the richest man in town, thousandaire Lord Lavender.

## SUSPECTS

**BARON MAROON**

An incredibly haughty man who holds a grudge. Nobody wants to offend the baron. At least, nobody who's still alive . . .

6'2" • RIGHT-HANDED • HAZEL EYES • RED HAIR

**EARL GREY**

He comes from a shorter (but still long) line of Earl Greys. And this Earl Grey does sign autographs, but he charges for the tea bags.

5'9" • RIGHT-HANDED • LIGHT BROWN EYES • WHITE HAIR

**VISCOUNT EMINENCE**

The oldest man you have ever seen. It is said that he outlived all of his sons and was born before his father.

5'2" • LEFT-HANDED • GRAY EYES • DARK BROWN HAIR

## LOCATIONS

**THE INVESTIGATION INSTITUTE**
INDOORS

A recently founded organization that investigates spiritualism and other related phenomena.

**A POTENTIALLY HAUNTED MANSION**
INDOORS

People keep seeing ghosts here, especially around the furnace in the basement.

**A COFFEE HOUSE**
INDOORS

Where you can drink coffee and discuss the latest ghastly happenings.

## WEAPONS

**A KNIFE**
MEDIUM-WEIGHT

Not a famous knife. Just a regular one. Maybe it'll be famous soon, though!

**THE PLAGUE**
LIGHT-WEIGHT

Well, not *the* plague, but one of them that's been going around.

**A JEWELED SCEPTER**
HEAVY-WEIGHT

Part of the crown jewels, and like most of them, it was stolen from another country.

## CLUES & EVIDENCE

- A knife was found in the headquarters of a recently founded organization.

- Viscount Eminence hated ghosts, so he had not been anywhere near the potentially haunted mansion.

- Baron Maroon's love affair with the person who brought the plague was the biggest subplot.

- Fingerprints on the jeweled scepter proved it was held by a left-handed suspect.

- **Lord Lavender's body was found next to a shattered cup of coffee.**

SUSPECTS  LOCATIONS

WEAPONS

LOCATIONS

WHO?

WHAT?

WHERE?

# 15. THE PERPLEXING PROBLEM OF THE PARROT 🔍

Arrr! The next Obsidian novel was set in the world of piracy, and it was full of thrills, chills, and multicolored beards. Logico was enthralled by the twist in the first act, when Blackbeard's parrot was murdered. Oh man, Logico thought, whoever crossed Blackbeard is in trouble!

## SUSPECTS

**BLACKBEARD**

Famous, feared, respected for the beard.

7'0" • RIGHT-HANDED • BLACK EYES • BLACK HAIR

**BLUEBEARD**

Actually a French wife-murderer, and not a pirate at all.

6'6" • LEFT-HANDED • BLUE EYES • BLUE HAIR

**NOBEARD**

His name used to be Redbeard, but then he shaved. A part-time pirate.

5'9" • RIGHT-HANDED • GREEN EYES • RED HAIR

## LOCATIONS

**THE GREAT WHIRLPOOL**
OUTDOORS

Apparently there's a big hole in the ocean and all the water's draining out.

**THE PIRATE COVE**
OUTDOORS

Where all the pirates go to drink and plan where to bury their treasure. (Maybe by those ancient ruins . . .)

**THE PIRATE SHIP**
OUTDOORS

Yo ho ho, a pirate's life for me—and also, inevitably, a pirate's death.

## WEAPONS

**A CANNON**
HEAVY-WEIGHT

Usually used to kill more than one person (or parrot), but exceptions can be made.

**A SCIMITAR**
MEDIUM-WEIGHT

Technically, it's just a bent sword, but if you call it a scimitar, it sounds cool.

**A FAKE TREASURE MAP**
LIGHT-WEIGHT

This map leads someone straight into a booby-trapped pit.

## CLUES & EVIDENCE

- Either Bluebeard brought a scimitar or a fake treasure map was in the pirate ship.

- The second tallest suspect was seen in the place where a pirate lives and dies.

- The fake treasure map was spinning around in giant circles out in the ocean, dissolving in the saltwater.

- The shortest suspect was suspicious of the person with the cannon.

- **The parrot was found floating in the waters of the pirate cove.**

SUSPECTS    LOCATIONS

WEAPONS

LOCATIONS

**WHO?**

**WHAT?**

**WHERE?**

# 16. FIFTEEN PERCENT OF MURDER 🔍

Deductive Logico went to Dame Obsidian's literary agency to look for a body. He found one, but it wasn't Dame Obsidian's. It was the body of a powerful agent, dead in his office.

## SUSPECTS

**EDITOR IVORY**

The greatest romance editor of all time. She invented the enemies-to-lovers genre, and she was the first person to put a naked man on the cover of a book.

**5'6" • LEFT-HANDED • LIGHT BROWN EYES • GRAY HAIR**

**ASSISTANT APPLEGREEN**

Her father is a principal, and she is making him proud. But you know what she's not making? Enough money.

**5'3" • LEFT-HANDED • BLUE EYES • BLOND HAIR**

**AGENT INK**

An agent with a heart of gold, but a mind for gold, too. If you like living, don't cross her.

**5'5" • RIGHT-HANDED • DARK BROWN EYES • BLACK HAIR**

## LOCATIONS

**THE BALCONY**
OUTDOORS

Standing on the balcony, you can look out over the city you run.

**THE BEST OFFICE**
INDOORS

The best-earning agent of the month gets this office. The worst is fired.

**THE UNSOLIC- ITED SUBMIS- SIONS ROOM**
INDOORS

It also doubles as an incinerator.

## WEAPONS

### AN ANTIQUE TYPEWRITER
**HEAVY-WEIGHT**

You can write your themes subtly, or you can hit them over the head with it.

### A GIANT STACK OF BOOKS
**HEAVY-WEIGHT**

You can shove this over and crush someone beneath it. But it's hard to carry around.

### A REAM OF PAPER
**MEDIUM-WEIGHT**

You could use these blank pages to give someone a thousand paper cuts or one paper bash.

## CLUES & EVIDENCE

- Editor Ivory and the person who brought a giant stack of books had known each other for years.

- Assistant Applegreen wasn't allowed to go out on the balcony.

- Logico received a clue from the Detective Club, written in their signature code: ZTVMG RMP SZW Z NVWRFN-DVRTSG DVZKLM. (See Exhibit A.)

- Whoever was in the unsolicited submissions room had to be right-handed, because otherwise you get burned.

- **The agent who died in his office had been the best-earning agent that month.**

# 17. THE CASE OF THE CONTRACT & THE CAPTAIN 🔍

On the yacht of legendary book publisher Chairman Chalk, Logico signed a contract for a book series and got to work solving the murder of a sailor, which he got to add to the book. Or, at least, he would, as soon as he cracked it.

## SUSPECTS

**BOOKIE-WINNER GAINSBORO**

He won the Bookington Award for his novel, which he will tell you within two minutes of meeting you. The book is six thousand pages long, and it's about dirt.

**6'0" • LEFT-HANDED • HAZEL EYES • LIGHT BROWN HAIR**

**CHAIRMAN CHALK**

He figured out the publishing business years ago and never looked back. He called ebooks a "fad" and still owns a rotary phone. He is worth a billion dollars.

**5'9" • RIGHT-HANDED • BLUE EYES • WHITE HAIR**

**AGENT INK**

An agent with a heart of gold, but a mind for gold, too. If you like living, don't cross her.

**5'5" • RIGHT-HANDED • DARK BROWN EYES • BLACK HAIR**

## LOCATIONS

**THE DECK**
OUTDOORS

Look out over the ocean, but not too far or someone might push you.

**THE ENGINE ROOM**
INDOORS

This is a green yacht: it's powered by a nuclear reactor. When the uranium rods are spent, just toss them into the ocean.

**THE DINING HALL**
INDOORS

They've hired an award-winning chef for cheap because he's banned from working on land.

## WEAPONS

**AN ANTIQUE ANCHOR**
HEAVY-WEIGHT

It's covered in moss and the chain is rusty: it looks awesome.

**A GOLDEN PEN**
LIGHT-WEIGHT

For signing contracts and stabbing competitors. Even the ink is gold.

**A BABY SHARK**
MEDIUM-WEIGHT

Just throw and go: toss it at your enemies and watch those baby teeth go.

## CLUES & EVIDENCE

- The second tallest suspect had never been in the engine room.

- Someone suffering from obvious seasickness wrote out this scrambled clue: WEEOHRV ASW NO HTE CDEK WSA TEFL HEDNAD.

- Bookie-Winner Gainsboro was jealous of the person with the golden pen. Why didn't I bring a golden pen? he wondered.

- The yacht had a strict no anchors in the dining hall policy, and nobody would have violated it, even to commit a murder.

- The tallest suspect didn't bring an antique anchor.

- **A tiny, sharp tooth was biting into the sailor's body.**

SUSPECTS     LOCATIONS

|  | 👓 | 👱 | 👩 | 🛥 | ⚙ | 🍽 |
|---|---|---|---|---|---|---|
| ⚓ |  |  |  |  |  |  |
| ✒ |  |  |  |  |  |  |
| 🦈 |  |  |  |  |  |  |
| 🛥 |  |  |  |  |  |  |
| ⚙ |  |  |  |  |  |  |
| 🍽 |  |  |  |  |  |  |

WEAPONS / LOCATIONS

**WHO?** _____

**WHAT?** _____

**WHERE?** _____

# 18. THROW THE (BOOKIE-WINNING) BOOK AT THEM! 🔍

That year, at the 138th annual Bookington Awards, Deductive Logico was nominated for one of the most prestigious awards: Best Debut Murder Mystery Puzzle Book Based on a True Story. Unfortunately, right after the winner was announced, the president of the Bookington Society was killed. But whodunit? And who won the Bookie?

## SUSPECTS

**PHILOSOPHER BONE**

A dashing, dark philosopher who pioneered the ethical theory that he is not responsible for his actions, but he should be paid for them.

**5'1" • RIGHT-HANDED • LIGHT BROWN EYES • BALD**

**DEDUCTIVE LOGICO**

He was finally there for the actual murder, which means he's a suspect.

**6'0" • RIGHT-HANDED • DARK BROWN EYES • BLACK HAIR**

**SILVERTON THE LEGEND**

An acclaimed actor of the Golden Age, now in his golden years.

**6'4" • RIGHT-HANDED • BLUE EYES • SILVER HAIR**

## LOCATIONS

**THE STAGE**
INDOORS

Where you accept your award at the lectern to the deafening applause of dozens of clapping hands.

**A NOMINEE TABLE**
INDOORS

Several of the nominees are seated together (for the sake of drama).

**BACKSTAGE**
INDOORS

Interns and assistants struggle with the ropes, levers, and control boards.

## WEAPONS

### A BOOKIE
MEDIUM-WEIGHT

The diminutive nickname of the most prestigious award in publishing. The fake gold is flaking off.

### A HEAVY BOOK
HEAVY-WEIGHT

Gainsboro's six-thousand-page dirt book.

### A FOUNTAIN PEN
LIGHT-WEIGHT

With this, you can sign checks or stab necks. Unfortunately, it leaks ink.

## CLUES & EVIDENCE

- Philosopher Bone hated the person who won the Bookie.

- A frantic fan gave Deductive Logico a piece of paper she had scrawled a scrambled clue on: NTVIROLSE ETH NGDELE ASW CIPUSISSUO OF HET PENSRO HWO HBTROGU A VHYEA KOBO.

- Whoever sat at the nominee table had a medium-weight weapon.

- Either Silverton the Legend brought a heavy book, or Silverton the Legend was behind a lectern.

- **The victim's body was found slumped over a control board.**

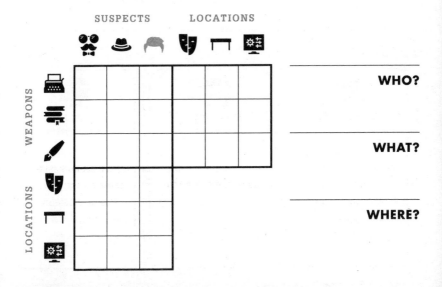

WHO?

WHAT?

WHERE?

# 19. DEATH ON THE BOOK TOUR 🔍

Deductive Logico's publisher asked him to go on a book tour to promote *Murdle,* but they had to cancel one of the stops because a bookstore owner had been murdered by one of their other authors. But due to ethics in publishing, they couldn't say which stop was canceled. He had to figure it out himself.

## SUSPECTS

**CHANCELLOR TUSCANY**

As the head of Deduction College, she has deduced the best ways to get away with murder. Only in theory, of course!

5'5" • LEFT-HANDED • GREEN EYES • GRAY HAIR

**SECRETARY CELADON**

The secretary of defense, and someone who is personally responsible for a number of war crimes, some of which are now named after her.

5'6" • LEFT-HANDED • GREEN EYES • LIGHT BROWN HAIR

**VICE PRESIDENT MAUVE**

A vice president of TekCo Futures. If she asks you to step into her metaverse, firmly refuse.

5'8" • RIGHT-HANDED • DARK BROWN EYES • BLACK HAIR

## LOCATIONS

**HOLLYWOOD**
OUTDOORS

Tinseltown, the City of Angels, La La Land, the Dream Factory.

**TEKTOPIA**
OUTDOORS

A billionaire built a fully automated city in the desert. His goal is to disrupt food. He will succeed.

**THE REPUBLIC OF DRAKONIA**
OUTDOORS

Previously the Holy Republic of Drakonia, now the Free Republic of Drakonia.

## WEAPONS

### A LAPTOP
MEDIUM-WEIGHT

The machine you work on. It's also connected to every distraction ever made.

### A POISONED CANDLE
MEDIUM-WEIGHT

If you light this candle, everyone in the room will die. But it has a nice lavender scent.

### A SEXTANT
MEDIUM-WEIGHT

Get your head out of the gutter and start thinking like a sailor.

## CLUES & EVIDENCE

- Everyone in the Dream Factory has a laptop.

- No sextant was in the Republic of Drakonia—that's right, not one in the whole country.

- Secretary Celadon refused to visit Hollywood until their movies treated the military better.

- The sextant was held by someone whose last name began with one of the letters in Deductive Logico's Detective Club member number. (See Exhibit A.)

- **The dead body smelled like lavender.**

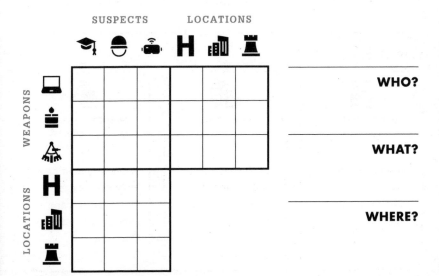

WHO?

WHAT?

WHERE?

# 20. DEAD TIRED 🔍

Once the book tour was over, Deductive Logico stumbled back to his office. It was small, but it seemed bigger than it was because of how orderly he kept it. Unfortunately for Logico, four things were disrupting his organizational system: the three people waiting on him, and the dead body between them.

## SUSPECTS

**COSMONAUT BLUSKI**

An ex-Soviet spaceman whose blood flows red. Sure, that's normal, but for him it's patriotic.

6'2" • LEFT-HANDED • DARK BROWN EYES • BLACK HAIR

**DR. CRIMSON**

She's the smartest doctor she's ever met, according to her, and she's probably right. Yeah, she skydives, but if something goes wrong, she'll calculate just how to fall.

5'9" • LEFT-HANDED • GREEN EYES • RED HAIR

**GENERAL COFFEE**

An espresso connoisseur who once made a pot of coffee so strong that it killed a man.

6'0" • RIGHT-HANDED • DARK BROWN EYES • BALD

## LOCATIONS

**THE MAIN OFFICE**
INDOORS

A desk, shelves of logic books, and a window with a view of a brick wall.

**THE CLOSET**
INDOORS

All of Logico's clothes are carefully sorted from A to Z.

**THE WAITING ROOM**
INDOORS

Logico doesn't have a receptionist so there's just a bell and a sign that says PLEASE WAIT.

## WEAPONS

**A DEDUCTION COLLEGE DIPLOMA**
HEAVY-WEIGHT

With its heavy oak frame, you could really do some damage. And they say a logic degree is useless.

**LEATHER GLOVES**
LIGHT-WEIGHT

Beware someone who wears leather gloves. They've already killed a cow: who's next?

**A MAGNIFYING GLASS**
MEDIUM-WEIGHT

You could use this to find a clue, read the fine print, or start a small fire.

## CLUES & EVIDENCE

- Cosmonaut Bluski hated the person who brought a magnifying glass.

- A magnifying glass was discovered near a window view of a brick wall.

- Dr. Crimson was seen behind alphabetically ordered jackets.

- Leather gloves were certainly not in the waiting room.

- **A logic degree was used to commit the murder.**

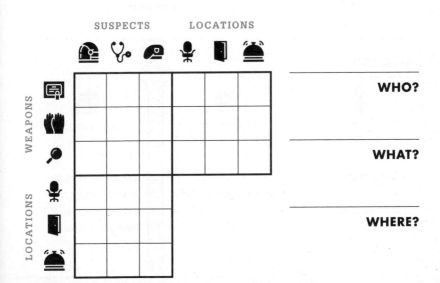

# 21. OIL KILL YOU FOR THIS 🔍

Deductive Logico followed the old pirate map: it led him to an oil field at the edge of an ocean. When he arrived at the *X*, he saw Dame Obsidian was already there, as were two other people, or three, if you counted the body.

## SUSPECTS

### CHAIRMAN CHALK

He figured out the publishing business years ago and never looked back. He called ebooks a "fad" and still owns a rotary phone. He is worth a billion dollars.

**5'9" • RIGHT-HANDED • BLUE EYES • WHITE HAIR**

### MIDNIGHT III

Maybe the only person capable of returning Midnight Movies to its former glory.

**5'8" • LEFT-HANDED • DARK BROWN EYES • DARK BROWN HAIR**

### DAME OBSIDIAN

Back from the dead! But Logico remembered when an interviewer asked her how she got all of her ideas for all of her fictional perfect murders, and she chuckled for two full minutes.

**5'4" • LEFT-HANDED • GREEN EYES • BLACK HAIR**

## LOCATIONS

### AN OIL DERRICK
OUTDOORS

They're digging another well right now with this massive derrick.

### THE OFFICES
INDOORS

Air-conditioned to such a low temperature that it uses most of the energy the field produces.

### THE ANCIENT RUINS
OUTDOORS

You can see them from the edge of the fields, silhouetted in the light of the setting sun.

## WEAPONS

**A CROWBAR**
MEDIUM-WEIGHT

Honestly, at this point, they're used more often for crime than anything else.

**A PIECE OF REBAR**
MEDIUM-WEIGHT

A long piece of metal. If this isn't a weapon, nothing is. Often used with powdered cement.

**AN OIL DRUM**
HEAVY-WEIGHT

Really more of a giant can than a drum: you've never seen a band feature one of these.

## CLUES & EVIDENCE

- Nobody ever put an oil drum anywhere near the ancient ruins. It was a superstition.

- Either Chairman Chalk brought an oil drum, or a crowbar was in an oil derrick.

- A trusted confidant gave Deductive Logico a piece of paper with a message written in what he called the Next Letter Code: SGD RGN-QSDRS RTRODBS VZR MNS AX SGD ZMBHDMS QThMR.

- Neither Midnight III nor Dame Obsidian had ever been in the offices.

- **Some powdered cement was found beside the victim.**

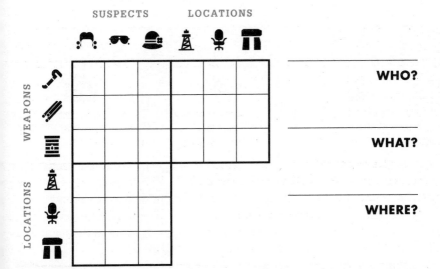

WHO?

WHAT?

WHERE?

# 22. THEY BILL YOU FOR DYING 🔍

Dame Obsidian contracted the most expensive law firm in the world—Blackstone & Blackstone—and one of them (Blackstone) required Logico to come to his office to be deposed. Unfortunately, when he got there, Blackstone was indisposed (AKA dead).

## SUSPECTS

**DAME OBSIDIAN**

Dame Obsidian had an army of attorneys. That's where she got the idea for her book *The Army of Attorneys I Have.*

**5'4" • LEFT-HANDED • GREEN EYES • BLACK HAIR**

**VICE PRESIDENT MAUVE**

A vice president of TekCo Futures. If she asks you to step into her metaverse, walk away quickly.

**5'8" • RIGHT-HANDED • DARK BROWN EYES • BLACK HAIR**

**BLACKSTONE, ESQ.**

The other one. Incredibly talented at the most important skill for an attorney: getting paid.

**6'0" • RIGHT-HANDED • BLACK EYES • BLACK HAIR**

## LOCATIONS

**THE LOBBY**
INDOORS

It has an enormous fountain, a marble desk, and a receptionist ready to call the police.

**AN ASSOCIATE'S OFFICE**
INDOORS

Tiny, cramped, cluttered, possibly a closet. Occupied by someone working too hard for too little.

**A PARTNER'S OFFICE**
INDOORS

Featuring pictures of the partner with every living US president, even the really bad ones.

## WEAPONS

**A MARBLE BUST**
HEAVY-WEIGHT

It's a bust of a famous lawyer, but don't look him up— you won't like what you find.

**CONFUSING CONTRACTS**
LIGHT-WEIGHT

Legalese so impenetrable it could give you an aneurysm.

**POISONED INKWELL**
LIGHT-WEIGHT

How was he poisoned? Well.

## CLUES & EVIDENCE

- Lawyers often use the Next Letter Code to make notes to themselves. Logico found one of them: SGD RTRODBS HM SGD ZRRNBHZSD'R NEEHBD GZC FQDDM DXDR.

- The suspect with a metaverse had never been in the partner's office.

- The tallest suspect had a crush on the person who brought a poisoned inkwell.

- Whoever had the confusing contracts was left-handed.

- **A bust of a . . . controversial figure was found beside the victim.**

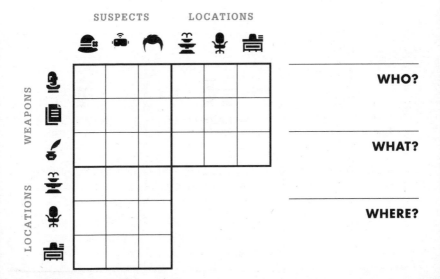

# 23. THE COURTHOUSE KILLING 🔍

It was finally the day of Dame Obsidian's trial, and Logico wore his finest raincoat to the courthouse. He hoped to see justice done. But instead of justice, he witnessed a murder. Was the death of this clerk connected to Dame Obsidian? Or just another everyday killing?

## SUSPECTS

**COACH RASPBERRY**

One of the best coaches this side of the Mississippi, regardless of which side you're on.

6'0" • LEFT-HANDED • BLUE EYES • BLOND HAIR

**OFFICER COPPER**

Ever since she murdered that guy, Officer Copper has been on administrative leave, which is when they leave the administrative work to her.

5'5" • RIGHT-HANDED • BLUE EYES • BLOND HAIR

**FATHER MANGO**

He has taken a vow of poverty, but he drives a BMW. He's taken a vow of obedience, but he has a staff of twenty-five. He's taken a vow of chastity, too, which is why he's on vacation.

5'10" • LEFT-HANDED • DARK BROWN EYES • BALD

## LOCATIONS

**THE ACTUAL COURTROOM**
INDOORS

Here is where Dame Obsidian's trial is going to be held.

**THE PARKING LOT**
OUTDOORS

More cop cars than Logico has seen since he got stuck behind that police parade.

**THE JUDGE'S CHAMBERS**
INDOORS

A nice desk, a good view out the window, and a closet filled with black robes.

## WEAPONS

### A NOTARY STAMP
**MEDIUM-WEIGHT**

Stamp a classic notary stamp on anything from papers to foreheads.

### THE SCALES OF JUSTICE
**HEAVY-WEIGHT**

Justice may be blind, but only because someone knocked her out with these scales.

### A HUGE PILE OF PAPERWORK
**HEAVY-WEIGHT**

A riddle: one piece of paper is too light to kill. But a big enough stack can. So, which single page turns it into a weapon?

## CLUES & EVIDENCE

- Someone with a shaky hand gave Logico a message: HET SUTSPEC IN EHT UCALTA ROOOTCUMR WAS HRIGT NDDAHE.

- The scales of justice were certainly not in the parking lot: that's where the cars go.

- Since Officer Copper committed murder, they had her doing notary work.

- Father Mango brought a huge pile of paperwork.

- **The body was found in the judge's chambers.**

SUSPECTS          LOCATIONS

WHO?

WHAT?

WHERE?

# 24. WILL THE FOREMAN PLEASE DIE? 🔍

Finally, it was time for the trial of the century, and Dame Obsidian put on a wonderful performance. But just when the jury was about to deliberate, the foreman was killed. Obviously, everyone thought Dame Obsidian did it. Did she?

## SUSPECTS

**JUDGE PINE**

Master of the courtroom and possessed of a firm belief in justice, as decided by her alone.

5'6" • RIGHT-HANDED • DARK BROWN EYES • BLACK HAIR

**OFFICER COPPER**

The best part of being a policewoman criminal is that you can cut out the middleman and fail to investigate your own crimes.

5'5" • RIGHT-HANDED • BLUE EYES • BLOND HAIR

**DAME OBSIDIAN**

Dame Obsidian looked very dignified all throughout the trial, and her book sales skyrocketed.

5'4" • LEFT-HANDED • GREEN EYES • BLACK HAIR

## LOCATIONS

**THE GALLERY**
INDOORS

Where all the family members sit beside the true-crime podcast enthusiasts.

**THE JUDGE'S BENCH**
INDOORS

You know the judge is in charge because she has the highest seat.

**THE JURY BOX**
INDOORS

In a sense, the entire trial is just a show performed for an audience of twelve.

## WEAPONS

**A BATON**
MEDIUM-WEIGHT

A great tool for brutalizing innocent people.

**A GAVEL**
MEDIUM-WEIGHT

Let's be frank: there's a reason they give the judge a big hammer. (Intimidation.)

**A FLAG**
HEAVY-WEIGHT

Flags have a long and respectable history of being used for violence.

## CLUES & EVIDENCE

- A gavel was nowhere near the true-crime enthusiasts.

- Deductive Logico received a message from the Detective Club written in Detective Code: QFWTV KRVM DZH HRGGRMT LM SVI YVMXS. (See Exhibit A.)

- Dame Obsidian had snuck in a baton "for self-defense," a dubious reason.

- Either Officer Copper brought a gavel, or Judge Pine was in the gallery.

- **Like many times before, a flag was used to commit this murder.**

WHO?

WHAT?

WHERE?

# 25. THE DEATH OF JUSTICE 🔍

Almost immediately after Dame Obsidian had been incarcerated, Logico got a call from the luxurious white-collar jail to which she had been sentenced, and he learned that she had been murdered herself. Was that justice? Was it fate? All he knew was it was a mystery.

## SUSPECTS

**SECRETARY CELADON**

The secretary of defense, and someone who is personally responsible for a number of international incidents, some of which are now named after her.

5'6" • LEFT-HANDED • GREEN EYES • LIGHT BROWN HAIR

**THE AMAZING AUREOLIN**

She blames Dame Obsidian for her incarceration, which makes sense, since Dame Obsidian framed her.

5'6" • LEFT-HANDED • GREEN EYES • BLOND HAIR

**MISS SAFFRON**

Miss Saffron also blames Dame Obsidian, though it's a little less sympathetic coming from her because she was actually guilty.

5'2" • LEFT-HANDED • HAZEL EYES • BLOND HAIR

## LOCATIONS

**THE SPA**
INDOORS

Built with money from the PTA (Prisoner Treats Association), although tax dollars do pay to heat it.

**THE PARKING LOT**
OUTDOORS

Prisoners can pay to park their luxury vehicles here for the duration of their stay.

**A PRIVATE SUITE**
INDOORS

If you have enough money, you can upgrade to a private suite with a big-screen TV, hot tub, and open bar.

## WEAPONS

**A QUARTER-MILLION-DOLLAR LAWYER**
HEAVY-WEIGHT

The most dangerous weapon of all. (And the most expensive.)

**A ROPE MADE OF DESIGNER CLOTHES**
MEDIUM-WEIGHT

When you need a rope but all you have are designer clothes.

**A PAIR OF GOLDEN HANDCUFFS**
HEAVY-WEIGHT

This is taking the metaphor too far, all right?

## CLUES & EVIDENCE

- Somebody passed Logico a slip of paper, on which a jumbled message was written: EW LLA SWA TEH ALWREY ROODISN.

- Secretary Celadon had a pair of custom-made golden handcuffs.

- The Detective Club sent Logico a card in Detective Code that read: GSV HSLIGVHG HFHKVXG DZH IVOZCRMT RM GSV HKZ WFIRMT GSV NFIWVI. (See Exhibit A.)

- The Amazing Aureolin could not afford the private suite on her magician's salary.

- **Dame Obsidian was found with a rope of designer clothes around her neck.**

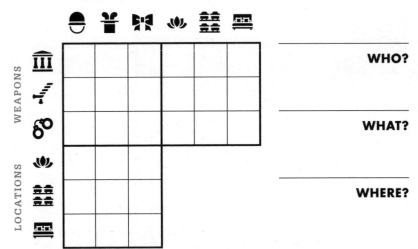

WHO?

WHAT?

WHERE?

# EXHIBIT B

| SIGN | ☉ | ELEMENT | DATES |
|------|-----|---------|-------|
| ARIES | ♈ | FIRE | MAR 21 – APRIL 19 |
| TAURUS | ♉ | EARTH | APRIL 20 – MAY 20 |
| GEMINI | ♊ | AIR | MAY 21 – JUNE 21 |
| CANCER | ♋ | WATER | JUNE 22 – JULY 22 |
| LEO | ♌ | FIRE | JULY 23 – AUG 22 |
| VIRGO | ♍ | EARTH | AUG 23 – SEP 22 |
| LIBRA | ♎ | AIR | SEP 23 – OCT 22 |
| SCORPIO | ♏ | WATER | OCT 23 – NOV 21 |
| SAGITTARIUS | ♐ | FIRE | NOV 22 – DEC 21 |
| CAPRICORN | ♑ | EARTH | DEC 22 – JAN 19 |
| AQUARIUS | ♒ | AIR | JAN 20 – FEB 18 |
| PISCES | ♓ | WATER | FEB 19 – MAR 20 |

## OTHER ALCHEMICAL SYMBOLS

| | | | | | |
|------|---|-----------|---|----------|---|
| MERCURY | ☿ | BRIMSTONE | 🜍 | HEMATITE | ♀ |
| IRON | ♂ | OIL | 🜆 | NITER | 🜕 |
| EARTH | 🜃 | FIRE | △ | RADIUM | ☢ |
| URANUS | ⛢ | DISSOLVE | 🜄 | YEAST | ♈ |

# INSPECTOR IRRATINO'S
# ASTROLOGICAL PRIMER

# OCCULT MEDIUM

Over the next twenty-five mysteries, Deductive Logico investigated some of the strangest phenomena in all the world, including astrology, alchemy, and aliens. But one thing remained the same: wherever Logico went, murder seemed to follow.

To help untangle the high strangeness of the next twenty-five puzzles, Logico was aided by this Astrological and Alchemical Primer (Exhibit B, seen to the left), which provided him with the key information he needed to solve these often unsettling cases.

Logico didn't believe in the occult, but he also didn't believe in turning down free help, because the mysteries were getting harder, too.

In these mysteries, you must examine the statements of the suspects, in addition to the clues and evidence. This can be rather confusing, but fortunately, you can count on this:

**The murderer will always lie, and the other suspects will always tell the truth.**

Sometimes, you'll be able to spot the lie right away. Other times, you might need to think through the logic of what one person lying would mean. Other times, you may need to test every suspect, to see if it's possible for them to be lying while everyone else is telling the truth.

The one and only liar will always be the murderer.

For those who want it to be even harder, feel free to take the Detective Club's All in the Mind Challenge: try to solve each of the following twenty-five puzzles without using a pencil, working entirely in your head, and without getting a single accusation wrong.

Prior to publication, we couldn't find a single detective who could. Can you?

# 26. THE MURDER OF A MAILMAN 🔍🔍

Deductive Logico went to check his PO box, but instead of finding a royalty check for *Murdle,* he found that a mailman had been killed, and the whole place was closed. Neither rain nor shine, thought Logico, but they close at the first sign of murder . . .

## SUSPECTS

**DR. CRIMSON**

She's the smartest doctor she's ever met, according to her, and she's probably right. Yeah, her diet is horrible, but if she has a heart attack, she'll operate on herself.

**5'9" • LEFT-HANDED • GREEN EYES • RED HAIR • AQUARIUS**

**MAYOR HONEY**

He knows where the bodies are buried, and he makes sure they always vote for him.

**6'0" • LEFT-HANDED • HAZEL EYES • LIGHT BROWN HAIR • SCORPIO**

**GENERAL COFFEE**

An espresso connoisseur who prefers the smell of coffee to napalm in the morning.

**6'0" • RIGHT-HANDED • DARK BROWN EYES • BALD • SAGITTARIUS**

## LOCATIONS

**A MAIL TRUCK**
INDOORS

Practically indestructible, so it's great for joyrides, so long as you're not the one paying for gas.

**THE LONG LINE**
OUTDOORS

People standing in line, waiting to mail their letters.

**THE SORTING ROOM**
INDOORS

Where the postal workers sort the junk mail, bills, and catalogs using a great machine.

## WEAPONS

### A LETTER OPENER
LIGHT-WEIGHT

A sharp knife used by people who won't just rip their letters open.

### A STAMP STAMP
MEDIUM-WEIGHT

A stamp for stamping over stamps.

### A HEAVY PACKAGE
HEAVY-WEIGHT

With a nice red ribbon that'll conceal blood stains.

## CLUES & EVIDENCE

- Letter openers were not allowed in the sorting room, ever since "the Incident," and that rule was not broken today.

- The suspect with the heavy package was self-conscious about their baldness and would prefer it not be mentioned in clues.

## STATEMENTS
(Remember: The murderer is lying. The others are telling the truth.)

**Dr. Crimson:** I brought a stamp stamp.
**Mayor Honey:** Dr. Crimson was not in a mail truck.
**General Coffee:** A letter opener was in a mail truck.

SUSPECTS      LOCATIONS

WHO?

WHAT?

WHERE?

# 27. A MYSTERIOUS MURDER IN THE MYSTERIOUS WOODS

Driving through the mysterious woods gave Deductive Logico the chills, but maybe that was because his AC was on full blast. Pretty soon, he had to pull over, partially to solve the murder of a hitchhiker, and partially because his car died.

## SUSPECTS

**COACH RASPBERRY**

One of the best coaches this side of the Mississippi, regardless of which side you're on.

6'0" • LEFT-HANDED • BLUE EYES • BLOND HAIR • ARIES

**OFFICER COPPER**

The best part of being a policewoman criminal is that you can cut out the middleman and fail to investigate your own crimes.

5'5" • RIGHT-HANDED • BLUE EYES • BLOND HAIR • ARIES

**GRANDMASTER ROSE**

A chess grand master who is always plotting his next move. Like how to bump off his next opponent! (1 . . . e5)

5'7" • LEFT-HANDED • DARK BROWN EYES • DARK BROWN HAIR • SCORPIO

## LOCATIONS

**THE SKULL ROCK**
OUTDOORS

A rock that looks like a skull. Is it natural, or did someone carve it?

**THE ANCIENT RUINS**
OUTDOORS

Wherever these stones appear, you know somebody is getting murdered nearby.

**THE ONLY ROAD**
OUTDOORS

A twisting, winding, half-paved road through the woods.

## WEAPONS

**A SHOVEL**
MEDIUM-WEIGHT

A multi-use tool: kill someone and bury them with the same shovel!

**A RITUAL DAGGER**
MEDIUM-WEIGHT

It's made out of some ancient metal that Logico can't identify.

**A POISONOUS SPIDER**
LIGHT-WEIGHT

Its unusual webbing shows it's not native to these woods.

## CLUES & EVIDENCE

- Logico caught a glimpse of the suspect with the shovel, but all he could see was that his eyes weren't blue.

- A poisonous spider was not on the only road.

## STATEMENTS
(Remember: The murderer is lying. The others are telling the truth.)

**Grandmaster Rose:** You must study the moves of the pieces. For example, Officer Copper was at the skull rock!

**Coach Raspberry:** Well, by golly, a shovel was at the ancient ruins.

**Officer Copper:** My statement? I brought a poisonous spider.

SUSPECTS    LOCATIONS

WEAPONS

LOCATIONS

**WHO?**

**WHAT?**

**WHERE?**

# 28. INVESTIGATION AT THE INVESTIGATION INSTITUTE 🔍🔍

Arriving at the Investigation Institute grounds, Deductive Logico was shocked by their budget. Their grounds had a hedge maze, an observatory, even a miniature golf course! This place could have hired half the detectives in the world. Why him? And who killed the groundskeeper?

## SUSPECTS

**CRYPTOZOOLO-GIST CLOUD**

He knows every sighting of Bigfoot, Yeti, Sasquatch, and also what the difference is.

5'7" • RIGHT-HANDED • GRAY EYES • WHITE HAIR • SCORPIO

**HERBALIST ONYX**

In her greenhouse, she's grown every kind of plant required in the culinary, magick, and poisoning arts.

5'0" • RIGHT-HANDED • DARK BROWN EYES • BLACK HAIR • VIRGO

**CHEF AUBERGINE**

It is said that she once killed her husband, cooked him, and then served him at her restaurant. It's not true, but just the fact that it's said about her tells you something.

5'2" • RIGHT-HANDED • BLUE EYES • BLOND HAIR • LIBRA

## LOCATIONS

**AN IMPOSSIBLE HEDGE MAZE**
OUTDOORS

This was designed by the legendary M. C. Escher, so good luck getting out.

**THE OBSERVATORY**
INDOORS

For studying the stars, or having a romantic evening, or committing a murder.

**THE MINIATURE GOLF COURSE**
OUTDOORS

Eighteen holes, featuring windmills, caves, and loop-de-loops. The works!

## WEAPONS

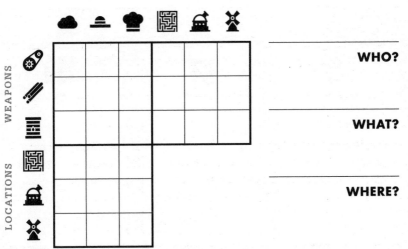

| A QUASI-PER-PETUAL MOTION MACHINE HEAVY-WEIGHT | A DOWSING ROD MEDIUM-WEIGHT | HYPER-ALLERGENIC OIL LIGHT-WEIGHT |
|---|---|---|
| It doesn't run forever. More like two or three minutes. | You can find water, oil, and suckers with this. | You read that right. *Everyone* is deathly allergic to this. |

## CLUES & EVIDENCE

- The second tallest suspect brought hyperallergenic oil.

- It turns out that a Libra was at the seventeenth hole when the murder was committed.

## STATEMENTS
**(Remember: The murderer is lying. The others are telling the truth.)**

**Cryptozoologist Cloud:** A dowsing rod was not in a hedge maze.

**Herbalist Onyx:** A quasi-perpetual motion machine was not in the observatory.

**Chef Aubergine:** Herbalist Onyx brought a quasi-perpetual motion machine.

SUSPECTS        LOCATIONS

WHO?

WHAT?

WHERE?

# 29. OH NO, NOT IN THE CHATEAU! 🔍🔍

"Hello!" Logico called. "I'm here to meet with the president!" Nobody answered, and he looked around. It seemed like the chateau was designed by Escher, too. Stairways and hallways twisted around each other, and every available surface was covered in books. Perhaps the least unexpected sight was the dead body.

## SUSPECTS

**SOCIOLOGIST UMBER**

As a representative from the hard sciences, she is always asking people to question their priors and if they've read Weber.

5'4" • LEFT-HANDED • BLUE EYES • BLOND HAIR • LEO

**PHILOLOGIST FLINT**

You can learn a lot about a word from its etymology, like where it came from, and what it used to mean.

5'2" • LEFT-HANDED • GREEN EYES • BLOND HAIR • AQUARIUS

**NUMEROLOGIST NIGHT**

A mathematical and esoteric prodigy. Not only do they know the value of X, they know the meaning of X.

5'9" • LEFT-HANDED • BLUE EYES • DARK BROWN HAIR • PISCES

## LOCATIONS

**THE FRONT DRIVEWAY**
OUTDOORS

Huge stone statues of various animals line the elegant drive to the chateau.

**THE ARCANE ATTIC**
INDOORS

Rumored to be haunted, guaranteed to contain a bunch of old junk.

**THE BALLROOM**
INDOORS

For grand parties and also basketball games.

## WEAPONS

**A CURSED DAGGER**
MEDIUM-WEIGHT

A dying duchess cursed this dagger when she used it to end her own life.

**A SELENITE WAND**
MEDIUM-WEIGHT

For casting spells and bashing skulls.

**AN EXCLUSIVE PIN**
LIGHT-WEIGHT

If this is pinned to someone's lapel, they're a member of a secret society.

## CLUES & EVIDENCE

- An Aquarius was standing beside a basketball goal.

- Numerologist Night calculated that the selenite wand corresponded to an inauspicious number, so they wouldn't touch it.

## STATEMENTS
(Remember: The murderer is lying. The others are telling the truth.)

**Sociologist Umber:** All I can say is I brought a cursed dagger.

**Philologist Flint:** If you consider the origin of the words, you could say: I was wearing an exclusive pin.

**Numerologist Night:** Based on the numbers, an exclusive pin was in the arcane attic.

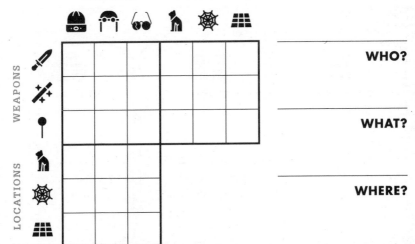

WHO?

WHAT?

WHERE?

# 30. THE CASE OF THE DEFINITELY DEAD PRESIDENT 🔍🔍

Deductive Logico went to the president's office and said, "I'm here to meet with the president." Unfortunately, they said, "The president's dead." But nobody had left the room. So instead of meeting with the president, he worked to solve his murder.

## SUSPECTS

**NUMEROLOGIST NIGHT**

A mathematical and esoteric prodigy. Not only do they know the value of $Z$, they know the meaning of $Z$.

5'9" • LEFT-HANDED • BLUE EYES • DARK BROWN HAIR • PISCES

**HERBALIST ONYX**

In her greenhouse, she's grown every kind of plant required in the culinary, magick, and poisoning arts.

5'0" • RIGHT-HANDED • DARK BROWN EYES • BLACK HAIR • VIRGO

**HIGH ALCHEMIST RAVEN**

There's an old joke that all alchemists are high alchemists. Raven hates it.

5'8" • RIGHT-HANDED • LIGHT BROWN EYES • DARK BROWN HAIR • PISCES

## LOCATIONS

**THE BOOK LADDER**
INDOORS

Climb up and grab a book, or just slide around the room yelling, "Wahoo!"

**THE COUCH**
INDOORS

A faux-leather couch, great for dozing off in the middle of the day.

**THE DESK**
INDOORS

Topped with lots of important paperwork and a computer from the eighties.

## WEAPONS

**A HYPNOTIC POCKET WATCH**
LIGHT-WEIGHT

If you look deeply into this watch, you can tell the time.

**A DECK OF MAROT CARDS**
LIGHT-WEIGHT

You can use these murder-themed tarot cards to tell your fortune.

**A PSEUDO-SCIENTIFIC APPARATUS**
HEAVY-WEIGHT

It measures quantonic currents to evaluate your inner blaxons.

## CLUES & EVIDENCE

- The suspect with the pseudo-scientific apparatus was born on September 7. (See Exhibit B.)

- A careful search revealed a fortune-telling card wedged between two faux-leather seat cushions.

## STATEMENTS
(Remember: The murderer is lying. The others are telling the truth.)

**Numerologist Night:** High Alchemist Raven was behind his desk.
**Herbalist Onyx:** Numerologist Night was on the book ladder.
**High Alchemist Raven:** Alchemically speaking, a pseudo-scientific apparatus was on the book ladder.

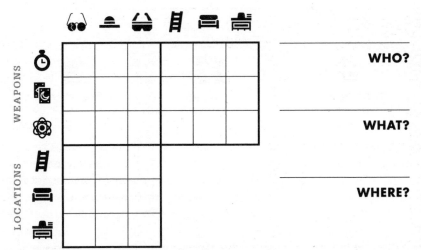

# 31. THE NEW MOON MURDER 🔍🔍

On his first case with the Investigation Institute, they sent Deductive Logico to the darkest woods he'd never seen. From the shadows, he watched a witches' sabbath, thinking he was totally hidden. So he was shocked when three witches stopped the ceremony, walked over to him, and asked him to solve the murder of their sister witch.

## SUSPECTS

**LADY VIOLET**

The heiress of the Violet Isles, the largest extra-judicial territory in the world.

5'0" • RIGHT-HANDED • BLUE EYES • BLOND HAIR • VIRGO

**VICE PRESIDENT MAUVE**

A vice president of TekCo Futures. If she asks you to step into her metaverse, run.

5'8" • RIGHT-HANDED • DARK BROWN EYES • BLACK HAIR • TAURUS

**THE DUCHESS OF VERMILLION**

A tall, old woman with tall, old secrets. If she is the murderer, it certainly wouldn't be the first time.

5'9" • LEFT-HANDED • GRAY EYES • WHITE HAIR • PISCES

## LOCATIONS

**THE CENTRAL FIRE**
OUTDOORS

Scry the pyre fire, friar. Say that three times fast.

**THE ANCIENT RUINS**
OUTDOORS

Covered in moss, but still recognizably those same ruins.

**THE THICK FOREST**
OUTDOORS

The woods are lovely, dark, and deep, but an owl finds it all a hoot.

## WEAPONS

### A CAULDRON
**HEAVY-WEIGHT**

If you can pick it up, you could hit someone with it. Or you can just give them a sip.

### A LOG
**HEAVY-WEIGHT**

A big, heavy oak log. Somebody killed the tree so that the tree could kill somebody.

### A BROOM
**MEDIUM-WEIGHT**

People say that witches fly on these, but Logico's only swept with them.

## CLUES & EVIDENCE

- A Virgo was standing beneath an owl, probably organizing something, because that's how they are.

- Surprisingly, a cauldron was not in the central fire.

## STATEMENTS
(Remember: The murderer is lying. The others are telling the truth.)

**Lady Violet:** Don't believe the commoners: the Duchess of Vermillion brought a broom.

**Vice President Mauve:** Well, I didn't bring a broom.

**The Duchess of Vermillion:** And I didn't bring a log.

SUSPECTS     LOCATIONS

WEAPONS

LOCATIONS

**WHO?**

**WHAT?**

**WHERE?**

# 32. THE CASE OF THE LAB WITH LEGAL ISSUES 🔍🔍

Next, the Investigation Institute sent Deductive Logico to a literal mad scientist's laboratory. To clarify, the scientist wasn't crazy: he was furious. His assistant had been killed, and his research had stalled.

## SUSPECTS

**VICE PRESIDENT MAUVE**

A vice president of TekCo Futures. If she asks you to step into her metaverse, get out now!

5'8" • RIGHT-HANDED • DARK BROWN EYES • BLACK HAIR • TAURUS

**PRINCIPAL APPLEGREEN**

A strict principal about everything except getting away with murder. His hands are always covered in chalk.

5'11" • RIGHT-HANDED • BLUE EYES • BLOND HAIR • LIBRA

**CAPTAIN SLATE**

A real-life astronaut. The first woman to travel around the dark side of the moon, and also the first to be suspected of murdering her copilot.

5'5" • LEFT-HANDED • DARK BROWN EYES • DARK BROWN HAIR • AQUARIUS

## LOCATIONS

**THE ROOFTOP**
OUTDOORS

A giant lightning rod is connected to millions of loose wires.

**THE GIANT LEVER**
INDOORS

All mad scientist laboratories have a giant lever you can flip from "OFF" to "ON."

**THE OPERATING TABLE**
INDOORS

Leather straps could restrain a person here, or a monster.

## WEAPONS

|  A BRAIN IN A JAR **HEAVY-WEIGHT** |  A GIANT MAGNET **MEDIUM-WEIGHT** |  A SOUP LADLE LIGHT-WEIGHT |
|---|---|---|
| The worst part is, it's oozing everywhere. | Keep it away from any fillings. It generates a powerful electromagnetic field. | Even a mad scientist loves soup. Particularly tomato bisque. |

## CLUES & EVIDENCE

- The shortest suspect was seen hanging around beneath a sign that says "OFF."

- Vice President Mauve never got near the operating table.

## STATEMENTS
(Remember: The murderer is lying. The others are telling the truth.)

**Vice President Mauve:** Captain Slate brought a giant magnet.
**Principal Applegreen:** A brain in a jar was not on the rooftop.
**Captain Slate:** It's as clear as the moon: Principal Applegreen brought a brain in a jar.

SUSPECTS  LOCATIONS

WHO?

WHAT?

WHERE?

# 33. A RECENT DEATH IN AN ANCIENT TEMPLE 🔍🔍

The Investigation Institute had been funding the excavation of an ancient temple, but while they were working on the project, one of the archeologists was killed—was it by ancient magick? They insisted Inspector Irratino accompany Logico, to make sure that magick got a fair shake.

## SUSPECTS

**INSPECTOR IRRATINO**

An esoteric detective. While Logico believes only what he can prove, Irratino believes only what he can't.

6'2" • LEFT-HANDED • GREEN EYES • DARK BROWN HAIR • AQUARIUS

**BISHOP AZURE**

A bishop in a local church, Azure has been known to pray for both her friends and her enemies. Of course, she asks for different things . . .

5'4" • RIGHT-HANDED • LIGHT BROWN EYES • DARK BROWN HAIR • GEMINI

**CHANCELLOR TUSCANY**

As the head of Deduction College, she has deduced the best way to get the most money from alumni. (Blackmail.)

5'5" • LEFT-HANDED • GREEN EYES • GRAY HAIR • LIBRA

## LOCATIONS

**THE GRAND ENTRANCE**
OUTDOORS

Thanks to the ravages of time, now more of a crumbling entrance.

**THE SACRED CHAMBER**
INDOORS

Who knows what happened in here behind these heavy iron doors?

**THE HIGH ALTAR**
INDOORS

A massive stone altar draped in rotting fabric.

## WEAPONS

**A CRYSTAL SKULL**
MEDIUM-WEIGHT

Made entirely of crystal. Maybe an ancient alien skull or maybe just a fun art project.

**A SKELETON ARM**
MEDIUM-WEIGHT

Cause the death of a person with the bones of a person who's dead.

**A RITUAL DAGGER**
MEDIUM-WEIGHT

It's made out of some ancient metal that Logico can't identify.

## CLUES & EVIDENCE

- Chancellor Tuscany did not trust the person who had the crystal skull.

- Logico discovered a splintered piece of bone outdoors, using the principle of rationality. (He tripped over it.)

## STATEMENTS
(Remember: The murderer is lying. The others are telling the truth.)

**Inspector Irratino:** A ritual dagger was at the high altar.
**Bishop Azure:** I brought a ritual dagger.
**Chancellor Tuscany:** Bishop Azure was not in the sacred chamber.

WHO?

WHAT?

WHERE?

# 34. THE BODY IN THE GRAVEYARD 🔍🔍

Next, Inspector Irratino wanted to go to a graveyard. So he used astrology to determine which graveyard they should visit, a method Deductive Logico detested.

There When they got to the graveyard, the caretaker had just been killed. Inspector Irratino elbowed Deductive Logico. "See!"

## SUSPECTS

**SIR RULEAN**

A sophisticated gentleman who was just recently knighted, if you believe the shoddy paperwork he carries with him.

**5'8" • RIGHT-HANDED • BLUE EYES • RED HAIR • LEO**

**VISCOUNT EMINENCE**

The oldest man you have ever seen. It is said that he was old when the old were young.

**5'2" • LEFT-HANDED • BLACK EYES • BLACK HAIR • PISCES**

**BROTHER BROWNSTONE**

A monk who has dedicated his life to the church, specifically to making money for it.

**5'4" • LEFT-HANDED • DARK BROWN EYES • DARK BROWN HAIR • CAPRICORN**

## LOCATIONS

**THE COLUMBARIUM**
INDOORS

A vault or wall where ashes are stored. (Now you've learned a new word.)

**THE HUGE MAUSOLEUM**
INDOORS

The rich members of the Midnight family are all buried in this pyramid-shaped tomb.

**THE GIFT SHOP**
INDOORS

You can buy little knickknack gravestones or a plushie of their mascot, Mr. Skull.

## WEAPONS

**A SKELETON ARM**
MEDIUM-WEIGHT

Cause the death of a person with the bones of a person who's dead.

**A VIAL OF A DEADLY POISON**
LIGHT-WEIGHT

Don't worry. It's safely contained by—hey, wait, where's the cork?!

**A STRING OF PRAYER BEADS**
MEDIUM-WEIGHT

Ivory prayer beads covered with tiny engraved symbols.

## CLUES & EVIDENCE

- Deductive Logico's forensics team discovered a drop of poison in a giant pyramid.

- Inspector Irratino found a finger bone in the columbarium. A telltale sign!

## STATEMENTS
(Remember: The murderer is lying. The others are telling the truth.)

**Sir Rulean:** I brought a string of prayer beads.
**Viscount Eminence:** Yes, well, I brought a skeleton arm.
**Brother Brownstone:** On the honor of my order, I was not in the gift shop.

| | SUSPECTS | | | LOCATIONS | | |
|---|---|---|---|---|---|---|
| WEAPONS | | | | | | | WHO? |
| | | | | | | | |
| | | | | | | | WHAT? |
| LOCATIONS | | | | | | | |
| | | | | | | | WHERE? |
| | | | | | | | |

# 35. MURDER AT THE CULT: A TRUE-CRIME DOCUMENTARY 🔍🔍

Inspector Irratino and Deductive Logico took the train upstate to a commune that Irratino had read about in a zine. When they got there, they discovered it was a leaderless society, but only because their supreme leader had just been murdered.

## SUSPECTS

**ASSISTANT APPLEGREEN**

She dropped out of the publishing game and moved to this commune. Her father is currently not proud.

5'3" • LEFT-HANDED • BLUE EYES • BLOND HAIR • VIRGO

**PHILOLOGIST FLINT**

You can learn a lot about a word from its etymology, like where it came from, and have you heard this before?

5'2" • LEFT-HANDED • GREEN EYES • BLOND HAIR • AQUARIUS

**NUMEROLOGIST NIGHT**

A mathematical and esoteric prodigy. Not only do they know the value of $E$, they know the meaning of $E$.

5'9" • LEFT-HANDED • BLUE EYES • DARK BROWN HAIR • PISCES

## LOCATIONS

**THE BARRACKS**
INDOORS

Where everyone sleeps except their leader. (Their leader never sleeps.)

**THE LIBRARY**
INDOORS

More books than you've ever seen. (But all by one guy.)

**THE ANCIENT RUINS**
INDOORS

They seem to hypnotize you. You get woozy around them.

## WEAPONS

**A SELENITE WAND**
MEDIUM-WEIGHT

For casting spells and bashing skulls.

**A SOUP LADLE**
LIGHT-WEIGHT

For serving soup at the commune.

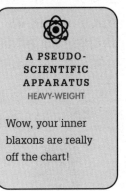

**A PSEUDO-SCIENTIFIC APPARATUS**
HEAVY-WEIGHT

Wow, your inner blaxons are really off the chart!

## CLUES & EVIDENCE

- The tallest suspect could not have fit in the library: it had low ceilings.

- Whoever was in the barracks had green eyes.

## STATEMENTS
(Remember: The murderer is lying. The others are telling the truth.)

**Assistant Applegreen:** I did not bring a selenite wand.

**Philologist Flint:** A pseudo-scientific apparatus was not by the ancient ruins.

**Numerologist Night:** Based on the numbers, I brought a selenite wand.

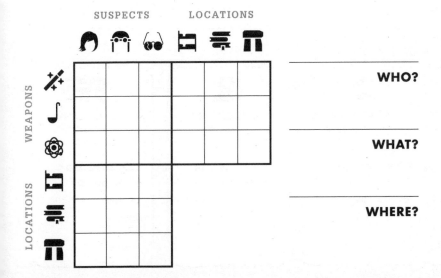

# 36. A CRUISE TO DIE FOR 🔍🔍

Deductive Logico was excited they were taking a cruise, but it turned out it was on a cargo ship in the Bermuda Triangle. When the first mate died, Irratino was ecstatic. Finally, proof of the paranormal!

## SUSPECTS

**MX. TANGERINE**

Proving that non-binary people can be murderers, too, they are an artist, poet, and suspect.

5'5" • LEFT-HANDED • HAZEL EYES • BLOND HAIR • PISCES

**ADMIRAL NAVY**

The firstborn son of an Admiral Navy who himself was the firstborn son of an Admiral Navy.

5'9" • RIGHT-HANDED • BLUE EYES • LIGHT BROWN HAIR • CANCER

**CAPTAIN SLATE**

A real-life astronaut. The first woman to travel around the dark side of the moon, and also the first to be suspected of murdering her copilot.

5'5" • LEFT-HANDED • DARK BROWN EYES • DARK BROWN HAIR • AQUARIUS

## LOCATIONS

**THE CAPTAIN'S QUARTERS**
INDOORS

Covered in posters of the captain's favorite waves.

**THE CARGO HOLD**
INDOORS

Millions of pounds of cargo, mostly cheap electronics and fast fashion.

**OVERBOARD**
OUTDOORS

Here you might get murdered by the sharks, too.

## WEAPONS

**POISONED RUM**
MEDIUM-WEIGHT

Yo ho ho and a bottle of arsenic.

**A SAILOR'S
ROPE**
MEDIUM-WEIGHT

Fraying into little white fibers.

**A FLARE**
LIGHT-WEIGHT

You could shoot a flare into the sky or into somebody's head.

## CLUES & EVIDENCE

- Much to his embarrassment, Admiral Navy had to call for help when he went overboard.

- The other person just as tall as Mx. Tangerine was seen playing with a flare.

## STATEMENTS
(Remember: The murderer is lying. The others are telling the truth.)

**Mx. Tangerine:** I was not in the cargo hold.
**Admiral Navy:** A sailor's rope was in the captain's quarters.
**Captain Slate:** What do you want me to say? I was in the captain's quarters.

SUSPECTS     LOCATIONS

WHO?

WHAT?

WHERE?

WEAPONS

LOCATIONS

# 37. LOGICO GOES HOME 🔍🔍

Deductive Logico got a call from his aunt: an uncle had died, and they had to figure out how to cover all of the funeral expenses. Also, someone had to solve his murder. So, for the first time in years, Deductive Logico went home. Thankfully, Irratino came with him, too.

## SUSPECTS

**FATHER MANGO**

He has taken a vow of poverty, but he drives a BMW. He's taken a vow of obedience, but he has a staff of twenty-five. He's taken a vow of chastity, too, which is why he's on vacation.

5'10" • LEFT-HANDED • DARK BROWN EYES • BALD • TAURUS

**MAYOR HONEY**

This is not the same mayor from Logico's first case: this is his totally innocent identical twin.

6'0" • LEFT-HANDED • HAZEL EYES • LIGHT BROWN HAIR • SCORPIO

**OFFICER COPPER**

The best part of being a policewoman criminal is that you can cut out the middleman and fail to investigate your own crimes.

5'5" • RIGHT-HANDED • BLUE EYES • BLOND HAIR • ARIES

## LOCATIONS

**A CHAIN RESTAURANT**
INDOORS

This opened up when the family diner couldn't afford their mortgage. They have a fried onion.

**A SECONDHAND SHOP**
INDOORS

Most of the stuff in here looks third-hand, even the moths.

**A USED CAR LOT**
OUTDOORS

The salesman tells you the cars will not explode, and that they're sold as is.

## WEAPONS

**AN OLD SWORD**
HEAVY-WEIGHT

This was used by the bad guys in some old war. It's all rusted.

**AN AXE**
MEDIUM-WEIGHT

A murder-mystery classic for a reason.

**A MAGNIFYING GLASS**
MEDIUM-WEIGHT

You could use this to find a clue or to read really small print.

## CLUES & EVIDENCE

- The suspect with the magnifying glass was seen examining their bald head with it.

- Officer Copper never set foot in a chain restaurant: they didn't give her discounts.

## STATEMENTS
(Remember: The murderer is lying. The others are telling the truth.)

**Father Mango:** Mayor Honey did not bring an axe.
**Mayor Honey:** An old sword was in a chain restaurant.
**Officer Copper:** An old sword was not in a used car lot.

SUSPECTS    LOCATIONS

WHO?

WHAT?

WHERE?

# 38. IRRATINO RETURNS TO HIS ESTATE 🔍🔍

While they were in Deductive Logico's hometown, Irratino had received a fax from his own. He needed to come right away—one of his (many) uncles had died. He had been murdered, and they needed to figure out whodunit to settle the will.

## SUSPECTS

**BROTHER BROWNSTONE**

A monk who has dedicated his life to the church, specifically to making money for it.

5'4" • LEFT-HANDED • DARK BROWN EYES • DARK BROWN HAIR • CAPRICORN

**THE DUKE OF VERMILLION**

Like his wife, he is full of secrets. Even some secrets from his wife.

5'9" • LEFT-HANDED • GRAY EYES • WHITE HAIR • PISCES

**ASTROLOGER AZURE**

A stargazer, full of wonder and questions about the exact time and place of your birth.

5'6" • RIGHT-HANDED • HAZEL EYES • LIGHT BROWN HAIR • CANCER

## LOCATIONS

**THE GROUNDS**
OUTDOORS

The grass is long, thick, and well-kempt, like Irratino's hair.

**THE FIFTY-CAR GARAGE**
INDOORS

Irratino's great-grandfather stored his show ponies here. Now they can only afford classic cars.

**THE ENORMOUS BEDROOM**
INDOORS

This bedroom is bigger than Logico's apartment building.

## WEAPONS

**A OUIJA BOARD**
LIGHT-WEIGHT

The most powerful magick artifact you can buy at the toy store.

**A CRYSTAL DAGGER**
MEDIUM-WEIGHT

It might have some kind of ritual purpose, but it might just look great on your mantle.

**A HEAVY CODEBOOK**
HEAVY-WEIGHT

Filled with keywords and ciphers, you can use it to crack codes or skulls.

## CLUES & EVIDENCE

- The suspect in the fifty-car garage did not have the crystal dagger.
- A Capricorn had a ouija board. (Capricorns are like that.)

## STATEMENTS
(Remember: The murderer is lying. The others are telling the truth.)

**Brother Brownstone:** In the name of God, the Duke of Vermillion brought a heavy codebook.

**The Duke of Vermillion:** Astrologer Azure was not in the grounds.

**Astrologer Azure:** Look at the stars! They say a heavy codebook was in the grounds.

WHO?

WHAT?

WHERE?

# 39. THE CASE OF THE HAUNTED HOTEL 🔍🔍

Deductive Logico and Inspector Irratino tried to check in to a hotel they had heard was haunted. But when they got there, it was a perfectly lovely hotel, albeit a bit old-fashioned. There was only one problem: the housekeeper had been murdered.

## SUSPECTS

**LORD LAVENDER**

A politically conservative MP in the House of Lords, as well as the musical theater composer behind such hits as *Good Stepsisters* and *Sunrise Ave.*

5'9" • RIGHT-HANDED • GREEN EYES • BLOND HAIR • VIRGO

**MISS SAFFRON**

Gorgeous and stunning, but maybe not all there in the brains department. Or maybe that's what she wants you to think. Or maybe she wants you to think that's what she wants you to think.

5'2" • LEFT-HANDED • HAZEL EYES • BLOND HAIR • LIBRA

**LADY VIOLET**

The heiress of the Violet Isles, the largest extra-judicial territory in the world.

5'0" • RIGHT-HANDED • BLUE EYES • BLOND HAIR • VIRGO

## LOCATIONS

**THE GRAND ENTRANCE**
INDOORS

There's a guest book with many people checking in, but none checking out.

**THE BOILER ROOM**
INDOORS

Supposedly the most haunted room. Definitely the room with the highest CO levels.

**THE BALLROOM**
INDOORS

Tons of beautiful couples, dancing to classical jazz.

## WEAPONS

**A POISONED MUFFIN**
LIGHT-WEIGHT

Not only poisoned, but rock hard. So you could use it two ways.

**A LAUNDRY BAG FILLED WITH KNIVES**
HEAVY-WEIGHT

Sometimes you gotta clean your knives.

**A GOLDEN PEN**
MEDIUM-WEIGHT

A solid gold pen (including the ink). It costs more than a house.

## CLUES & EVIDENCE

- The suspect with the laundry bag filled with knives was born on October 13. (See Exhibit B.)

- The tallest suspect was seen uttering some kind of incantation in the boiler room.

## STATEMENTS
**(Remember: The murderer is lying. The others are telling the truth.)**

**Lord Lavender:** Lady Violet was not in the grand entrance.

**Miss Saffron:** I'm not sure if this means anything, but a poisoned muffin was in the ballroom.

**Lady Violet:** As a lady, I'll say this: a golden pen was in the grand entrance.

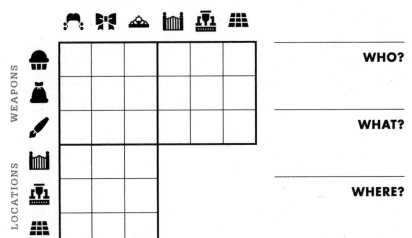

# 40. THE BIG-MONEY BIG-BANK MURDER 🔍🔍

"Follow the money!" Inspector Irratino said as he led Deductive Logico to the biggest bank he'd ever seen. "Wherever there's money, there's murder."

The teller's body attested to the truth of that.

## SUSPECTS

**THE DUKE OF VERMILLION**

He's learning that his wife has secrets, too, because his money is missing.

5'9" • LEFT-HANDED • GRAY EYES • WHITE HAIR • PISCES

**SIGNOR EMERALD**

An Italian jeweler of great renown, Signor Emerald has traveled the world in search of rare, precious stones, which are always falling out of his pockets.

5'8" • LEFT-HANDED • LIGHT BROWN EYES • BLACK HAIR • SAGITTARIUS

**VISCOUNT EMINENCE**

The oldest man you have ever seen. It is said that he remembers what everyone else has forgotten.

5'2" • LEFT-HANDED • BLACK EYES • BLACK HAIR • PISCES

## LOCATIONS

**THE CLOCK ROOM**
INDOORS

Cogs and gears and brass that operate the outdoor clock. Explore at your own risk!

**THE BACK ROOM**
INDOORS

There's a printing press back here, and the money looks funny. Franklin has a mustache.

**THE VAULT**
INDOORS

Safe-deposit boxes full of cash money, gold, and secrets.

## WEAPONS

**A LAPTOP**
MEDIUM-WEIGHT

The machine you work on. It's connected to every distraction ever made.

**A GLOBE**
HEAVY-WEIGHT

For plotting world domination or storing drinks.

**LEATHER GLOVES**
LIGHT-WEIGHT

Beware someone who wears leather gloves. They've already killed a cow: who's next?!

## CLUES & EVIDENCE

- A cowhide glove was discovered in the vault.

- A Sagittarius was in the clock room.

## STATEMENTS
(Remember: The murderer is lying. The others are telling the truth.)

**The Duke of Vermillion:** I was in the back room.
**Signor Emerald:** I promise you this: a globe was in the back room.
**Viscount Eminence:** Outrageous! I did not bring a globe!

SUSPECTS       LOCATIONS

WHO?

WHAT?

WHERE?

# 41. THE PSYCHIC WHO DIDN'T FORESEE HIS DEATH

"The Institute has seen some promising data out of the PRL," Irratino said, using an acronym Logico didn't recognize. "If they can prove this psychic is real, we're going to give them one million dollars." Unfortunately, all they could prove was that their psychic was dead.

## SUSPECTS

**THE AMAZING AUREOLIN**

Currently in a prisoners-in-the-arts program where they allow incarcerated magicians to evaluate self-proclaimed psychics.

5'6" • LEFT-HANDED • GREEN EYES • BLOND HAIR • ARIES

**DR. CRIMSON**

She's the smartest doctor she's ever met, according to her, and she's probably right. Yeah, she flies single-engine planes, but if she crashes, she'll set her own bones.

5'9" • LEFT-HANDED • GREEN EYES • RED HAIR • AQUARIUS

**THE DUCHESS OF VERMILLION**

A tall, old woman with tall, old secrets. Like how much money she's given the PRL.

5'9" • LEFT-HANDED • GRAY EYES • WHITE HAIR • PISCES

## LOCATIONS

**THE GROUNDS**
OUTDOORS

Filled with holes as a result of dowsing experiments.

**THE ROOF**
OUTDOORS

Where they've done successful experiments with astral projection and failed ones with actual levitation.

**THE ISOLATION CHAMBER**
INDOORS

A water tank in a dark room. In it, you can regress in time or just be really bored.

## WEAPONS

**A QUASI-PER-
PETUAL MOTION
MACHINE**
HEAVY-WEIGHT

It doesn't run for-
ever. This one's re-
cord is two hours.

**A DOWSING
ROD**
MEDIUM-WEIGHT

You can find water,
oil, and suckers
with this.

**A CRYSTAL
BALL**
HEAVY-WEIGHT

If you look into it, it
will tell you your fu-
ture, so long as your
future is a crystal
ball.

## CLUES & EVIDENCE

- A quasi-perpetual motion machine was discovered inside a freshly dug hole.

- The suspect with the dowsing rod was born on February 1. (See Exhibit B.)

## STATEMENTS
(Remember: The murderer is lying. The others are telling the truth.)

**The Amazing Aureolin:** Magician's code: I did not bring a crystal ball.
**Dr. Crimson:** Trust me: the Amazing Aureolin was standing on the roof.
**The Duchess of Vermillion:** I was relaxing in the isolation chamber.

SUSPECTS          LOCATIONS

WHO?

WHAT?

WHERE?

# 42. THE RETURN OF THE COFFEE SHOP KILLER 🔍🔍

Deductive Logico told Inspector Irratino that he knew of a place where there were numerous occult phenomena, and he took him to a coffee shop. But the moment they got there, they found the barista was dead.

## SUSPECTS

**SISTER LAPIS**

A nun who travels the world, doing God's work on His dime. Her habit is cashmere, and her habit is spending.

**5'2" • RIGHT-HANDED • LIGHT BROWN EYES • LIGHT BROWN HAIR • CANCER**

**GRANDMASTER ROSE**

A chess grand master who is always plotting his next move. Like what kind of latte to get. (2. Qh5)

**5'7" • LEFT-HANDED • DARK BROWN EYES • DARK BROWN HAIR • SCORPIO**

**GENERAL COFFEE**

An espresso connoisseur who has murdered several people but is still allowed to visit this coffee shop because of how well he tips. (A lesson!)

**6'0" • RIGHT-HANDED • DARK BROWN EYES • BALD • SAGITTARIUS**

## LOCATIONS

**THE PARKING LOT**
OUTDOORS

There's no drive-thru, because this is a fancy coffee shop. People have to get out of their cars to drink coffee.

**THE BATHROOM**
INDOORS

It's a coffee shop. So obviously, it's going to have a bathroom. This one is always out of paper towels.

**THE COURTYARD**
OUTDOORS

Sun-dappled tables and chairs sit beneath a magnificent oak. A great place for conversation . . . or murder.

## WEAPONS

**A BUTTER KNIFE**
LIGHT-WEIGHT

An embarrassing way to be killed, honestly.

**A METAL STRAW**
LIGHT-WEIGHT

Better for the planet than a plastic straw, but more deadly!

**A BOILING POT**
HEAVY-WEIGHT

Hot and heavy! For murderers, that's called a double feature.

## CLUES & EVIDENCE

- The suspect who tips well was sitting in the courtyard.

- The tallest suspect was suspicious of the person who had the butter knife.

## STATEMENTS
(Remember: The murderer is lying. The others are telling the truth.)

**Sister Lapis:** Grandmaster Rose was not in the parking lot.
**Grandmaster Rose:** A metal straw was in the bathroom.
**General Coffee:** Hmm . . . a butter knife was in the courtyard.

|  | SUSPECTS | | | LOCATIONS | | |
|---|---|---|---|---|---|---|
| WEAPONS 🔪 |  |  |  |  |  |  |
| 🥤 |  |  |  |  |  |  |
| 🍲 |  |  |  |  |  |  |
| LOCATIONS 🏢 |  |  |  |  |  |  |
| 🚽 |  |  |  |  |  |  |
| 🌳 |  |  |  |  |  |  |

**WHO?**

**WHAT?**

**WHERE?**

# 43. THE HEINOUS CRIME OF PENGUICIDE 🔍🔍

Deductive Logico found Inspector Irratino weeping, and he asked him what was wrong. "An endangered penguin was killed!" bawled the inspector.

Logico grabbed his shoulder and said, "We're going to solve his murder."

## SUSPECTS

**CHANCELLOR TUSCANY**

As the head of Deduction College, she is respected for her power, her knowledge, and the fact that she's never been caught.

5'5" • LEFT-HANDED • GREEN EYES • GRAY HAIR • LIBRA

**THE DUCHESS OF VERMILLION**

A tall, old woman with tall, old secrets. How many times am I going to tell you this?

5'9" • LEFT-HANDED • GRAY EYES • WHITE HAIR • PISCES

**MX. TANGERINE**

Proving that non-binary people can be murderers, too: they are a scientist, skier, and suspect.

5'5" • LEFT-HANDED • HAZEL EYES • BLOND HAIR • PISCES

## LOCATIONS

**THE PING-PONG ROOM**
INDOORS

For letting off steam, or (perhaps more aptly) for breaking the ice. There are snacks!

**THE FROZEN WASTELANDS**
OUTDOORS

A vast, unforgiving wilderness, but at least you can get some alone time.

**THE BARRACKS**
INDOORS

Where everybody sleeps under incredibly cozy blankets.

## WEAPONS

### POISONED HOT CHOCOLATE
LIGHT-WEIGHT

Drink up, and it's the last warm tummy you'll ever have.

### AN ICE AXE
MEDIUM-WEIGHT

For climbing and killing and anything else where you need to make a small hole.

### AN ICICLE DAGGER
LIGHT-WEIGHT

The perfect weapon. You stab someone and only leave a puddle behind.

## CLUES & EVIDENCE

- The suspect in the frozen wastelands had white hair.

- The scientist/skier/suspect did not bring an icicle dagger.

## STATEMENTS
(Remember: The murderer is lying. The others are telling the truth.)

**Chancellor Tuscany:** As the holder of seven PhDs, let me just say: I was in the ping-pong room.

**The Duchess of Vermillion:** Do you want to know what I think? Chancellor Tuscany brought poisoned hot chocolate.

**Mx. Tangerine:** If I had to say something, an ice axe was in the barracks.

|  | SUSPECTS | | | LOCATIONS | | |
|---|---|---|---|---|---|---|
| WEAPONS | | | | | | |
| ☕ | | | | | | |
| ⛏ | | | | | | |
| 🔻 | | | | | | |
| 🏓 | | | | | | |
| ❄ | | | | | | |
| 🏳 | | | | | | |

**WHO?**

**WHAT?**

**WHERE?**

# 44. MURDER ON THE STAGE 🔍🔍

Deductive Logico and Inspector Irratino saw a play in a theater in the woods, and Logico was surprised to discover it was an interactive, immersive whodunit, until he was informed that it was actually a crime scene. The director had been killed.

## SUSPECTS

**EARL GREY**

He comes from a long line of Earl Greys. Yes, of the tea. No, he doesn't sign autographs. But he'll give you a free bag if you ask.

5'9" • RIGHT-HANDED • LIGHT BROWN EYES • WHITE HAIR • CAPRICORN

**SISTER LAPIS**

A nun who travels the world, doing God's work on His dime. Her habit is cashmere, and her habit is spending.

5'2" • RIGHT-HANDED • LIGHT BROWN EYES • LIGHT BROWN HAIR • CANCER

**JUDGE PINE**

Master of the courtroom and possessed of a firm belief in justice, as decided by her alone.

5'6" • RIGHT-HANDED • DARK BROWN EYES • BLACK HAIR • TAURUS

## LOCATIONS

**THE STAGE**
OUTDOORS

Made from wood from the surrounding trees, now in plank form.

**THE FRONT TREE**
OUTDOORS

Like the front desk, but a tree. It's decorated so you know where to check in.

**THE BACKSTAGE WOODS**
OUTDOORS

Dark and spooky and perfect for surprise entrances.

## WEAPONS

### A TOXIC PROGRAM
LIGHT-WEIGHT

Not only are the bios toxic, but the ink is, too.

### POISONED POPCORN
MEDIUM-WEIGHT

Freshly popped and freshly poisoned, too. Almond flavored!

### A STAGE SWORD
MEDIUM-WEIGHT

It's dulled a little for the safety of the performers. But not enough . . .

## CLUES & EVIDENCE

- Earl Grey was terrified of the dark, so he would never go in the back-stage woods.

- A Taurus had the weapon that was poorly dulled.

## STATEMENTS
(Remember: The murderer is lying. The others are telling the truth.)

**Earl Grey:** Take my word as the honorable Earl of Grey: poisoned popcorn was by the front tree.

**Sister Lapis:** A toxic program was on the stage.

**Judge Pine:** All I know is that Sister Lapis was on the stage.

# 45. FADE IN TO A MURDER MYSTERY 🔍🔍

After Deductive Logico requested no more live theater, Inspector Irratino took him to see a murder-mystery movie at a supposedly haunted drive-in theater. But as far as Logico could tell, it was a perfectly normal drive-in theater. There had to be something spooky about it. Maybe it was the fact that the ticket taker had been killed.

## SUSPECTS

**EDITOR IVORY**

The greatest romance editor of all time. She invented the enemies-to-lovers genre, and she was the first person to put a naked man on the cover of a book.

5'6" • LEFT-HANDED • LIGHT BROWN EYES • GRAY HAIR • SCORPIO

**SUPERFAN SMOKY**

He knows the shooting locations of every Midnight mystery, but not how to make friends.

5'10" • LEFT-HANDED • DARK BROWN EYES • BLACK HAIR • VIRGO

**SILVERTON THE LEGEND**

An acclaimed actor of the Golden Age, now in his golden years.

6'4" • RIGHT-HANDED • BLUE EYES • SILVER HAIR • LEO

## LOCATIONS

**THE SCREEN**
OUTDOORS

If you don't like the movie, turn on your lights and it'll get washed out.

**THE CONCESSION STAND**
OUTDOORS

You can get all the regular stuff: soda, cabbage, a raw egg. Whatever!

**THE BOX OFFICE**
OUTDOORS

It's a drive-thru. They charge per car, so a lot of clowns come.

## WEAPONS

**A SPARE TIRE**
HEAVY-WEIGHT

Where the rubber meets your head!

**A SHOVEL**
MEDIUM-WEIGHT

A multi-use tool: kill someone and bury them with the same shovel!

**POISONED POPCORN**
MEDIUM-WEIGHT

Freshly popped and freshly poisoned, too. Almond flavored!

## CLUES & EVIDENCE

- A heavy-weight weapon was left at the drive-thru.
- Superfan Smoky used to stalk the person who brought poisoned popcorn.

## STATEMENTS
(Remember: The murderer is lying. The others are telling the truth.)

**Editor Ivory:** Well, Silverton the Legend brought a shovel.
**Superfan Smoky:** Oh, wow! Editor Ivory was in the concession stand.
**Silverton the Legend:** Let me tell you how it is: I was by the screen.

SUSPECTS        LOCATIONS

WEAPONS

LOCATIONS

**WHO?**

**WHAT?**

**WHERE?**

# 46. A CRUISE TO DIE FOR 2 🔍🔍

Inspector Irratino had the Institute's (new) numerologist run the numbers, and she found it was cheaper to take an all-expenses-paid cruise than it was to keep flying everywhere. And so, finally, Irratino took Deductive Logico on that cruise. Their favorite memory was when they solved the murder of the first mate.

## SUSPECTS

**ADMIRAL NAVY**

The firstborn son of an Admiral Navy who himself was the firstborn son of an Admiral Navy.

5'9" • RIGHT-HANDED • BLUE EYES • LIGHT BROWN HAIR • CANCER

**VICE PRESIDENT MAUVE**

A vice president of TekCo Futures. If she asks you to step into her metaverse—my God! Get out now!

5'8" • RIGHT-HANDED • DARK BROWN EYES • BLACK HAIR • TAURUS

**PRINCIPAL APPLEGREEN**

His daughter quit her high-paying job in publishing and moved to a commune, so you could say he's taking this cruise to relax.

5'11" • RIGHT-HANDED • BLUE EYES • BLOND HAIR • LIBRA

## LOCATIONS

**THE DECK**
OUTDOORS

You can play cribbage up here, but nobody seems to know what cribbage is, exactly.

**THE DINING HALL**
INDOORS

Probably the best dining hall anywhere in the entire boat.

**THE CAPTAIN'S QUARTERS**
INDOORS

The captain keeps his door locked shut so that nobody else sees how much space he has.

## WEAPONS

**A TOXIC BLOWFISH**
LIGHT-WEIGHT

Prepared carefully, it's safe to eat. Prepared even more carefully, it can kill.

**A FISHING SPEAR**
MEDIUM-WEIGHT

Tourists can pay to have the fish pre-attached to the end.

**THE STEERING WHEEL**
MEDIUM-WEIGHT

The worst part of using this to kill is that now the boat will crash.

## CLUES & EVIDENCE

- The Investigation Institute was able to transmit a message to Irratino about the case (See Exhibit B): ♉ ♒ ♓ ♐ ♓ ♏ ☿ ♈ ♅ ♐ ♓ ♄ ♒ ♐
- No toxic blowfishes were permitted in the dining hall.

## STATEMENTS
(Remember: The murderer is lying. The others are telling the truth.)

**Admiral Navy:** Principal Applegreen was on the deck.
**Vice President Mauve:** Admiral Navy brought the steering wheel.
**Principal Applegreen:** The steering wheel was in the captain's quarters.

SUSPECTS    LOCATIONS

WEAPONS

LOCATIONS

**WHO?**

**WHAT?**

**WHERE?**

# 47. THE MYSTERY OF THE MYSTERIOUS ISLAND 🔍🔍

The ship had crashed on an island filled with mysteries, like why was the lighthouse not lit, and what was the point of having a lighthouse if you weren't going to light it, and who just screamed, and who killed the captain?

## SUSPECTS

**MX. TANGERINE**

Proving that non-binary people can be murderers, too: they are a sailor, chef, and suspect.

5'5" • LEFT-HANDED • HAZEL EYES • BLOND HAIR • PISCES

**BARON MAROON**

An incredibly haughty man who holds a grudge. Nobody wants to offend the baron. At least, nobody who's still alive . . .

6'2" • RIGHT-HANDED • HAZEL EYES • RED HAIR • SCORPIO

**ASTROLOGER AZURE**

A stargazer, full of wonder and questions about the exact time and place of your birth.

5'6" • RIGHT-HANDED • HAZEL EYES • LIGHT BROWN HAIR • CANCER

## LOCATIONS

**THE DEAD WOODS**
OUTDOORS

All of the trees are dead. But still, something lives in these woods.

**THE CLIFFSIDE LIGHTHOUSE**
INDOORS

They discovered why the flame wasn't lit: the keeper was long dead.

**THE RUINED CHURCH**
INDOORS

The roof has caved in and the church has spoiled.

## WEAPONS

| AN OLD SWORD | A SPOILED TOXIC BLOWFISH | A SHOVEL |
|---|---|---|
| HEAVY-WEIGHT | MEDIUM-WEIGHT | MEDIUM-WEIGHT |
| This was used by the bad guys in some old war. It's all rusted. | It's gone bad now, so even the non-toxic parts are poisonous. | A multi-use tool: kill someone and bury them with the same shovel! |

## CLUES & EVIDENCE

- The weapon at the cliffside lighthouse was not rusted.
- A trusted informant handed Logico a note written in a shaky hand: A OCSPIRO SAW IN HET AEDD OOWSD.

## STATEMENTS

(Remember: The murderer is lying. The others are telling the truth.)

**Mx. Tangerine:** Well, if you ask me, Astrologer Azure brought a shovel.
**Baron Maroon:** A toxic blowfish was in the ruined church.
**Astrologer Azure:** Look at the stars! They say Mx. Tangerine brought a toxic blowfish.

SUSPECTS    LOCATIONS

WHO?

WHAT?

WHERE?

# 48. THE BODY IN THE MOONLIT RUINS 🔍🔍

As the night came on the island, Logico and Irratino split up to cover more ground, looking for clues and a way to radio for help. Logico stumbled upon a ruined church, bathed in the moonlight. Then, he stumbled over a dead body. It was the second first mate.

## SUSPECTS

**PHILOSOPHER BONE**

A dashing, dark philosopher who pioneered the ethical theory that he is not responsible for his actions, but he should be paid for them.

5'1" • RIGHT-HANDED • LIGHT BROWN EYES • BALD • TAURUS

**BROTHER BROWNSTONE**

A monk who has dedicated his life to the church, specifically to making money for it.

5'4" • LEFT-HANDED • DARK BROWN EYES • DARK BROWN HAIR • CAPRICORN

**SISTER LAPIS**

A nun who travels the world, doing God's work on His dime. Her habit is cashmere, and her habit is spending.

5'2" • RIGHT-HANDED • LIGHT BROWN EYES • LIGHT BROWN HAIR • CANCER

## LOCATIONS

**THE FLOODED PEWS**
INDOORS

The wood of the pews is rotten and warped.

**THE OVER-GROWN ORGAN**
INDOORS

Vines and weeds have covered the organ, and bugs skitter out of the pipes.

**THE CRACKED ALTAR**
INDOORS

A huge crack runs through the middle of the stone altar.

## WEAPONS

**A ROCK**
MEDOIUM-WEIGHT

When you can't find
another weapon,
a rock is always
nearby. This one's
chipped.

**A STRING OF
PRAYER BEADS**
LIGHT-WEIGHT

Ivory prayer beads
covered with tiny
engraved symbols.

**A HOLY RELIC**
MEDIUM-WEIGHT

It's a totem of some
long forgotten god
with a terrifying
visage.

## CLUES & EVIDENCE

- Philosopher Bone never set foot in the flooded pews: he wouldn't get
  his feet wet.

- The suspect at the cracked altar was born on December 25. (See Exhibit B.)

## STATEMENTS
(Remember: The murderer is lying. The others are telling the truth.)

**Philosopher Bone:** Sister Lapis did not bring a rock.
**Brother Brownstone:** A holy relic was not in the overgrown organ.
**Sister Lapis:** Philosopher Bone brought a rock.

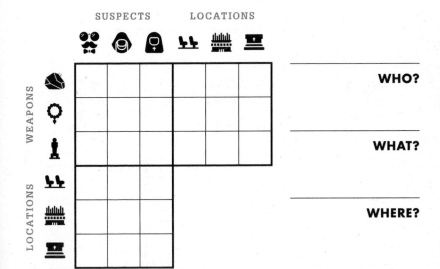

WHO?

WHAT?

WHERE?

# 49. DEATH IN THE DEAD WOODS 🔍🔍

Logico didn't like this island. There was something wrong with it. And there was something wrong about the way they'd been brought here. And there was something wrong with Irratino, who didn't seem to be enjoying any of these mysteries. Logico went on a walk, and he saw someone dart into the dead woods. He followed, but when he caught up to her, she was dead!

## SUSPECTS

**CHANCELLOR TUSCANY**

As the head of Deduction College, she knows every possible way that a person can die. Most in theory.

**5'5" • LEFT-HANDED • GREEN EYES • GRAY HAIR • LIBRA**

**SIR RULEAN**

A sophisticated gentleman who was just recently knighted, if you believe the shoddy paperwork he carries with him.

**5'8" • RIGHT-HANDED • BLUE EYES • RED HAIR • LEO**

**EARL GREY**

He comes from a long line of Earl Greys. Yes, of the tea. No, he doesn't sign autographs. But he'll give you a free bag if you ask.

**5'9" • RIGHT-HANDED • LIGHT BROWN EYES • WHITE HAIR • CAPRICORN**

## LOCATIONS

**THE ANCIENT RUINS**
OUTDOORS

They seem to pulse with some sort of ineffable aura.

**THE GNARLED TREE**
OUTDOORS

Bent and twisted at impossible angles. It looks like a witch.

**THE MOVING CAVE**
INDOORS

Every time you find this cave, it seems to be in a different spot.

## WEAPONS

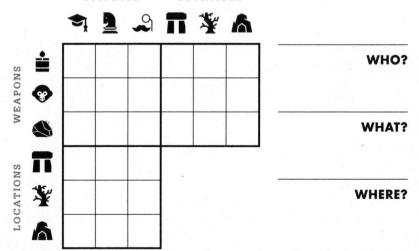

| A PRAYER CANDLE | A TRAINED MONKEY | A ROCK |
|---|---|---|
| MEDOIUM-WEIGHT | HEAVY-WEIGHT | MEDIUM-WEIGHT |
| If you were praying that somebody died, your wish came true. | He's lurking in the woods . . . He may be watching us right now. | A regular rock. But weirdly, not from this island. Chipped. |

## CLUES & EVIDENCE

* You would think the monkey would be up in that gnarled tree: you'd be wrong.

* Someone scrambled to give Logico an important message: UNACSYT DHA HET ROKC.

## STATEMENTS
(Remember: The murderer is lying. The others are telling the truth.)

**Chancellor Tuscany:** As an academic I can tell you that Sir Rulean brought a prayer candle.

**Sir Rulean:** A prayer candle was in the ancient ruins.

**Earl Grey:** I was not in the ancient ruins.

WHO?

WHAT?

WHERE?

# 50. THE KILLING OF IRRATINO

As Deductive Logico was walking back from the dead woods, he saw that someone had lit the light of the lighthouse! And then, he heard a scream, unmistakably the scream of Inspector Irratino! Logico raced toward the lighthouse, but he was too late. Irratino was unconscious and badly hurt. While the castaways tended to him, Logico worked to crack the case.

## SUSPECTS

**BARON MAROON**

An incredibly haughty man who holds a grudge. Nobody wants to offend the baron. At least, nobody who's still alive . . .

6'2" • RIGHT-HANDED • HAZEL EYES • RED HAIR • SCORPIO

**SIR RULEAN**

A sophisticated gentleman who was just recently knighted, if you believe the shoddy paperwork he carries with him.

5'8" • RIGHT-HANDED • BLUE EYES • RED HAIR • LEO

**SISTER LAPIS**

A nun who travels the world, doing God's work on His dime. Her habit is cashmere, and her habit is spending.

5'2" • RIGHT-HANDED • LIGHT BROWN EYES • LIGHT BROWN HAIR • CANCER

## LOCATIONS

**THE LIGHT ITSELF**
INDOORS

Now shining with a terrible fire that warns all seafarers: stay away!

**A SECLUDED COVE**
OUTDOORS

A sandy cove where the castaways have Irratino on a stretcher. He's still too dazed to speak.

**THE GENERATOR**
INDOORS

A massive machine that powers the island with coal.

## WEAPONS

**A ROCK**
MEDIUM-WEIGHT

Used to commit the first-ever murder, and probably the last.

**A BOTTLE OF OIL**
LIGHT-WEIGHT

Enough oil to keep the fire going or to smash over someone's head.

**A SAILOR'S ROPE**
MEDIUM-WEIGHT

Obviously whoever tied these people up didn't use sailing knots.

## CLUES & EVIDENCE

- Sir Rulean never liked the person who brought a bottle of oil.

- Another message was slipped to Deductive Logico from a representative of the Investigation Institute: ♏ ⚏ ♌ ♓ ♓ ♂ ♌
  ☿ ♒ ♍ ♓ ♌ ♓ ♅

## STATEMENTS
**(Remember: The murderer is lying. The others are telling the truth.)**

**Baron Maroon:** Sister Lapis was not near the light itself.
**Sir Rulean:** A bottle of oil was in the generator.
**Sister Lapis:** A rock was not in the generator.

|  | SUSPECTS | | | LOCATIONS | | |
|---|---|---|---|---|---|---|
| (rock) |  |  |  |  |  |  |
| (oil) |  |  |  |  |  |  |
| (rope) |  |  |  |  |  |  |
| (fire) |  |  |  |  |  |  |
| (crab) |  |  |  |  |  |  |
| (tower) |  |  |  |  |  |  |

**WHO?**

**WHAT?**

**WHERE?**

# EXHIBIT C

# HARD BOILED

Deductive Logico had lost everything.

His friend, his rival, his maybe something more. His source of funds.

With Inspector Irratino gone, he was alone against the world. But he was a man with a mission, too. And he wasn't going to let anything get in the way of it.

In these twenty-five mysteries, he pushed himself to the limit to solve the riddle of Irratino's murder. There were more suspects, but he stopped getting their statements. He tried to get inside their heads instead.

In these mysteries, you have to find not only who, what, and where each murder was committed, but why, too. **Everybody has a possible motive, but only one of them is guilty.**

Logico had never cared about motives before, but Irratino had. Maybe this was his way of keeping him around. Or maybe he now just saw everyone as a potential killer.

He was a man on a mission. He had to figure out what these ancient ruins were, what the symbols stamped upon them meant (Exhibit C, seen to the left), and what they had to do with Irratino's killing.

Because he knew Sir Rulean was just a tool of a larger conspiracy. Someone behind him, someone else was calling the shots. And Logico was going to find that person.

And when he found that person, he was going to get revenge.

The Detective Club Challenge for these mysteries is to figure out what the ancient ruins truly are before Logico does. Can you do it?

# 51. THE GRAVE DEATH AT THE GRAVEYARD 🔍🔍🔍

Deductive Logico could not believe that Irratino was really dead. But he had seen him die, and he had seen him be buried, and there was really no denying it now. He was dead. And so, it turned out, was the parson who was supposed to speak at his funeral.

## SUSPECTS

**ASTROLOGER AZURE**

A stargazer, full of wonder and questions about the exact time and place of your birth.

**5'6" • RIGHT-HANDED • HAZEL EYES • LIGHT BROWN HAIR • CANCER**

**EARL GREY**

He comes from a long line of Earl Greys. Yes, of the tea. No, he doesn't sign autographs. But he'll give you a free bag if you ask.

**5'9" • RIGHT-HANDED • LIGHT BROWN EYES • WHITE HAIR • CAPRICORN**

**MX. TANGERINE**

Proving that non-binary people can be murderers, too, they are a gravedigger, pallbearer, and suspect.

**5'5" • LEFT-HANDED • HAZEL EYES • BLOND HAIR • PISCES**

**CRYPTOZOOLO- GIST CLOUD**

He knows every sighting of the Jersey Devil, Mothman, and Boggy Creek Monster, and also what the difference is.

**5'7" • RIGHT-HANDED • GRAY EYES • WHITE HAIR • SCORPIO**

## LOCATIONS

### THE WEIRD SHACK
INDOORS

A wooden shack in the corner of the graveyard that you just know contains a secret.

### THE GIFT SHOP
INDOORS

You can buy little knickknack gravestones or a plushie of their mascot, Mr. Skull.

### THE HUGE MAUSOLEUM
INDOORS

The rich members of a single family get this pyramid-shaped tomb.

### THE ENTRANCE GATE
OUTDOORS

A giant wrought-iron gate with just the right amount of rust for ominous vibes.

## WEAPONS

### A CAULDRON
HEAVY-WEIGHT • MADE OF METAL

If you can pick it up, you can hit someone with it. Or you can just give them a sip.

### A GHOST DETECTOR
MEDIUM-WEIGHT • MADE OF METAL & TECH

It's not great at detecting ghosts, but it's pretty good at electrocuting people.

### A BROOM
MEDIUM-WEIGHT • MADE OF WOOD & STRAW

People say that witches fly on these, but Logico's only swept with them.

### A SKELETON ARM
MEDIUM-WEIGHT • MADE OF BONE

Cause the death of a person with the bones of a person who's dead.

## MOTIVES

 TO ROB THE VICTIM

 TO SEE IF THEY COULD

 TO HIDE AN AFFAIR

 TO STEAL A BODY

## CLUES & EVIDENCE

- Astrologer Azure did not bring a broom.

- Earl Grey would not kill to see if he could, nor to hide an affair.

- A ghost detector was discovered wedged between wrought-iron bars.

- Logico found a single broom bristle next to a plush skeleton.

- The person waving around a skeleton arm was trying desperately to hide their affair.

- Mx. Tangerine had always wanted to steal a body. Maybe tonight was the night?

- The person lugging the cauldron around wanted to rob the parson.

- Cryptozoologist Cloud was seen poking around in the weird shack.

- **The body was found inside a giant pyramid.**

SUSPECTS    MOTIVES    LOCATIONS

WEAPONS

LOCATIONS

MOTIVES

WHO?

WHAT?

WHERE?

WHY?

# 52. A RETURN TO THE INSTITUTE 🔍🔍🔍

Deductive Logico headed back to the Investigation Institute to find that the grounds were overgrown with weeds. With Irratino gone, nobody was taking care of the place, and it seemed quiet—too quiet. Logico realized that was because the only guard had been murdered.

## SUSPECTS

**NUMEROLOGIST NIGHT**

A mathematical and esoteric prodigy. Not only do they know the value of *V*, they know the meaning of *V*.

5'9" • LEFT-HANDED • BLUE EYES • DARK BROWN HAIR • PISCES

**HIGH ALCHE-MIST RAVEN**

There's an old joke that all alchemists are high alchemists. Raven hates it.

5'8" • RIGHT-HANDED • LIGHT BROWN EYES • DARK BROWN HAIR • PISCES

**HERBALIST ONYX**

In her greenhouse, she's grown every kind of plant required in the culinary, magick, and poisoning arts.

5'0" • RIGHT-HANDED • DARK BROWN EYES • BLACK HAIR • VIRGO

**PHILOLOGIST FLINT**

You can learn a lot about a word from its etymology, like where it came from, and what it used to mean.

5'2" • LEFT-HANDED • GREEN EYES • BLOND HAIR • AQUARIUS

## LOCATIONS

### THE GRAND CHATEAU
INDOORS

The tree growing in the middle has started to wilt and die.

### THE GREAT TOWER
INDOORS

A towering tower specifically built to drop things for experimental purposes.

### THE MINIATURE GOLF COURSE
OUTDOORS

Eighteen holes. Windmills, caves, and loop-de-loops. But no one wants to play.

### AN IMPOSSIBLE HEDGE MAZE
OUTDOORS

People have to be rescued from the hedge maze all the time.

## WEAPONS

### A DOWSING ROD
MEDIUM-WEIGHT • MADE OF WOOD

You can find water, oil, and suckers with this.

### A HYPNOTIC POCKET WATCH
LIGHT-WEIGHT • MADE OF METAL

If you look deeply into this watch, you can tell the time.

### A QUASI-PERPETUAL MOTION MACHINE
HEAVY-WEIGHT • MADE OF METAL

It doesn't run forever. This one made it a day.

### A CRYSTAL BALL
HEAVY-WEIGHT • MADE OF CRYSTAL

If you look into it, you will see your fortune, so long as your fortune is a crystal ball.

## MOTIVES

 TO PROVE THEY'RE TOUGH

 TO INHERIT A FORTUNE

 TO FIGHT FOR LOVE

 BECAUSE THEY COULD

## CLUES & EVIDENCE

- The shortest suspect brought a dowsing rod to reach things.

- High Alchemist Raven was seen hanging around high above the grounds.

- The suspect with a quasi-perpetual motion machine deeply desired to fight for love.

- No one with blue eyes was in the grand chateau.

- A fortune-telling tool was found beside a tiny windmill.

- The suspect who would kill because they could was in the grand chateau.

- The Aquarius wanted to inherit a fortune.

- The suspect with a time-telling device did not want to prove they're tough.

- **The guard's body was found between twisting hedge rows.**

|  | SUSPECTS | | | | MOTIVES | | | | LOCATIONS | | | |
|---|---|---|---|---|---|---|---|---|---|---|---|---|
| WEAPONS | | | | | | | | | | | | |
| | | | | | | | | | | | | |
| | | | | | | | | | | | | |
| | | | | | | | | | | | | |
| LOCATIONS | | | | | | | | | | | | |
| | | | | | | | | | | | | |
| | | | | | | | | | | | | |
| | | | | | | | | | | | | |
| MOTIVES | | | | | | | | | | | | |
| | | | | | | | | | | | | |
| | | | | | | | | | | | | |
| | | | | | | | | | | | | |

_____

**WHO?**

_____

**WHAT?**

_____

**WHERE?**

_____

**WHY?**

# 53. THE WALK IN THE MYSTERIOUS WOODS 🔍🔍🔍

Deductive Logico walked away from the Institute, down the lone and lonely road, until eventually, he wandered off the road and into the woods, where he found the body of a woman wearing strange, cultic robes.

## SUSPECTS

**CRYPTOZOOLO-GIST CLOUD**

He knows every sighting of the Barghest, Dobhar-chú, Beast of Bodmin Moor, and also what the difference is.

**5'7" • RIGHT-HANDED • GRAY EYES • WHITE HAIR • SCORPIO**

**BARON MAROON**

An incredibly haughty man who holds a grudge. Nobody wants to offend the baron. At least, nobody who's still alive . . .

**6'2" • RIGHT-HANDED • HAZEL EYES • RED HAIR • SCORPIO**

**JUDGE PINE**

Master of the courtroom and possessed of a firm belief in justice, as decided by her alone.

**5'6" • RIGHT-HANDED • DARK BROWN EYES • BLACK HAIR • TAURUS**

**SOCIOLOGIST UMBER**

As a representative from the hard sciences, she is always asking people to question their priors and if they've read Durkheim.

**5'4" • LEFT-HANDED • BLUE EYES • BLOND HAIR • LEO**

## LOCATIONS

### THE GNARLED TREE
OUTDOORS

Bent and twisted at impossible angles. It reminds Logico of Irratino's logic.

### THE MOVING CAVE
INDOORS

Every time you find this cave, it seems to be in a different spot.

### THE ANCIENT RUINS
OUTDOORS

Your legs seem unsteady around them, like they're sinking into the ground.

### THE LITTLE HILL
OUTDOORS

A nice little hill for sitting on and having picnics at. Or mourning your partner.

## WEAPONS

### A HEAVY CANDLE
HEAVY-WEIGHT • MADE OF WAX

It's heavy, yet it lightens the room.

### AN OLD SWORD
HEAVY-WEIGHT • MADE OF METAL

This was used by the bad guys in an old war. It's all rusted.

### A LOG
HEAVY-WEIGHT • MADE OF WOOD

A big, heavy oak log. Somebody killed the tree so that the tree could kill somebody.

### AN AXE
MEDIUM-WEIGHT • MADE OF WOOD & METAL

This axe could chop a tree down. If only it could cut out bad memories.

## MOTIVES

 TO SCARE A BEAR AWAY

 TO STEAL A PRIZED BOOK

 FOR THE REVOLUTION

 TO GET REVENGE

## CLUES & EVIDENCE

- Logico found a red hair wrapped around the log.

- The person carrying a heavy candle wanted to steal a prized book.

- Whoever wanted to get revenge was a Scorpio. (Typical.)

- Whoever wanted to scare a bear away would've had to have been right-handed.

- The suspect who had a motive to kill for the revolution was seen plotting indoors.

- Analysts discovered traces of a weapon made (at least in part) of metal on the clothing of Sociologist Umber.

- It seemed like somebody was going to chop down a strange and twisted tree, because an axe was leaning against it.

- Someone at a great picnic spot would obviously need to scare a bear away.

- The second shortest suspect had never been on the little hill.

- **A rusted blade was found beside the cultist.**

|  | SUSPECTS | | | | MOTIVES | | | | LOCATIONS | | | |
|---|---|---|---|---|---|---|---|---|---|---|---|---|

WHO?

WHAT?

WHERE?

WHY?

# 54. AND THEN THERE WAS ANOTHER ONE AGAIN 🔍🔍🔍

Deductive Logico returned to the secluded island to investigate the ancient ruins that were there. But when he got there, the new caretaker had been murdered. This did not seem like a safe job.

## SUSPECTS

**VICE PRESIDENT MAUVE**

A vice president of TekCo Futures. If she asks you to step into her metaverse, scream at the top of your lungs.

5'8" • RIGHT-HANDED • DARK BROWN EYES • BLACK HAIR • TAURUS

**ADMIRAL NAVY**

Also, his grandfather was the firstborn son of an Admiral Navy, and his grandfather was, too!

5'9" • RIGHT-HANDED • BLUE EYES • LIGHT BROWN HAIR • CANCER

**AGENT INK**

An agent with a heart of gold, but a mind for gold, too. She knows how to make a killing.

5'5" • RIGHT-HANDED • DARK BROWN EYES • BLACK HAIR • VIRGO

**GRANDMASTER ROSE**

A chess grand master who is always plotting his next move. Like how to stop being a suspect in a murder mystery. (2 . . . Ke7??)

5'7" • LEFT-HANDED • DARK BROWN EYES • DARK BROWN HAIR • SCORPIO

## LOCATIONS

### THE DOCKS
OUTDOORS

Old, rotting docks that have certainly seen better days. Look out for the sharks!

### THE HAUNTED GROVE
OUTDOORS

A grove of trees on the corner of the island. Visitors have reported hearing voices whispering.

### THE ANCIENT RUINS
OUTDOORS

New hypothesis: it's ancient installation art.

### THE CLIFFS
OUTDOORS

It's a long drop, but on the bright side, the jagged rocks would break your fall.

## WEAPONS

### AN ORDINARY BRICK
MEDIUM-WEIGHT • MADE OF BRICK

Just a regular, ordinary brick. Nothing special. Just a brick.

### AN AXE
MEDIUM-WEIGHT • MADE OF WOOD & METAL

This axe could chop a tree down. Or a person down!

### AN OAR
HEAVY-WEIGHT • MADE OF WOOD

You could use this to paddle a boat, but be careful of splinters.

### A BEAR TRAP
HEAVY-WEIGHT • MADE OF METAL

If you think it's too gruesome for a person, then think how the bears feel!

## MOTIVES

 TO AVENGE THEIR FATHER

 TO STEAL A TREASURE MAP

 TO IMPRESS A LADY

 OUT OF MADNESS

## CLUES & EVIDENCE

- The person with a bear trap did not want to steal a treasure map.

- The suspect who wanted to impress a lady had a weapon made at least partially of metal.

- Only a person who would kill out of madness would use an ordinary brick.

- Vice President Mauve was seen studying what might be installation art.

- A Virgo had the oar. Virgos love oar-der.

- The tallest suspect had a weapon made (at least in part) with wood.

- The person who wanted to impress a lady was on the cliffs.

- The second tallest suspect had a weapon made (at least in part) with metal.

- Whoever was in the haunted grove was left-handed.

- **An axe was used to kill the caretaker.**

SUSPECTS   MOTIVES   LOCATIONS

WEAPONS

LOCATIONS

MOTIVES

WHO?

WHAT?

WHERE?

WHY?

# 55. UNUSUAL WEBBING, UNNATURAL CRIMES 🔍🔍🔍

Camping alone in a national park, Deductive Logico dreamt about ancient ruins and a park ranger being murdered. When he woke up, he saw the dream had come true.

## SUSPECTS

**MAYOR HONEY**

He's on a retreat in the woods to reevaluate his political prospects in the wake of the latest scandal (murder).

**6'0" • LEFT-HANDED • HAZEL EYES • BROWN HAIR • SCORPIO**

**PRINCIPAL APPLEGREEN**

A strict principal about everything except getting away with murder. His hands are always covered in chalk.

**5'11" • RIGHT-HANDED • BLUE EYES • BLOND HAIR • LIBRA**

**COACH RASPBERRY**

One of the best coaches this side of the Mississippi, regardless of which side you're on.

**6'0" • LEFT-HANDED • BLUE EYES • BLOND HAIR • ARIES**

**CHANCELLOR TUSCANY**

As the head of Deduction College, she has deduced the best way to play the game of academic power politics: reward your allies, punish your enemies, and don't be afraid to kill.

**5'5" • LEFT-HANDED • GREEN EYES • GRAY HAIR • LIBRA**

## LOCATIONS

### THE ANCIENT RUINS
OUTDOORS

Maybe they are some kind of marker to tell aliens locations of interest?

### THE HOT SPRINGS SPA
INDOORS

People travel from hundreds of miles to take pictures of themselves in these hot springs.

### THE PARTY LAKE
OUTDOORS

People have been known to drown in this lake, so people have been known to hide bodies in its ice-cold waters, too.

### THE ENTRANCE GATE
OUTDOORS

A huge gate that advertises a place where you can disconnect from the modern world, for a price.

## WEAPONS

### A POISONOUS SPIDER
LIGHT-WEIGHT • MADE OF A LIVE ANIMAL

Definitely not an accident: its unusual webbing shows that this spider is not native to these woods.

### A PAIR OF GARDENING SHEARS
MEDIUM-WEIGHT • MADE OF METAL

Rusty, heavy, and dangerous. You could trim a hedge or years off someone's life.

### A BOW AND ARROW
MEDIUM-WEIGHT • MADE OF CERAMIC, LINEN, & FEATHERS

Look at this thing: what a beauty! Look at the feathers on the arrows as they fly toward your head.

### A CLIMBING AXE
HEAVY-WEIGHT • MADE OF METAL & WOOD

You could climb up a cliff and behold the beauty of the natural landscape. Or kill someone.

## MOTIVES

 TO ROB THE VICTIM

 AS PART OF A REAL ESTATE SCAM

 TO SEE IF THEY COULD

 TO ESCAPE BLACKMAIL

## CLUES & EVIDENCE

- Logico had seen poisoned spiders used before, but only ever as part of a real estate scam.

- Principal Applegreen was not at the entrance gate.

- The shortest suspect had a climbing axe.

- Traces of a weapon made of a live animal were found in the ancient ruins.

- The suspect who wanted to see if they could had a weapon made at least partially of ceramic.

- Coach Raspberry was seen swimming in ice-cold water.

- The gardening shears were right-handed.

- The suspect who wanted to escape blackmail was seen outdoors.

- **Some unusual webbing was found beside the forest ranger.**

SUSPECTS        MOTIVES        LOCATIONS

WEAPONS

LOCATIONS

MOTIVES

WHO?

WHAT?

WHERE?

WHY?

# 56. THE RUINS OF A VILLAGE 🔍🔍🔍

Deductive Logico returned to the quaint little village where he had first followed Dame Obsidian. Now, half the houses were for sale. The other half were empty. A mysterious figure was running around the town, and nobody knew where the shopkeep was. Then Logico found a murder weapon, and he knew what had happened to the shopkeep.

## SUSPECTS

**MISTER SHADOW**

A silhouette in shadow. He moves like the wind and he looks like the night.

▮▮▮ • LEFT-HANDED • GREEN EYES • ▮▮▮▮▮▮▮ • ▮▮▮ • AQUARIUS

**FATHER MANGO**

He has taken a vow of poverty, but he drives a BMW. He's taken a vow of obedience, but he has a staff of twenty-five. He's taken a vow of chastity, too, which is why he's on vacation.

5'10" • LEFT-HANDED • DARK BROWN EYES • BALD • TAURUS

**LORD LAVENDER**

A politically conservative MP in the House of Lords, as well as the musical theater composer behind such hits as *The Shadow of the Orchestra: Everything Dies.*

5'9" • RIGHT-HANDED • GREEN EYES • GRAY HAIR • VIRGO

**OFFICER COPPER**

The best part of being a policewoman criminal is that you can cut out the middleman and fail to investigate your own crimes.

5'5" • RIGHT-HANDED • BLUE EYES • BLOND HAIR • ARIES

## LOCATIONS

### THE NEW DEVELOPMENT
OUTDOORS

This new development will either revitalize the community or ruin it, depending on who you ask.

### THE ANCIENT RUINS
OUTDOORS

Is it possible they were some kind of beacon?

### THE CHAPEL
INDOORS

A tiny church with stained-glass windows and secrets.

### THE QUAINT GARDEN
OUTDOORS

A quaint little garden for growing herbs and flowers. But there might have been some new mounds of dirt lately, of a suspicious size and shape.

## WEAPONS

### YARN
LIGHT-WEIGHT • MADE OF WOOL

Sometimes, when you realize you've missed a stitch, you could just strangle somebody.

### AN ANTIQUE FLINTLOCK
MEDIUM-WEIGHT • MADE OF WOOD & METAL

It takes only twenty-five minutes to load this.

### A KNITTING NEEDLE
LIGHT-WEIGHT • MADE OF METAL

You could knit a sweater or a garrote.

### A BOTTLE OF CYANIDE
LIGHT-WEIGHT • MADE OF GLASS & CHEMICALS

Almond-scented poison in a quaint little bottle.

## MOTIVES

 TO STEAL AN IDEA

 AS PART OF A REAL ESTATE SCAM

 TO STEAL A BODY

 TO SCARE A BEAR AWAY

## CLUES & EVIDENCE

- Whoever had yarn was right-handed.

- Lord Lavender had not been in the quaint garden.

- Whoever wanted to steal an idea had green eyes.

- Father Mango was seen hanging around beneath a stained-glass window.

- The person who wanted to steal a body was in the ancient ruins.

- Whoever was in the new development had a medium-weight weapon.

- Whoever might kill as part of a real estate scam was an Aquarius.

- If you are going to scare a bear away, you are going to need a weapon made of metal.

- **Logico found a knitting needle that was covered in blood.**

SUSPECTS        MOTIVES        LOCATIONS

WEAPONS

LOCATIONS

MOTIVES

_____
WHO?

_____
WHAT?

_____
WHERE?

_____
WHY?

# 57. SING A HYMN OF HORROR 🔍🔍🔍

Father Mango claimed sanctuary in his chapel, and he closed the doors. Almost immediately, however, a parishioner was murdered, and he opened the doors again and said that Logico should figure out who did it, so that he could kick out the other murderer.

## SUSPECTS

**FATHER MANGO**

He has taken a vow of poverty, but he drives a BMW. He's taken a vow of obedience, but he has a staff of twenty-five. He didn't take a vow not to murder, though, and he did that, too.

5'10" • LEFT-HANDED • DARK BROWN EYES • BALD • TAURUS

**BISHOP AZURE**

A bishop in the church, Azure has been known to pray for both her friends and her enemies. Of course, she asks for different things . . .

5'4" • RIGHT-HANDED • LIGHT BROWN EYES • DARK BROWN HAIR • GEMINI

**DEACON VERDIGRIS**

A deacon of the church. She handles the parishioners' donations and, sometimes, their secrets.

5'3" • LEFT-HANDED • BLUE EYES • GRAY HAIR • LEO

**BROTHER BROWNSTONE**

A monk who has dedicated his life to the church, specifically to making money for it.

5'4" • LEFT-HANDED • DARK BROWN EYES • DARK BROWN HAIR • CAPRICORN

## LOCATIONS

### THE CHOIR LOFT
**INDOORS**

There's no one singing there now: it's quiet. But during the services, you should hear the organ!

### THE FRONT STEPS
**OUTDOORS**

Kind of a hassle to walk up and down, but it adds to the ambience.

### THE GRAVEYARD
**OUTDOORS**

A small graveyard next to the church. Most of the graves are old, but perhaps, one is more recent . . .

### THE VESTIBULE
**INDOORS**

An entrance room with many doors and a table covered in fliers for church events.

## WEAPONS

### AN ANTIQUE FLINTLOCK
**MEDIUM-WEIGHT • MADE OF WOOD & METAL**

It can fire a bullet as far as four feet and cover you in gunpowder.

### A BOTTLE OF WINE
**MEDIUM-WEIGHT • MADE OF GLASS**

Watch out for stains, because the red doesn't come out.

### A HOLY RELIC
**MEDIUM-WEIGHT • MADE OF BONE**

It's a totem of a loving god with a beauteous visage.

### YARN
**LIGHT-WEIGHT • MADE OF WOOL**

Sometimes, when you realize you've missed a stitch, you could just strangle somebody.

## MOTIVES

 BECAUSE THEY WERE BE-
COMING THEIR PARENTS

 A GHOST MADE THEM

 AS PRACTICE

 FOR RELIGIOUS
REASONS

## CLUES & EVIDENCE

- Whoever had a bottle of wine was left-handed.

- Gunpowder was found on the church fliers.

- The person who wanted to kill for religious reasons was not in the graveyard.

- Father Mango was outside when the murder happened.

- A weapon made of bone was brought by the person who wanted to kill as practice.

- A Gemini was standing on the front steps.

- Whoever might kill because they were becoming their parents had blue eyes. (Just like their parents!)

- The suspect with the same height as Bishop Azure was seen with yarn.

- **The parishioner's body was found in the choir loft.**

|  | SUSPECTS | | | | MOTIVES | | | | LOCATIONS | | | |
|---|---|---|---|---|---|---|---|---|---|---|---|---|

WHO?

WHAT?

WHERE?

WHY?

# 58. A MAZE OF DEATH AND HEDGES 🔍🔍🔍

Deductive Logico walked through the hedge maze at Dame Obsidian's abandoned manor house. Like the ones at the Investigation Institute, these hedges had grown wild, and the paths were no longer straight. It turns out the gardener had been murdered.

## SUSPECTS

**VISCOUNT EMINENCE**

The oldest man you have ever seen. It is said that he was old when your grandfather was born, and he'll be old when your grandchildren die.

5'2" • LEFT-HANDED • GRAY EYES • DARK BROWN HAIR • PISCES

**LORD LAVENDER**

A politically conservative MP in the House of Lords, as well as the musical theater composer behind such hits as *Mary and the Wonderful Black-and-White Pantsuit* and *Mirta*.

5'9" • RIGHT-HANDED • GREEN EYES • BLOND HAIR • VIRGO

**THE DUCHESS OF VERMILLION**

A tall, old woman with tall, old secrets. If she is the murderer, then it wouldn't be the first time.

5'9" • LEFT-HANDED • GRAY EYES • WHITE HAIR • PISCES

**BARON MAROON**

An incredibly haughty man who holds a grudge. Nobody wants to offend the baron. At least, nobody who's still alive . . .

6'2" • RIGHT-HANDED • HAZEL EYES • RED HAIR • SCORPIO

## LOCATIONS

### THE LOOKOUT TOWER
INDOORS

From above the garden, you can see everything. Plus, there's a map of the maze on the wall.

### THE ANCIENT RUINS
OUTDOORS

Since these were already falling apart, they had a head start on the rest of the maze.

### THE FOUNTAIN
OUTDOORS

A fountain at the center of the maze. It's bone dry.

### THE SECRET GARDEN
OUTDOORS

A secret garden in the center of the maze, featuring every flower you can name and hundreds you cannot.

## WEAPONS

### POISONED TEA
HEAVY-WEIGHT
MADE OF CERAMIC, WATER, & LEAVES

Enjoy a nice sip of tea, followed by a long, long nap.

### A PAIR OF GARDENING SHEARS

MEDIUM-WEIGHT • MADE OF METAL

You could trim a hedge or years off someone's life.

### AN ORDINARY BRICK
HEAVY-WEIGHT • MADE OF CLAY

Just a regular, ordinary brick. Nothing special. Just a brick.

### A FLOWERPOT
MEDIUM-WEIGHT • MADE OF CERAMIC

If you use this to kill, please repot the flowers first.

## MOTIVES

 TO PROTECT A SECRET

 TO STEAL A PRIZED BOOK

 TO SEE WHAT IT FELT LIKE TO KILL

 AS A SCIENTIFIC EXPERIMENT

## CLUES & EVIDENCE

- Forensics found traces of a metal weapon by the ancient ruins.

- Whoever wanted to steal a prized book was left-handed.

- Whoever wanted to see what it felt like to kill had dark brown hair.

- A single red hair was found in the secret garden.

- Whoever wanted to kill as a scientific experiment was a Virgo.

- An informant told Logico, "A tea bag was indoors." He could be no more specific.

- The suspect who was just as tall as the Duchess of Vermillion was not in the lookout tower.

- The Duchess of Vermillion had brought a brick she could barely carry.

- **A flowerpot was used to commit the murder.**

SUSPECTS MOTIVES LOCATIONS

WEAPONS

LOCATIONS

MOTIVES

WHO?

WHAT?

WHERE?

WHY?

# 59. I YACHT TO KILL YOU FOR THIS 🔍🔍🔍

Deductive Logico was invited back onto the yacht to have a talk with Chairman Chalk about his book sales. They were selling, but they weren't selling enough. "If only," the Chairman said, "we had some way of getting publicity. Oh! One of my sailors was murdered! You could solve that!"

## SUSPECTS

**BOOKIE-WINNER GAINSBORO**

He won the Bookington Award for his novel, which he will tell you within two minutes of meeting you. The book is six thousand pages long, and it's about dirt.

6'0" • LEFT-HANDED • HAZEL EYES • LIGHT BROWN HAIR • GEMINI

**CHAIRMAN CHALK**

He figured out the publishing business years ago and never looked back. He called ebooks a "fad" and still owns a rotary phone. He is worth a billion dollars.

5'9" • RIGHT-HANDED • BLUE EYES • WHITE HAIR • SAGITTARIUS

**EDITOR IVORY**

The greatest romance editor of all time. She invented the enemies-to-lovers genre, and she was the first person to put a naked man on the cover of a book.

5'6" • LEFT-HANDED • LIGHT BROWN EYES • GRAY HAIR • SCORPIO

**AGENT INK**

An agent with a heart of gold, but a mind for gold, too. She sells more books than Amazon.

5'5" • RIGHT-HANDED • DARK BROWN EYES • BLACK HAIR • VIRGO

## LOCATIONS

### THE ENGINE ROOM
INDOORS

This is a green yacht: it's powered by a nuclear reactor. When the uranium rods are spent, just toss them into the ocean.

### THE DECK
OUTDOORS

Look out over the ocean, but not too far or someone might push you.

### OVERBOARD
OUTDOORS

The open ocean. Home of some of history's favorite drowning victims.

### THE DINING HALL
INDOORS

They've got an award-winning chef because he's banned from working on land.

## WEAPONS

### A COMMEMORATIVE PEN
LIGHT-WEIGHT • MADE OF METAL & INK

To commemorate that special event . . . whatever it was. It leaks expensive ink.

### CONFUSING CONTRACTS
LIGHT-WEIGHT • MADE OF PAPER

Legalese so impenetrable it could give you an aneurysm.

### A TOTE BAG
MEDIUM-WEIGHT • MADE OF CANVAS

Bibliophile mafiosos use these canvas bags for hits. You can also carry books in them.

### AN ANTIQUE ANCHOR
HEAVY-WEIGHT • MADE OF METAL

It's covered in moss and the chain is rusty: it looks awesome.

## MOTIVES

 BY THE ORDER OF A
CULT

 TO STEAL A PRIZED
BOOK

 TO COMFORT LOGICO

 TO IMPROVE BOOK
SALES

## CLUES & EVIDENCE

- Impenetrable legalese was discovered on the deck.

- Logico received a message written by an obviously seasick tipster: ORIETD OYVRI EWNATD TO LAETS A PEDRZI KOOB.

- The person with a commemorative pen wanted to improve book sales.

- A rusty chain was found next to a nuclear reactor. Is that a safety hazard?

- Bookie-Winner Gainsboro wanted to kill by the order of a cult.

- Chairman Chalk did not want to comfort Logico.

- Editor Ivory had not been on the deck.

- Agent Ink was swimming around in a vast, uncaring ocean.

- **The sailor was found face down in award-winning food.**

SUSPECTS   MOTIVES   LOCATIONS

WEAPONS

LOCATIONS

MOTIVES

_____

**WHO?**

_____

**WHAT?**

_____

**WHERE?**

_____

**WHY?**

Deductive Logico remembered something about that commune: on the edge of their lands, there were ancient ruins. So he traveled back upstate, and not only were there ancient ruins, but there was a murder, too. A long-time cultist had been killed.

## SUSPECTS

**COMRADE CHAMPAGNE**

A communist and a rich one. Comrade Champagne likes nothing more than to travel the world, sharing the message of communism while sipping on the finest sparkling wines.

5'11" • LEFT-HANDED • HAZEL EYES • BLOND HAIR • CAPRICORN

**MX. TANGERINE**

Proving that non-binary people can be murderers, too, they are a communalist, farmer, and potential suspect.

5'5" • LEFT-HANDED • HAZEL EYES • BLOND HAIR • PISCES

**ASSISTANT APPLEGREEN**

Her father is a principal, and the more time she spends on this commune, the less proud he is.

5'3" • LEFT-HANDED • BLUE EYES • BLOND HAIR • VIRGO

**PRINCIPAL APPLEGREEN**

A strict principal about everything except getting away with murder. His hands are always covered in chalk.

5'11" • RIGHT-HANDED • BLUE EYES • BALD • LIBRA

## LOCATIONS

### THE MEETING HOUSE
INDOORS

Where the official discussion is done, and where absolutely nothing is accomplished.

### THE OLD MILL
INDOORS

A great place to grind grain or hide secrets.

### THE ANCIENT RUINS
OUTDOORS

Do they have religious significance? Maybe to the old gods . . .

### THE LIBRARY
INDOORS

More books than you've ever seen. (But all by one guy.)

## WEAPONS

### AN ALUMINUM PIPE
HEAVY-WEIGHT • MADE OF METAL

Safer than lead, unless it hits you in the head.

### AN ANTIQUE CLOCK
HEAVY-WEIGHT • MADE OF WOOD & METAL

Tick, tock, tick, tock. Technically, time is killing us all slowly.

### A MAGNIFYING GLASS
MEDIUM-WEIGHT • MADE OF METAL & GLASS

You could use this to find a clue or identify a bug.

### AN OLD SWORD
HEAVY-WEIGHT • MADE OF METAL

This was used by the bad guys in some old war. It's all rusted.

## MOTIVES

 BY THE ORDER OF A
CULT

 TO TEACH THEM A
LESSON

 TO MOTIVATE LOGICO

 TO PREVENT A CHANGE
IN THE WILL

## CLUES & EVIDENCE

- A magnifying glass was used as a prop during the official discussion.

- Principal Applegreen brought an antique clock to tell time.

- The person with an aluminum pipe wanted to motivate Logico.

- Whoever was in the library was right-handed.

- A Capricorn was milling about the old mill.

- A Pisces was a member of the Deep Well of Wisdom.

- All members of the Deep Well of Wisdom desire to kill by the order of their cult.

- Whoever wanted to teach the long-time cultist a lesson was holding a medium-weight weapon.

- **The body of the long-time cultist was found draped upon the ancient ruins.**

SUSPECTS    MOTIVES    LOCATIONS

WEAPONS

LOCATIONS

MOTIVES

_____

WHO?

_____

WHAT?

_____

WHERE?

_____

WHY?

# 61. THE ISLAND OF BAD DREAMS 🔍🔍🔍

Deductive Logico never wanted to again lay eyes upon the island where Inspector Irratino had died, but when he closed his eyes, it was all he could see. He had to go back, and when he did, there was another murder for him to solve, and another mysterious figure running around.

## SUSPECTS

**MISTER SHADOW**

A silhouette in shadow. He moves like the wind and he looks like the night.

▇▇▇ • LEFT-HANDED • GREEN EYES • ▇▇▇▇▇▇▇
▇▇▇ • AQUARIUS

**PRÉSIDENT AMARANTH**

The literal French *président*, Amaranth loves spending time with his constituents, especially a certain one percent of them.

5'10" • RIGHT-HANDED • GRAY EYES • RED HAIR • GEMINI

**CAPTAIN SLATE**

A real-life astronaut. The first woman to travel around the dark side of the moon, and also the first to be suspected of murdering her copilot.

5'5" • LEFT-HANDED • DARK BROWN EYES • DARK BROWN HAIR • AQUARIUS

**MIDNIGHT III**

He learned filmmaking from his father and business from his grandfather. But at murder, he's a natural.

5'8" • LEFT-HANDED • DARK BROWN EYES • DARK BROWN HAIR • LIBRA

## LOCATIONS

### THE DEAD WOODS
OUTDOORS

You can almost feel the ancient ruins buried within these dead woods.

### THE WRECKED CRUISE SHIP
OUTDOORS

Once a fashionable cruise liner, now wrecked and rusted.

### THE RUINED CHURCH
INDOORS

The roof has caved in and the church is spoiled.

### THE CLIFFSIDE LIGHTHOUSE
INDOORS

They have now replaced the fire with an automatic LED light that is significantly cheaper.

## WEAPONS

### AN AXE
MEDIUM-WEIGHT • MADE OF WOOD & METAL

Left on the island. Maybe for good reason.

### A BROOM
MEDIUM-WEIGHT • MADE OF WOOD & STRAW

People say that witches fly on these, but Logico's only swept with them.

### A CRYSTAL SKULL
MEDIUM-WEIGHT • MADE OF CRYSTAL

Maybe an actual alien's skull, or maybe just a fun art project.

### AN "ALIEN" ARTIFACT
HEAVY-WEIGHT • MADE OF PLASTIC

Maybe real, probably fake. Definitely made of plastic.

## MOTIVES

 TO CLOSE A BUSINESS DEAL

 TO SAVE FACE

 TO ROB A GRAVE

 TO HELP WIN A WAR

## CLUES & EVIDENCE

- The suspect who wanted to help win a war had a weapon made of plastic.

- An Aquarius was lit by an LED light. It was not flattering.

- Captain Slate was found babbling in the dead woods.

- Midnight III did not want to save face. He didn't care about face.

- Whoever was beneath a caved-in roof was right-handed.

- An axe was found near a rusted hull.

- Whoever wanted to rob a grave was a Gemini.

- A crystal skull was glittering in the moonlight of the outdoors.

- **A piece of straw was found by the body.**

WEAPONS

LOCATIONS

MOTIVES

WHO?

WHAT?

WHERE?

WHY?

# 62. YOU CAN GO HOME AGAIN 🔍🔍🔍

Deductive Logico thought about giving up, moving back home, and becoming an insurance adjuster. And actually, there was a job opening in town: an insurance adjuster had just been killed. Logico thought about whether he wanted the job while he investigated.

## SUSPECTS

**FORMER MAYOR HONEY**

Yes, when he was mayor, he murdered somebody, but once he resigned it all blew over.

**6'0" • LEFT-HANDED • HAZEL EYES • LIGHT BROWN HAIR • SCORPIO**

**OFFICER COPPER**

Ever since she killed that person, her employ-ability as a cop has been mildly reduced.

**5'5" • RIGHT-HANDED • BLUE EYES • BLOND HAIR • ARIES**

**MR. ORDINARY BLUE SKY**

Totally ordinary American man with thick Russian accent. Pay no mind.

**6'2" • LEFT-HANDED • DARK BROWN EYES • BLACK HAIR • ARIES**

**DR. CRIMSON**

She's the smartest doctor she's ever met, according to her, and she's probably right. But as a murderer, even she can't figure out a way to get a job somewhere else.

**5'9" • LEFT-HANDED • GREEN EYES • RED HAIR • AQUARIUS**

## LOCATIONS

### A USED CAR LOT
INDOORS

The salesman tells you the cars will not explode, and that they're also sold as is.

### THE RUN-DOWN MALL
INDOORS

The fountain is dry and only two stores are open: a payday loan company and one that buys gold.

### THE OLD FACTORY
INDOORS

They used to build gadgets and gizmos, but now the gadgets and gizmos are all apps.

### A SECONDHAND SHOP
INDOORS

Most of the stuff in here looks third-hand, even the moths.

## WEAPONS

### A FORK
LIGHT-WEIGHT • MADE OF METAL

A lot more gruesome than a knife, if you think about it.

### AN ANTIQUE ANCHOR
HEAVY-WEIGHT • MADE OF METAL

It's covered in moss and the chain is rusty: it looks pretty cool.

### AN ALUMINUM PIPE
HEAVY-WEIGHT • MADE OF METAL

Safer than lead, unless it hits you in the head.

### AN ORDINARY BRICK
MEDIUM-WEIGHT • MADE OF BRICK

Just a regular, ordinary brick. Nothing special. Just a brick.

## MOTIVES

 FOR MONEY

 TO PROTECT A SECRET

#! TO RETURN AN INSULT

WHILE BLACKED OUT

## CLUES & EVIDENCE

- Mr. Ordinary Blue Sky wanted to protect a secret. But what could his secret be?

- The suspect in the run-down mall was a member of the Underground Power.

- Whoever had an ordinary brick was right-handed. (It was a right-handed brick.)

- A Scorpio had the fork. Scorpios collect forks.

- An Aquarius was beside a vehicle they had been assured would not explode.

- The brick had clearly been in the old factory.

- Members of the Underground Power were not allowed to touch aluminum.

- The person with an antique anchor wanted to return an insult.

- Whoever might have killed while blacked out was right-handed.

- **The body of the insurance adjuster was covered in moths.**

| | SUSPECTS | | | | MOTIVES | | | | LOCATIONS | | | |
|---|---|---|---|---|---|---|---|---|---|---|---|---|
| WEAPONS | | | | | | | | | | | | |
| | | | | | | | | | | | | |
| | | | | | | | | | | | | |
| | | | | | | | | | | | | |
| LOCATIONS | | | | | | | | | | | | |
| | | | | | | | | | | | | |
| | | | | | | | | | | | | |
| | | | | | | | | | | | | |
| MOTIVES | | | | | | | | | | | | |
| | | | | | | | | | | | | |
| | | | | | | | | | | | | |
| | | | | | | | | | | | | |

_____

**WHO?**

_____

**WHAT?**

_____

**WHERE?**

_____

**WHY?**

# 63. THE BODY IN THE SNOWDRIFT 🔍🔍🔍

Deductive Logico received a letter in the mail from a monastery. Brother Brownstone wanted to speak to him about something of grave importance. But when Logico got to the monastery, Brother Brownstone had been killed!

## SUSPECTS

**FATHER MANGO**

Father Mango could have enjoyed being a priest in the church for years. They just had one rule: don't get caught murdering people. Now, he was confined to this monastery.

5'10" • LEFT-HANDED • DARK BROWN EYES • BALD • TAURUS

**DEACON VERDIGRIS**

A deacon of the church. She handles the parishioners' donations and, sometimes, their secrets.

5'3" • LEFT-HANDED • BLUE EYES • GRAY HAIR • LEO

**SISTER LAPIS**

A nun who travels the world, doing God's work on His dime. Her habit is cashmere, and her habit is spending.

5'2" • RIGHT-HANDED • LIGHT BROWN EYES • LIGHT BROWN HAIR • CANCER

**BROTHER BROWNSTONE**

Brother Brownstone's brother, who is not a brother of the church, just Brownstone's.

5'4" • LEFT-HANDED • DARK BROWN EYES • DARK BROWN HAIR • CAPRICORN

## LOCATIONS

### THE COURTYARD
OUTDOORS

There's a snowdrift there right now, but usually it's pretty nice.

### THE FORBIDDEN LIBRARY
INDOORS

Where they store the books the monks aren't allowed to read.

### THE CHAPEL
INDOORS

You can hear the monks praying well and singing poorly.

### THE CLIFFS
OUTDOORS

Why do people keep building on the side of cliffs? And always over jagged rocks?

## WEAPONS

### A STRING OF PRAYER BEADS
LIGHT-WEIGHT • MADE OF IVORY

Ivory prayer beads covered with tiny engraved symbols.

### A PRAYER CANDLE
MEDIUM-WEIGHT • MADE OF WAX

If you were praying that somebody died, your wish came true.

### SACRAMENTAL WINE
MEDIUM-WEIGHT • MADE OF GLASS & WINE

A great way to show your devotion is to drink a lot of this holy red wine.

### A BOTTLE OF SACRED OIL
LIGHT-WEIGHT • MADE OF OIL & TOXINS

It's not, like, massage oil. It's petroleum oil. But it's still sacred.

## MOTIVES

 TO AVENGE THEIR
FATHER

 TO PROVE THEY'RE
TOUGH

 OUT OF MADNESS

 FOR RELIGIOUS
REASONS

## CLUES & EVIDENCE

- Whoever would kill out of madness was right-handed.

- The person with a bottle of sacred oil wanted to kill to avenge their father. It was their father's sacred oil, you see.

- A Taurus was loving the sacramental wine. Maybe too much.

- The prayer beads were not allowed outside, and nobody broke that rule.

- Deacon Verdigris was found wandering outdoors.

- A weapon covered in tiny engraved symbols was brought by the person who had a motive to kill for religious reasons.

- The suspect who was on the cliffs had light brown eyes.

- The second tallest suspect was listening to the sounds of off-key singing.

- **The body was found in a snowdrift.**

|  | SUSPECTS | | | | MOTIVES | | | | LOCATIONS | | | |
|---|---|---|---|---|---|---|---|---|---|---|---|---|
| WEAPONS | | | | | | | | | | | | |
| | | | | | | | | | | | | |
| | | | | | | | | | | | | |
| | | | | | | | | | | | | |
| LOCATIONS | | | | | | | | | | | | |
| | | | | | | | | | | | | |
| | | | | | | | | | | | | |
| | | | | | | | | | | | | |
| MOTIVES | | | | | | | | | | | | |
| | | | | | | | | | | | | |
| | | | | | | | | | | | | |
| | | | | | | | | | | | | |

_____ **WHO?**

_____ **WHAT?**

_____ **WHERE?**

_____ **WHY?**

# 64. DEDUCTION COLLEGE 🔍🔍🔍

If the answers Logico needed were in the past, he was going to have to hit the books. So he went to his old alma mater, the College of Deduction, to do some research. But someone was trying to stop him. Either that or the librarian was killed for unrelated reasons.

## SUSPECTS

**DEAN GLAUCOUS**

The dean of some such and such department at Deduction College. What does he do? Well, he handles the money, for one . . .

**5'6" • RIGHT-HANDED • LIGHT BROWN EYES • LIGHT BROWN HAIR • VIRGO**

**MISTER SHADOW**

A silhouette in shadow. He moves like the wind and he looks like the night.

**▆▆▆ • LEFT-HANDED • ▆▆▆▆ • ▆▆▆▆ ▆▆▆ • AQUARIUS**

**CHANCELLOR TUSCANY**

As the head of Deduction College, she has deduced the best way to prevent herself from being killed by a rival. (Kill them first.)

**5'5" • LEFT-HANDED • GREEN EYES • GRAY HAIR • LIBRA**

**MISS SAFFRON**

Gorgeous and stunning, but maybe not all there in the brains department. Or maybe that's what she wants you to think. Or maybe she wants you to think that's what she wants you to think.

**5'2" • LEFT-HANDED • HAZEL EYES • BLOND HAIR • LIBRA**

## LOCATIONS

### THE BOOKSTORE
INDOORS

The biggest moneymaker on campus. A sign offers a deal on textbooks, three for $750.

### OLD MAIN
INDOORS

The first building on campus, the most important, and the least maintained. Paint is peeling off the walls!

### THE STADIUM
OUTDOORS

The field features the absolute highest-quality fake grass money can buy.

### THE ARBORETUM
OUTDOORS

An arboretum in the middle of campus. They've got oak, pine—all the trees!

## WEAPONS

### A CRYSTAL SKULL
MEDIUM-WEIGHT • MADE OF CRYSTAL

Maybe an actual alien's skull or maybe just a hoax.

### A GRADUATION CORD
LIGHT-WEIGHT • MADE OF CLOTH

It would be an honor to be strangled by one of these.

### A SHARP PENCIL
LIGHT-WEIGHT • MADE OF WOOD & METAL

Back then, they used actual lead. One stab and you'd die from lead poisoning.

### A HEAVY BACKPACK
HEAVY-WEIGHT • MADE OF CLOTH & BOOKS

Finally, a use for all of those logic textbooks.

## MOTIVES

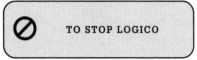

**TO PROVE A POINT**

**TO STOP LOGICO**

**FOR THE GREATER GOOD**

**TO CREATE A DIVERSION**

## CLUES & EVIDENCE

- The person who wanted to create a diversion was in the stadium.

- Mister Shadow did not want to kill for the greater good.

- A Virgo was looking at a pine tree. It was pretty.

- In the labyrinth engraved on the ancient ruins, chamber 1 is connected with the chamber bearing the second letter of the last name of the suspect in the bookstore. (See Exhibit C.)

- Logico found a shard of a crystal in Old Main.

- Whoever wanted to prove a point was right-handed.

- A graduation cord was seen lying on the ground outdoors.

- Miss Saffron was seen with a sharp pencil—maybe she *is* smart!

- **A heavy backpack was found beside the librarian.**

|  | SUSPECTS | MOTIVES | LOCATIONS |
|---|---|---|---|

WEAPONS

LOCATIONS

MOTIVES

WHO?

WHAT?

WHERE?

WHY?

# 65. LIKE OLD TIMES IN OLD MAIN 🔍🔍🔍

Chancellor Tuscany led Deductive Logico to the archives in Old Main. Unfortunately, when he got there, he found that the assistant librarian had been killed, too. Maybe this one was about him. Either way, he had to investigate before he could research.

## SUSPECTS

**DEAN GLAUCOUS**

The dean of some such and such department at Deduction College. What does he do? Well, he handles the money, for one . . .

5'6" • RIGHT-HANDED • LIGHT BROWN EYES • LIGHT BROWN HAIR • VIRGO

**PHILOSOPHER BONE**

A dashing, dark philosopher who pioneered the ethical theory that he is not responsible for his actions, but he should be paid for them.

5'1" • RIGHT-HANDED • LIGHT BROWN EYES • BALD • TAURUS

**EDITOR IVORY**

The greatest romance editor of all time. She invented the enemies-to-lovers genre, and she was the first person to put a naked man on the cover of a book.

5'6" • LEFT-HANDED • LIGHT BROWN EYES • GRAY HAIR • SCORPIO

**CRYPTOZOOLO-GIST CLOUD**

He knows every sighting of Bigfoot, Yeti, Sasquatch, and also what the difference is.

5'7" • RIGHT-HANDED • GRAY EYES • WHITE HAIR • SCORPIO

## LOCATIONS

### THE CHANCELLOR'S OFFICE
INDOORS

Behind the chancellor's desk is a painting of Chancellor Tuscany.

### THE ROOF
OUTDOORS

You can look out over the whole campus and even see the arboretum!

### THE TEACHER'S LOUNGE
INDOORS

Lots of apples. Like, way, way too many apples.

### THE FRONT STEPS
OUTDOORS

These stone steps represent the endless climb of human knowledge. (Or something.)

## WEAPONS

### A MARBLE BUST
HEAVY-WEIGHT • MADE OF MARBLE

It's a bust of a famous academic, but don't look him up—you won't like what you find.

### AN OLD COMPUTER
HEAVY-WEIGHT • MADE OF PLASTIC & TECH

A monitor, a giant tower, a heavy keyboard with clacking keys, a rollerball mouse—it's an antique!

### A LAPTOP
MEDIUM-WEIGHT • MADE OF METAL & TECH

The machine you work on. It's connected to every distraction ever made.

### A HEAVY BOOK
HEAVY-WEIGHT • MADE OF PAPER

A reference book about standing stones.

## MOTIVES

 FOR POLITICAL
PURPOSES

 BECAUSE THEY COULD

 AS A SCIENTIFIC
EXPERIMENT

 TO IMPRESS A LADY

## CLUES & EVIDENCE

- A weapon made of paper was not found on the roof.

- The suspect who knew too much about Bigfoot wanted to impress a lady.

- Philosopher Bone was a member of the Path of the Ancient Dead.

- The person with a marble bust wanted to kill for political purposes.

- The suspect on the roof had gray hair.

- Right-handed fingerprints were found on the weapon partially made of metal.

- A reference book was found outdoors.

- Members of the Path of the Ancient Dead never desired to conduct scientific experiments.

- A student handed Logico a scrambled note: A RIVGO DAH EHT LDO RTMEPOCU.

- The person who would kill because they could was in the teacher's lounge.

- **The assistant librarian's body was found beneath a painting of the chancellor.**

SUSPECTS  MOTIVES  LOCATIONS

WEAPONS

LOCATIONS

MOTIVES

WHO?

WHAT?

WHERE?

WHY?

# 66. VIVE LA RÉVOLUTION ! 🔍🔍🔍

When Logico studied the archives, he found that in one of the many, many French revolutions, the ancient ruins seemed to play a minor part in an otherwise major event: a single murder in a revolution is like a single spark in a fire. This time, a minor royal had been killed.

## SUSPECTS

**PRÉSIDENT AMARANTH**

The legendary Président Amaranth, with whom the current president shares a name. He loves spending time with his constituents, especially a certain class of them.

5'10" • RIGHT-HANDED • GRAY EYES • RED HAIR • GEMINI

**AMIRAL MARINE**

Amiral Marine is the son of an Amiral Marine who was himself the son of an Amiral Marine.

5'9" • RIGHT-HANDED • BLUE EYES • LIGHT BROWN HAIR • CANCER

**VISCOUNT EMINENCE**

This can't be possible, but the history books seem to suggest that this is not an ancestor of Viscount Eminence, but the same man.

5'2" • LEFT-HANDED • GRAY EYES • DARK BROWN HAIR • PISCES

**COMRADE CHAMPAGNE**

Not the present-day Comrade Champagne, mind you, or even an ancestor. Just another comrade who also likes his bubbly.

5'11" • LEFT-HANDED • HAZEL EYES • BLOND HAIR • CAPRICORN

# LOCATIONS

### THE ANCIENT RUINS
OUTDOORS

The texts reference these stones in cryptic ways, like they're hiding something.

### THE BARRICADES
OUTDOORS

The kind of guerrilla fortification you can write a musical about.

### THE BASTILLE
INDOORS

At any point in French history, you were either storming this fortress or defending it.

### THE SEINE
OUTDOORS

At the time, an incredibly polluted river. Do not drink it, swim in it, touch it, or look at it.

# WEAPONS

### A POLITICAL TREATISE
MEDIUM-WEIGHT • MADE OF PAPER

The densest jargon you've ever read justifying violence, so it's fitting to use it to kill.

### A BALLOT BOX
HEAVY-WEIGHT • MADE OF WOOD & PAPER

Voting matters, especially to the weight of this box.

### A TORCH
MEDIUM-WEIGHT • MADE OF WOOD & FIRE

A torch of freedom or tyranny depending on who's holding it.

### A SACRED SCEPTER
HEAVY-WEIGHT • MADE OF GLASS & TOXINS

An ancient sacred scepter, revered by all French people. It's missing a jewel.

## MOTIVES

 TO STOP THE
REVOLUTION

 TO BECOME KING

 FOR THE GREATER
GOOD

 FOR THE REVOLUTION

## CLUES & EVIDENCE

- A torch lit the halls of a great fortress.

- The person who wanted to stop the revolution was scheming in the ancient ruins.

- Amiral Marine was a member of the Drinkers of the Dark Wine.

- In the labyrinth engraved on the ancient ruins, the L is connected with the first letter of the last name of the suspect who wanted to kill for the revolution. (See Exhibit C.)

- A ballot-stuffed box was found by the barricades: democracy in action!

- Comrade Champagne was a man of the people: he did not want to become king.

- The person with a torch did not want to kill for the revolution.

- The second tallest suspect was seen hanging around a toxic river.

- Members of the Drinkers of the Dark Wine were required to carry a political treatise with them at all times.

- **A single jewel was found beside the victim.**

SUSPECTS     MOTIVES     LOCATIONS

WEAPONS

LOCATIONS

MOTIVES

WHO?

WHAT?

WHERE?

WHY?

# 67. KING ARTHUR AND THE MURDER OF A JESTER 🔍🔍🔍

Deductive Logico delved more deeply into the past, into early, early history, where he found the pieces of a lesser legend of King Arthur. A decades-long war was reportedly started because of the murder of a court jester, but Logico thought there was something funny going on.

## SUSPECTS

**LORD LAVENDER**

A steadfast ultra-royalist in the Court, as well as the bardic composer behind *The Ghost of the Castle* and *Starlight Carriage*.

5'9" • RIGHT-HANDED • GREEN EYES • GRAY HAIR • VIRGO

**LADY VIOLET**

The discoverer of the Violet Isles, which are named after her.

5'0" • RIGHT-HANDED • BLUE EYES • BLOND HAIR • VIRGO

**THE DUKE OF VERMILLION**

The current Duke of Vermillion's great-times-seventy-three grandfather.

5'9" • LEFT-HANDED • GRAY EYES • WHITE HAIR • PISCES

**SIR RULEAN**

The old knight that the fake Sir Rulean probably stole his name from.

5'8" • RIGHT-HANDED • BLUE EYES • RED HAIR • LEO

## LOCATIONS

### AVALON
OUTDOORS

A magical and mysterious island, as most legendary islands seem to be.

### THE ANCIENT RUINS
OUTDOORS

Even in the times of Arthurian legends, these stones still stood.

### CAMELOT
INDOORS

The great court of King Arthur, where inequality was only slightly less than it is now.

### THE ENCHANTED LAKE
OUTDOORS

A lady lives in a pond, and she throws swords at passersby. Life was dangerous back then.

## WEAPONS

### A BOTTLE OF WINE
MEDIUM-WEIGHT • MADE OF GLASS & ALCOHOL

Watch out for stains, because the red doesn't come out.

### AN ANTIQUE HELMET
HEAVY-WEIGHT • MADE OF METAL

It's rusty and it looks awesome.

### EXCALIBUR
HEAVY-WEIGHT • MADE OF METAL

The ancient sword of legend. Either thrown from the lake or pulled from a stone—not sure.

### THE GRAIL
MEDIUM-WEIGHT • MADE OF METAL

The Holy Grail or maybe just a golden cup. But valuable either way!

## MOTIVES

 BECAUSE IT WAS LOGICAL

 TO STEAL A BODY

 FOR RELIGIOUS REASONS

 ON A DARE

## CLUES & EVIDENCE

- Lord Lavender was seen carousing with an underwater woman.

- The person with an antique helmet did not want to kill on a dare.

- The person with the grail had a motive to kill for religious reasons.

- One piece of the text was scrambled: ETH KUED OF LIVINMLERO WAS ENSE WHTI LRBIUCXAE.

- The second shortest suspect was seen in the ancient ruins.

- The person with a bottle of wine drank enough to want to steal a body.

- Lord Lavender did not want to steal a body. He was above that!

- The person who would kill because it was logical was being logical in Avalon.

- **The body was found in Camelot.**

|  | SUSPECTS | MOTIVES | LOCATIONS |
| --- | --- | --- | --- |

WEAPONS

LOCATIONS

MOTIVES

_____ **WHO?**

_____ **WHAT?**

_____ **WHERE?**

_____ **WHY?**

# 68. HOUSTON, WE HAVE A BODY 🔍🔍🔍

Rearranging the letters in the labyrinth engraved on the ancient ruins (see Exhibit C), Logico found they spelled LUNAR ONE I. He hacked into a government database about the recently built lunar base, and he learned two unbelievable things: they had discovered ancient ruins on the moon, and they had also been covering up a moon murder.

## SUSPECTS

**COACH RASPBERRY**

One of the best coaches this side of the Mississippi, regardless of which side you're on.

**6'0" • LEFT-HANDED • BLUE EYES • BLOND HAIR • ARIES**

**CAPTAIN SLATE**

A real-life astronaut. The first woman to travel around the dark side of the moon, and also the first to be suspected of murdering her copilot.

**5'5" • LEFT-HANDED • DARK BROWN EYES • DARK BROWN HAIR • AQUARIUS**

**COSMONAUT BLUSKI**

An ex-Soviet spaceman whose blood flows red. Sure, that's normal, but for him it's patriotic.

**6'2" • LEFT-HANDED • DARK BROWN EYES • BLACK HAIR • ARIES**

**GENERAL COFFEE**

An espresso connoisseur who could not have become the war criminal he is today if not for coffee.

**6'0" • RIGHT-HANDED • DARK BROWN EYES • BALD • SAGITTARIUS**

## LOCATIONS

### THE ANCIENT RUINS
OUTDOORS

In space, they are perfectly preserved. But how are they up there? And why?

### THE LUNAR ROVER
OUTDOORS

A great buggy to cruise around in, maybe meet some moon babes or moon bros.

### THE LUNAR BASE
INDOORS

Your home away from home-world. Enjoy feeling super strong in the low-G environment.

### THE LUNAR LANDER
OUTDOORS

This bad boy can fly back up to the orbiting spacecraft with its space jets.

## WEAPONS

### AN AIR TANK
HEAVY-WEIGHT • MADE OF METAL & AIR

You can use it to breathe or to stop someone from breathing.

### A BIG BATTERY
HEAVY-WEIGHT • MADE OF METAL & TECH

It can power your space tools with ten thousand volts, or kill!

### A HUMAN SKULL
MEDIUM-WEIGHT • MADE OF BONE

"Alas, poor Yorick, I knew him. And now I'm swinging his skull at people."

### A MOON ROCK
MEDIUM-WEIGHT • MADE OF ROCK

When you can't find another weapon, a rock is always nearby.

## MOTIVES

 TO GET REVENGE

 AS A SCIENTIFIC EXPERIMENT

 FOR POLITICAL PURPOSES

 OUT OF SPACE MADNESS

## CLUES & EVIDENCE

- According to the government records, the person with an air tank would kill out of space madness, which is a real thing.

- An Aries was confirmed to be carrying the moon rock.

- A Sagittarius, meanwhile, possessed the big battery.

- The suspect with the same height as General Coffee and the person who brought an air tank ran around with the same group of friends at space camp.

- Being cooped up in the lunar base made that person want to get revenge.

- The remains of a human head were seen outdoors.

- The person who wanted to kill as a scientific experiment was driving the lunar rover.

- According to secret, scrambled records: TMASUONCO KBISUL ADH UOHTRBG OT EHT NOMO TEH KULSL OF A EGATR ELOATNYRIV-UOR REHO.

- Whoever was visiting the ancient ruins was right-handed.

- **The murder took place underneath a space jet.**

SUSPECTS  MOTIVES  LOCATIONS

WEAPONS

LOCATIONS

MOTIVES

WHO?

WHAT?

WHERE?

WHY?

# 69. THE MAGICAL MYSTERY MURDER 🔍🔍🔍

Deductive Logico realized "AUREOLIN" was an anagram of the letters on the ancient ruins, and that couldn't be a coincidence. So, he bought tickets to the Magic Palace to confront her. But when he got there, the booker had been killed. Was it Aureolin? Or were there two murderers at the Palace that night?

## SUSPECTS

**MISTER SHADOW**

A silhouette in shadow. He moves like the wind, and he looks like the night.

▇▇▇▇ • LEFT-HANDED • ▇▇▇▇▇▇▇▇ • ▇▇▇▇▇▇▇
▇▇▇▇ • AQUARIUS

**HIGH ALCHE-MIST RAVEN**

There's an old joke that all alchemists are high alchemists. Raven hates it.

5'8" • RIGHT-HANDED • LIGHT BROWN EYES • DARK BROWN HAIR • PISCES

**THE AMAZING AUREOLIN**

She got out of jail a while ago, because she was a master of escape.

5'6" • LEFT-HANDED • GREEN EYES • BLOND HAIR • ARIES

**SUPERFAN SMOKY**

He knows the shooting locations of every Midnight mystery, but not how to make friends.

5'10" • LEFT-HANDED • BLACK EYES • DARK BROWN HAIR • VIRGO

## LOCATIONS

### THE PIANO ROOM
INDOORS

In this mysterious room is a piano that plays itself! Is it a ghost, or uncredited low-wage labor?

### THE CLOSE-UP TABLE
INDOORS

Where you watch card and coin tricks . . . and if you're smart, your wallet!

### THE MAIN STAGE
INDOORS

Where only the best or most well-connected magicians perform classics, like the milk can escape (which leaves milk everywhere).

### THE PARKING LOT
OUTDOORS

There is only valet parking and it costs a fortune.

## WEAPONS

### THE ACE OF SPADES
LIGHT-WEIGHT • MADE OF PAPER

Thrown hard enough, it can slice a human throat. Even worse, it can be used for a card trick.

### A SAW
MEDIUM-WEIGHT • MADE OF METAL & WOOD

For sawing a woman in two, or honestly, for sawing anyone in two.

### A TRAINED VICIOUS RABBIT
MEDIUM-WEIGHT • MADE OF RABBIT

Check your hats before you put them on. There might be a furry white menace inside.

### A BOTTLE OF CHEAP LIQUOR
LIGHT-WEIGHT • MADE OF GLASS & CHEMICALS

Denatured and deadly, with only the faintest taste of methanol.

## MOTIVES

 TO STEAL AN IDEA

 TO PROTECT A MAGI-CAL SECRET

 BECAUSE THEY BROKE THE CODE

 A GHOST MADE THEM

## CLUES & EVIDENCE

- Whoever might have killed because a ghost made them was right-handed.

- Logico found a receipt with a huge bill and a scrambled note: A RIVGO DAH A FYRRU HWEIT ANEECM.

- In the labyrinth engraved on the ancient ruins, chamber 2 is connected to the first letter of the last name of a suspect who did not want to steal an idea. (See Exhibit C.)

- Whoever was in the piano room had a light-weight weapon.

- High Alchemist Raven brought a medium-weight weapon.

- The suspect who wanted to protect a magical secret had a weapon made of paper.

- The Amazing Aureolin was standing in a puddle of milk.

- The person who would kill because they broke the code was at the close-up table.

- **The booker had been sawed in two.**

SUSPECTS       MOTIVES        LOCATIONS

WEAPONS

LOCATIONS

MOTIVES

WHO?

WHAT?

WHERE?

WHY?

# 70. DEATH IN AN EVEN DARKER ALLEY 🔍🔍🔍

Stumbling out of the Magic Palace, having found no leads in his quest for understanding (and—don't forget!—revenge), Deductive Logico instead found himself in an even darker alley than the previous one. And there, on the ground, was (are you even surprised?) another dead body.

## SUSPECTS

**BABYFACE BLUE**

This is absolutely one fully grown man, and not two kids in a trench coat. They can do adult things like see R-rated movies, buy beer, and stay out way past bedtime.

**7'8" • RIGHT-HANDED • BLUE EYES • BLOND HAIR • GEMINI**

**BLACKSTONE, ESQ.**

Incredibly talented at the most important skill for an attorney: getting paid.

**6'0" • RIGHT-HANDED • BLACK EYES • BLACK HAIR • SCORPIO**

**MISTER SHADOW**

A silhouette in shadow. He moves like the wind, and he looks like the night.

**▮▮▮ • LEFT-HANDED • ▮▮▮▮▮▮▮ • DARK BROWN HAIR • ▮▮▮▮▮**

**SILVERTON THE LEGEND**

An acclaimed actor of the Golden Age, now in his golden years.

**6'4" • RIGHT-HANDED • BLUE EYES • SILVER HAIR • LEO**

## LOCATIONS

### A METAL FENCE
OUTDOORS

Your typical chain-link fence. What more do you want?

### A BURNT-OUT CAR HUSK
OUTDOORS

It looks like someone smashed a car to bits and then set it on fire.

### A DUMPSTER
OUTDOORS

It does not smell good. No, it does not.

### THE DISTRACTING GRAFFITI
OUTDOORS

The dragon-riding-a-motorcycle mural has been painted over by an ominous image of ruins.

## WEAPONS

### A SCIMITAR
MEDIUM-WEIGHT • MADE OF METAL

Technically, it's just a bent sword, but if you call it scimitar, it sounds cooler.

### A SHOVEL
MEDIUM-WEIGHT • MADE OF METAL & WOOD

The great thing about using a shovel for murder is it can also dig a hole to help hide the body.

### A RED HERRING
MEDIUM-WEIGHT • MADE OF FISH

If you hold it by the tail, you can get some real momentum behind it.

### A VIAL OF POISON
LIGHT-WEIGHT • MADE OF GLASS & TOXINS

Your typical vial of poison. Don't underestimate the classics.

## MOTIVES

 TO STEAL AN IDEA

 OUT OF BLOODLUST

 TO TEACH THEM A LESSON

 TO SILENCE A WITNESS

## CLUES & EVIDENCE

- The suspect with the red herring also had black hair.

- The suspect who wanted to steal an idea had a weapon made at least partially of metal.

- A gossip columnist gave Logico a scrambled note that read: A OGD-NLE EAG ORATC AETNDW TO LLIK OTU FO TOUSLOBLD EFATR NGIEB NESE NI A UTRBN OTU RAC KHSU.

- Babyface Blue had cut themselves on a bent sword and begun to cry.

- Silverton the Legend had a vial of poison.

- The person who wanted to steal an idea was not near the distracting graffiti.

- Whoever was at the metal fence was right-handed.

- Mister Shadow was not next to the distracting graffiti.

- The person who wanted to silence a witness was in the dumpster.

- **A blood-stained shovel was found by the body.**

SUSPECTS    MOTIVES    LOCATIONS

WEAPONS

LOCATIONS

MOTIVES

_____
WHO?

_____
WHAT?

_____
WHERE?

_____
WHY?

# 71. NEW AGE, NEW MURDER! 🔍🔍🔍

New Aegis was a relaxed, hippie town with wide roads, funky shops, and a robust tourist-enlightenment industry. Irratino would have loved this place, so Logico loved it a little, too. Even though he wasn't sure about their claims of "scientifically proven spiritual transcendence guaranteed." For example, how did that square with the deputy mayor being murdered?

## SUSPECTS

**UNCLE MIDNIGHT**

When his dad died, he bought a desert mansion with a pool and retired. He was seventeen.

5'8" • LEFT-HANDED • BLUE EYES • DARK BROWN HAIR • SAGITTARIUS

**BOOKIE-WINNER GAINSBORO**

He won the Bookington Award for his novel, which he will tell you within two minutes of meeting you. The book is six thousand pages long, and it's about dirt.

6'0" • LEFT-HANDED • HAZEL EYES • LIGHT BROWN HAIR • GEMINI

**MAYOR HONEY**

This is actually a third identical Mayor Honey. Totally not a multiple murderer.

6'0" • LEFT-HANDED • HAZEL EYES • LIGHT BROWN HAIR • SCORPIO

**THE CRYSTAL GODDESS**

Her followers regard her as a divine being, which is why they give her money.

5'9" • LEFT-HANDED • BLUE EYES • WHITE HAIR • LEO

## LOCATIONS

### A KITSCHY RESTAURANT
INDOORS

An ancient-alien-themed restaurant with entrees like the UFOmelette.

### THE TOWN SQUARE
OUTDOORS

Here you can find a well, which they discovered by dowsing. (It's dry.)

### A CRYSTAL SHOP
INDOORS

They sell only your finest and most expensive crystals here. All guaranteed to have good vibes.

### A UFO CRASH SITE
OUTDOORS

The town's moneymaker. A tourist destination that rivals the Eiffel Tower (according to the pamphlets, at least).

## WEAPONS

### A SELENITE WAND
MEDIUM-WEIGHT • MADE OF CRYSTAL

For casting spells and bashing skulls.

### A DOWSING ROD
MEDIUM-WEIGHT • MADE OF WOOD

You can find water, oil, and suckers with this.

### A BENT SPOON
LIGHT-WEIGHT • MADE OF METAL

Was it twisted by the mysterious powers of the mind, or when you weren't looking?

### A PRAYER CANDLE
MEDIUM-WEIGHT • MADE OF WAX

If you were praying that somebody died, your wish came true.

## MOTIVES

 WHILE TRIPPIN' OUT, MAN

 OUT OF JEALOUSY

 TO PROTECT A SECRET

 AS A SCIENTIFIC EXPERIMENT

## CLUES & EVIDENCE

- The person with a prayer candle might have killed while trippin' out, man.

- A Leo had the bent spoon. (Typical.)

- A Sagittarius had the prayer candle. (Of course.)

- Either Mayor Honey was at a UFO crash site, or Bookie-Winner Gainsboro was in a kitschy restaurant.

- The suspect who might kill out of jealousy was seen indoors.

- The person who wanted to kill as a scientific experiment was in the town square.

- Bookie-Winner Gainsboro hated kitsch: he would never, ever set foot in a kitschy restaurant, not even to murder.

- Someone had used the Next Letter Code in some spray-painted graffiti: Z RDKDMHSD VZMC VZR RDDM HMCNNQR.

- **A bloody dowsing rod was found beside the body of the deputy mayor.**

SUSPECTS     MOTIVES     LOCATIONS

WEAPONS

LOCATIONS

MOTIVES

WHO?

WHAT?

WHERE?

WHY?

# 72. PRISM OR PRISON? 🔍🔍🔍

Deductive Logico stepped into the crystal shop, and his first thought was that he should get a present for Inspector Irratino. His second thought was sadness, because he wouldn't be able to do that ever again. His third thought was that the crystal salesman was dead.

## SUSPECTS

**SUPREME MAS-TER COBALT**

He has a long, white beard and he wears long, white robes.

5'9" • RIGHT-HANDED • BLUE EYES • SILVER HAIR • AQUARIUS

**NUMEROLOGIST NIGHT**

A mathematical and esoteric prodigy. Not only do they know the value of *H*, they know the meaning of *H*.

5'9" • LEFT-HANDED • BLUE EYES • DARK BROWN HAIR • PISCES

**BLACKSTONE, ESQ.**

Incredibly talented at the most important skill for an attorney: getting paid.

6'0" • RIGHT-HANDED • BLACK EYES • BLACK HAIR • SCORPIO

**DR. SEASHELL, DDS**

He's an amateur physicist with a new theory of the universe, and also, he's a working dentist.

5'7" • RIGHT-HANDED • GREEN EYES • GRAY HAIR • PISCES

## LOCATIONS

### THE SAGE SECTION
INDOORS

Sustainably harvested cultural appropriation. (But it does work!)

### THE GIANT SAFE
INDOORS

The money's kept in the cash register. The only thing in here is more crystals.

### THE ROOFTOP BAR
OUTDOORS

On top of the crystal shop is a bar where you can drink crystal-infused cocktails.

### THE OUTDOOR MEDITATION SPACE
OUTDOORS

A place to calmly meditate about how much money you're willing to spend here.

## WEAPONS

### A CRYSTAL DAGGER
MEDIUM-WEIGHT • MADE OF CRYSTAL

It might have some kind of ritual purpose, but it might just look great on your mantle.

### A DECK OF MAROT CARDS
LIGHT-WEIGHT • MADE OF PAPER

You can use these murder-themed tarot cards to read your future.

### A CRYSTAL BALL
HEAVY-WEIGHT • MADE OF CRYSTAL

If you look into it, it will tell you your future, so long as your future is a crystal ball.

### A CHANNELED TEXT
HEAVY-WEIGHT • MADE OF PAPER

This book is longer than Gainsboro's masterpiece and was supposedly written by ghosts.

## MOTIVES

 FOR MONEY

 BECAUSE THE VIBES WERE OFF

 TO PROVE THEIR LOVE

 TO STEAL A CRYSTAL

## CLUES & EVIDENCE

- The person with a crystal dagger wanted to prove their love.

- All members of the Order of the Holy Earth carried a copy of a channeled text.

- Forensics determined a weapon made out of paper was present in the sage section.

- Whoever would kill because the vibes were off had blue eyes.

- A scrambled note recorded the movements of a suspect: PMREESU ESRMTA BLACOT WSA UDFNO DROOTOSU.

- The suspect with the same height as Supreme Master Cobalt was in love with the person who brought a deck of marot cards.

- Dr. Seashell, DDS, was a member of the Order of the Holy Earth.

- Whoever wanted to steal a crystal was also giving off real Pisces vibes.

- Whoever was in the outdoor meditation space had a heavy-weight weapon.

- A Pisces was literally inside the giant safe.

- Analysts discovered traces of a weapon made of crystal on the clothing of Blackstone, Esq.

- **The crystal salesman was killed by a crystal ball. Is that ironic?**

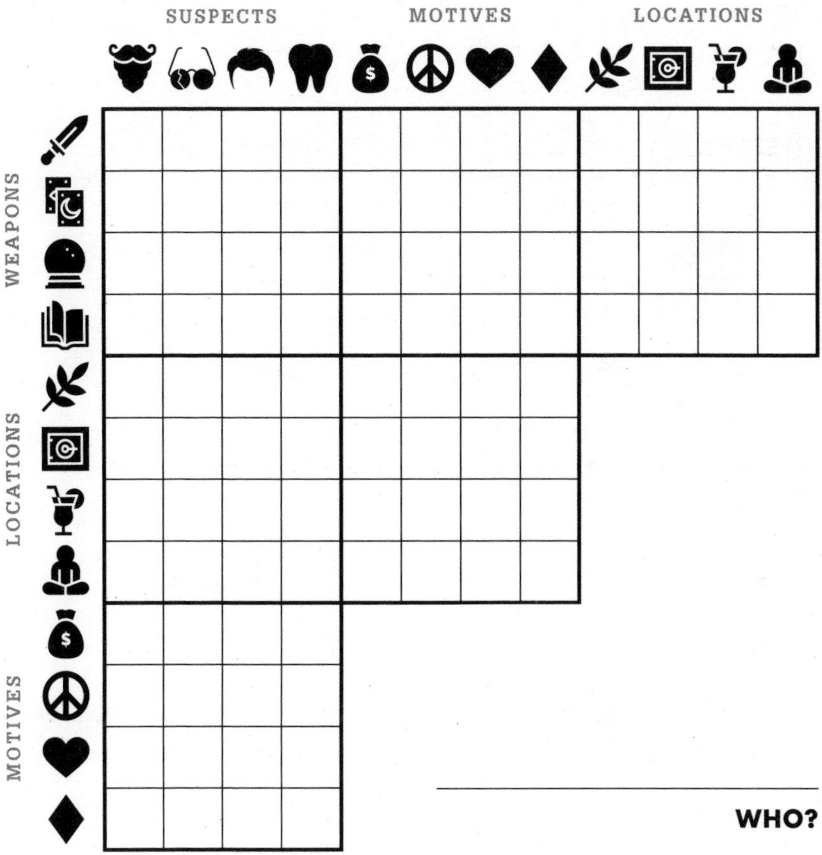


WHO?

WHAT?

WHERE?

WHY?

# 73. KITSCHY KITSCHY KILLING 🔍🔍🔍

Logico went to a nice little diner, decorated with mementos of the town, like its hot springs and its ancient ruins and its UFO crash site. He tried to order a sandwich but was informed this was impossible, as the sandwich chef had been murdered.

## SUSPECTS

### COACH RASPBERRY

One of the best coaches this side of the Mississippi, regardless of which side you're on.

6'0" • LEFT-HANDED • BLUE EYES • BLOND HAIR • ARIES

### GENERAL COFFEE

An espresso connoisseur who has been missing his favorite coffee cup for a long time. If he finds the person who took it, he'll kill them.

6'0" • RIGHT-HANDED • DARK BROWN EYES • BALD • SAGITTARIUS

### CHEF AUBERGINE

It is said that she once killed her husband, cooked him, and then served him at her restaurant. It's not true, but just the fact that it's said about her tells you something.

5'2" • RIGHT-HANDED • BLUE EYES • BLOND HAIR • LIBRA

### EARL GREY

He comes from a long line of Earl Greys. Yes, of the tea. No, he doesn't sign autographs. But he'll give you a free bag if you ask.

5'9" • RIGHT-HANDED • LIGHT BROWN EYES • WHITE HAIR • CAPRICORN

# LOCATIONS

### THE KITCHEN
INDOORS

You honestly don't want to see how the food is made here.

### THE BATHROOM
INDOORS

As much as you don't want to go into the kitchen, you really don't want to go in here.

### THE BOOTHS
INDOORS

Sure, the booths are torn up and the stuffing is coming out. But it's a booth!

### THE FRONT PATIO
OUTDOORS

The front patio has a view of the town square so you can do great people watching.

# WEAPONS

### A WALL KNICKKNACK
HEAVY-WEIGHT • MADE OF METAL

An old knickknack is hanging on the wall. It's some kind of old tool.

### A VIAL OF POISON
LIGHT-WEIGHT • MADE OF GLASS & TOXINS

Your typical vial of poison. Don't underestimate the classics.

### A SPOON
LIGHT-WEIGHT • MADE OF METAL

If a fork is more gruesome than a knife, think how bad killing someone with a spoon would be.

### HYPERALLERGENIC OIL
LIGHT-WEIGHT • MADE OF OIL

You read that right. Everyone is deathly allergic to this.

## MOTIVES

 TO PROVE A POINT

 TO GET A BETTER SEAT

 TO LIVEN UP A PARTY

 OUT OF JEALOUSY

## CLUES & EVIDENCE

- The person who wanted to liven up a party was not in the kitchen (even though cooking is a great way to liven up a party).

- Whoever wanted to prove a point was right-handed.

- An Aries had an old tool. That sounds like an insult, but it's just a fact.

- Chef Aubergine was a member of the Order of Steel.

- Someone had scrawled a scrambled clue on the plastic menu: ENN-AOY IWHT A LVIA FO NOIPOS OWDLU KILL TOU OF LEJYSUAO.

- A drop of oil was discovered in the bathroom.

- A Sagittarius was sitting on the front patio.

- Members of the Order of Steel only carried metal weapons.

- Whoever wanted to get a better seat was a Capricorn.

- **A spoon was used to commit the murder.**

SUSPECTS     MOTIVES     LOCATIONS

WEAPONS

LOCATIONS

MOTIVES

_____
WHO?

_____
WHAT?

_____
WHERE?

_____
WHY?

# 74. UFO, WHAT'D YOU KNOW? 🔍🔍🔍

Deductive Logico traveled to the locally famous UFO crash site. Some tourists believed it was a real crash of a real UFO. Other tourists thought it had been faked. And one tourist didn't agree with either of these positions, because he was dead.

## SUSPECTS

**SECRETARY CELADON**

The secretary of defense, and someone who is personally responsible for a number of global crises, some of which are now named after her.

5'6" • LEFT-HANDED • GREEN EYES • LIGHT BROWN HAIR • LEO

**SOCIOLOGIST UMBER**

As a representative from the hard sciences, she is always asking people to question their priors and if they've read Adorno.

5'4" • LEFT-HANDED • BLUE EYES • BLOND HAIR • LEO

**HERBALIST ONYX**

In her greenhouse, she's grown every kind of plant required in the culinary, magick, and poisoning arts.

5'0" • RIGHT-HANDED • DARK BROWN EYES • BLACK HAIR • VIRGO

**DR. SEASHELL, DDS**

He's an amateur physicist with a new theory of the universe, and also a working dentist.

5'7" • RIGHT-HANDED • GREEN EYES • GRAY HAIR • PISCES

## LOCATIONS

### THE CRATER
OUTDOORS

At the middle is some metal equipment that looks like it might be extraterrestrial (if you squint).

### THE MOUTH OF THE CAVE
OUTDOORS

A faint light and a pulsing sound seem to come from inside.

### THE GIFT SHOP
INDOORS

You can buy a little plush alien doll, a local timeshare, or an abductee NFT.

### THE GOVERNMENT VAN
INDOORS

If it is a hoax, then why is there a white government van loitering nearby?

## WEAPONS

### A PSEUDO-SCIENTIFIC APPARATUS
HEAVY-WEIGHT • MADE OF METAL

This one has been upgraded to measure your parquons in addition to your blaxons.

### A CAULDRON
HEAVY-WEIGHT • MADE OF METAL

If you can pick it up, you can hit someone with it. Or you can just give them a sip.

### A SELENITE WAND
MEDIUM-WEIGHT • MADE OF SELENITE

For casting spells and bashing skulls.

### A HYPNOTIC POCKET WATCH
LIGHT-WEIGHT • MADE OF METAL

If you look deeply into this watch, you can tell the time.

## MOTIVES

 AS A SCIENTIFIC EXPERIMENT

 BECAUSE THE VIBES WERE OFF

 BY THE ORDER OF A CULT

 TO STEAL THE UFO

## CLUES & EVIDENCE

- Secretary Celadon was a member of the Order of the Tar and Feather.

- Whoever wanted to kill by the order of a cult was a Virgo.

- A parquon-measuring device was found beside a plush doll.

- Sociologist Umber had a cauldron. (In addition to being a sociologist, she was a witch.)

- A scrambled message was left in the guestbook: A ELO WSA NI HET ARCERT.

- Members of the Order of the Tar and Feather were not allowed to touch selenite or stand in the mouths of caves.

- Whoever would kill because the vibes were off had a heavy-weight weapon.

- Whoever wanted to steal the UFO was left-handed.

- Either Dr. Seashell, DDS, brought a selenite wand, or he was in the mouth of the cave.

- Herbalist Onyx brought a pseudo-scientific apparatus.

- **The tourist's body was found inside a white van.**

SUSPECTS    MOTIVES    LOCATIONS

WEAPONS

LOCATIONS

MOTIVES

_____
**WHO?**

_____
**WHAT?**

_____
**WHERE?**

_____
**WHY?**

# 75. REVENGE IN THE CAVE 🔍🔍🔍

Deductive Logico crept through the tunnels of the mysterious cave. Suddenly, he heard a scream, so he stopped creeping and started running. He didn't find a body. He found something else: some kind of underground workshop, and the secret hideout of the last three murderers.

What was this place, and who was Mister Shadow, really?

## SUSPECTS

**MISTER SHADOW**

A silhouette in shadow. He moves like the wind, and he looks like the night.

**6'2" • LEFT-HANDED • GREEN EYES • DARK BROWN HAIR • AQUARIUS**

**MAYOR HONEY**

He knows where the bodies are buried, and he makes sure they always vote for him.

**6'0" • LEFT-HANDED • HAZEL EYES • LIGHT BROWN HAIR • SCORPIO**

**BLACKSTONE, ESQ.**

Incredibly talented at the most important skill for an attorney: getting paid.

**6'0" • RIGHT-HANDED • BLACK EYES • BLACK HAIR • SCORPIO**

**DR. SEASHELL, DDS**

He's an amateur physicist with a new theory of the universe, and also a working dentist.

**5'7" • RIGHT-HANDED • GREEN EYES • GRAY HAIR • PISCES**

# LOCATIONS

### A BIG MACHINE
INDOORS

It looks like this machine is manufacturing the so-called ancient ruins!

### THE NEW RUINS
INDOORS

Identical to the ancient ruins, except new and unruined, and with *SdW* stamped on the side of them.

### A TABLE
INDOORS

The table is covered in maps of the ruin locations, plus forged historical documents.

### A DEAD END
INDOORS

A long tunnel that leads to a stone wall and nothing else.

# WEAPONS

### A GIANT BONE
HEAVY-WEIGHT • MADE OF BONE

What size animal could such a bone come from? And what size dog would eat it?!

### A GIANT MAGNET
MEDIUM-WEIGHT • MADE OF METAL

Keep it away from any fillings.

### A ROCK
MEDIUM-WEIGHT • MADE OF MINERALS

A regular rock. But weirdly, not from this desert. And chipped.

### A GLOBE
HEAVY-WEIGHT • MADE OF METAL

For plotting world domination or storing drinks.

## MOTIVES

 FOR MONEY

 TO PROMOTE THE OCCULT

 TO HELP WIN A WAR

 TO PROMOTE THE TOWN

## CLUES & EVIDENCE

- Whoever was standing by the table was right-handed.

- A member of the Rite of the Flaming Earth wanted to promote the town.

- The person who wanted to kill for money was not in a dead end.

- Mister Shadow kept swinging his weapon, and from the sparks when it hit something, Logico could tell it was made of metal.

- Whoever wanted to help win a war was giving off real Pisces vibes.

- To join the Rite of the Flaming Earth, you have to be a Scorpio.

- A giant bone was next to a stamp that read *SdW*. What does that stand for?

- Either Mayor Honey brought a globe, or a globe was by a big machine.

- A member of the Rite of the Flaming Earth had the globe.

- A scrambled note was scrawled on the cave wall: RHVWEOE TWEADN OT LLIK FRO EYOMN LDEH A GBELO IN HEITR HDNA.

- **The person with the giant magnet was clearly the one responsible.**

SUSPECTS     MOTIVES     LOCATIONS

WEAPONS

LOCATIONS

MOTIVES

WHO?

WHAT?

WHERE?

WHY?

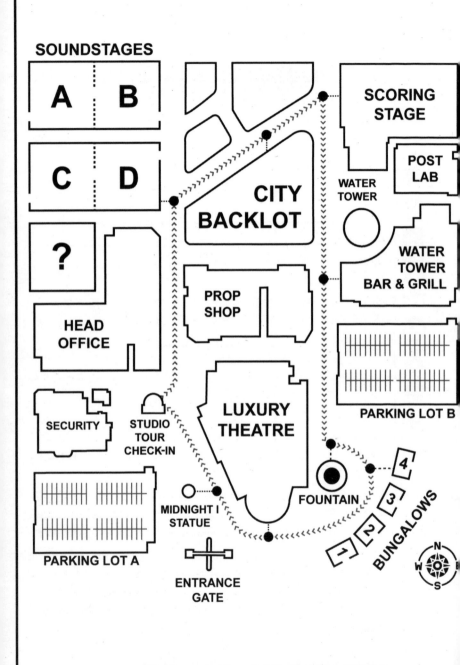

# EXHIBIT D

SOUNDSTAGES

A B

C D

?

HEAD OFFICE

SECURITY

STUDIO TOUR CHECK-IN

PARKING LOT A

MIDNIGHT I STATUE

ENTRANCE GATE

CITY BACKLOT

PROP SHOP

LUXURY THEATRE

FOUNTAIN

SCORING STAGE

POST LAB

WATER TOWER

WATER TOWER BAR & GRILL

PARKING LOT B

BUNGALOWS

1 2 3 4

N W E S

# A MAP OF MIDNIGHT MOVIE STUDIOS

# IMPOSSIBLE

Deductive Logico retired from detective work.

Revenge had driven him through the last twenty-five mysteries, but when he had solved them all, he learned that the person he wanted revenge for and the person he wanted revenge on were the exact same person. And so, he gave up detective work and began to focus on purely logical problems, like how many sides a triangle could have before it became a square.

But then, one day, he received a call from a former suspect: Midnight III, the heir to Midnight Movies, the oldest independent studio in Hollywood. (Their facilities can be seen in the map to the left, presented as Exhibit D.)

"Would you be interested in making *Murdle: The Movie?*" he asked.

Logico was unsure. Not only was he retired from mysteries, he had never loved mystery movies anyway, because they never stopped to give you time to think.

"Never mind if it's a good idea," Midnight III said, "let me tell you what it pays."

Logico listened, heard, and immediately agreed.

But when he went to Hollywood, he found that it was more isolating than an island, more confusing than a hedge maze, and more surprising than a Dame Obsidian novel. He found himself confronted with mysteries that seemed almost impossible.

Can you use everything you've learned until now to solve these final twenty-five impossible mysteries? And if you're looking for an even harder challenge, try to solve the real Hollywood mystery: Why are so many movies so bad?

# 76. HOORAY FOR HOLLYWOOD! 🔍🔍🔍🔍

When Logico arrived in Hollywood, he struggled to get his bearings. And once he had his bearings, he struggled to solve a murder: a Hollywood historian had been made history.

## SUSPECTS

**EXECUTIVE PRODUCER STEEL**

The richest, smartest, and meanest producer in Hollywood. For now.

5'6" • RIGHT-HANDED • GRAY EYES • WHITE HAIR • ARIES

**HACK BLAXTON**

He's one of the best paid writers in Hollywood, and one of the worst.

6'0" • RIGHT-HANDED • LIGHT BROWN EYES • BALD • SAGITTARIUS

**SUPERFAN SMOKY**

He knows the shooting locations of every Midnight mystery, but not how to make friends.

5'10" • LEFT-HANDED • BLACK EYES • DARK BROWN HAIR • VIRGO

**BACKGROUND MARENGO**

You'll never remember her, which is why she's a good extra, and a great murderer.

5'5" • LEFT-HANDED • LIGHT BROWN EYES • DARK BROWN HAIR • GEMINI

## LOCATIONS

**MIDNIGHT MOVIE STUDIOS**
INDOORS

Once the biggest studio in Hollywood. They're producing *Murdle: The Movie,* which might turn things around.

**THE GREAT PARK**
OUTDOORS

Actually named after a murderer (look it up), so we'll just call it the Great Park.

**THE ARGYLE TALENT AGENCY**
INDOORS

The most powerful institution in Hollywood history that doesn't control the water supply.

**THE MAGIC PALACE**
INDOORS

A magicians-only nightclub. To Logico, this place is famous mostly for its murders.

## WEAPONS

**A BOTOX NEEDLE**
LIGHT-WEIGHT • MADE OF PLASTIC & TOXINS

Botox is a poison, which means it could be used as a weapon.

**A FILM STRIP**
LIGHT-WEIGHT • MADE OF PLASTIC

Ironically, this film strip depicts a man being strangled.

**A GOLF CLUB**
MEDIUM-WEIGHT • MADE OF METAL

Studio executives work hard, too. Look at all the business golf they do.

**AN AWARD**
MEDIUM-WEIGHT • MADE OF METAL

An incredibly prestigious Hollywood award.

## MOTIVES

 **TO PROVE THEY'RE TOUGH**

 **TO GET THEIR MOVIE MADE**

 **TO HELP SELL A SCRIPT**

 **TO BREAK INTO THE INDUSTRY**

## CLUES & EVIDENCE

- Superfan Smoky wanted to break into the Industry.

- Background Marengo wanted to get her movie made. (Good luck!)

- The suspect who wanted to prove they're tough was outdoors.

- Forensics found a drop of Botox in the most powerful non-water-related institution in town.

- Executive Producer Steel would never ever want to help sell a script.

- Hack Blaxton had a grudge against the person who had the golf club.

- The award was held by someone who was right-handed.

- Logico was handed a scrambled message by one of the historian's fellow academics: RWOHVEE WAS NI HTE AIGMC ACLAPE ADH A MIMDEU HIEWGT AWNPOE.

## STATEMENTS

(Remember: The murderer is lying. The others are telling the truth.)

**Executive Producer Steel:** Superfan Smoky did not bring a golf club.

**Hack Blaxton:** Picture it: Background Marengo was in the Argyle Talent Agency.

**Superfan Smoky:** Oh, wow! A film strip was at the Midnight Movie Studios.

**Background Marengo:** Ooh! A golf club was in the Great Park.

SUSPECTS        MOTIVES         LOCATIONS

WEAPONS

LOCATIONS

MOTIVES

_____

**WHO?**

_____

**WHAT?**

_____

**WHERE?**

_____

**WHY?**

# 77. LOGICO GOES TO A HOLLYWOOD PARTY 🔍🔍🔍🔍

Logico's first meeting was not at a production house in Hollywood, but at a producer's house in the Hollywood Hills. The producer was not a good host, but it wasn't his fault: he was dead.

## SUSPECTS

**MIDNIGHT III**

The heir to Midnight Movies with plans to turn it into the number one studio in the world again. Right now, his dad only lets him select the award nominees.

5'8" • LEFT-HANDED • DARK BROWN EYES • DARK BROWN HAIR • LIBRA

**AGENT ARGYLE**

Unlike Agent Ink, Argyle does not have a heart of gold, or a heart at all.

6'4" • RIGHT-HANDED • LIGHT BROWN EYES • DARK BROWN HAIR • VIRGO

**EXECUTIVE PRODUCER STEEL**

The richest, smartest, and meanest producer in Hollywood. For now.

5'6" • RIGHT-HANDED • GRAY EYES • WHITE HAIR • ARIES

**UNCLE MIDNIGHT**

When his dad died, he bought a desert mansion with a pool and retired. He was seventeen.

5'8" • LEFT-HANDED • BLUE EYES • DARK BROWN HAIR • SAGITTARIUS

## LOCATIONS

### THE BASEMENT BAR
INDOORS

It has a fully stocked bar, a pinball machine, and a whole bunch of cardboard boxes.

### THE ROOFTOP BALCONY
OUTDOORS

You can look out over the Hollywood Hills and feel so smug and powerful.

### THE GREAT HALL
INDOORS

An enormous spiral staircase winds around a huge statue of the producer himself.

### THE COURTYARD POOL
OUTDOORS

A perfect pool to stand around while drinking and name-dropping.

## WEAPONS

### A RARE VASE
HEAVY-WEIGHT • MADE OF CERAMIC

Ceramic art from an ancient Hollywood era—the 1930s.

### PIANO WIRE
LIGHT-WEIGHT • MADE OF METAL

Somewhere out there, there's a piano missing a wire, and it's about to ruin a concert.

### AN ANTIQUE TYPEWRITER
HEAVY-WEIGHT • MADE OF METAL

From the 1970s, which, in Hollywood, is the early modern era.

### A GIANT SCREENPLAY
HEAVY-WEIGHT • MADE OF PAPER

It sets up a franchise, so it's got an extra fifty pages of tedious exposition.

## MOTIVES

TO FINISH THEIR
MOVIE

TO LIVEN UP A PARTY

TO CLOSE A BUSINESS
DEAL

FOR COLD HARD CASH

## CLUES & EVIDENCE

- The person who wanted to close a business deal was not on the rooftop balcony.

- A member of the Ancient Song of Pitch was in the basement bar with a giant screenplay, and they wanted to liven up the party, as well.

- Someone who had had a bit too much to drink gave Logico a scrambled note: EHT SEORNP WHTI A AERR VSEA ADWNET OT SFHNII HTRIE VOMEI.

- Only a Sagittarius could join the Ancient Song of Pitch.

- A dark brown hair was found on a weapon from the early modern era.

- Whoever was in the courtyard pool was left-handed.

## STATEMENTS

(Remember: The murderer is lying. The others are telling the truth.)

**Midnight III:** Let me jump in: Agent Argyle brought an antique typewriter.

**Agent Argyle:** Here is the deal: an antique typewriter was on the rooftop balcony.

**Executive Producer Steel:** Look, a rare vase was in the great hall.

**Uncle Midnight:** Hey now, Midnight III was in the courtyard pool.

|  | SUSPECTS | | | | MOTIVES | | | | LOCATIONS | | | |
|---|---|---|---|---|---|---|---|---|---|---|---|---|
| WEAPONS | | | | | | | | | | | | |
| | | | | | | | | | | | | |
| | | | | | | | | | | | | |
| | | | | | | | | | | | | |
| LOCATIONS | | | | | | | | | | | | |
| | | | | | | | | | | | | |
| | | | | | | | | | | | | |
| | | | | | | | | | | | | |
| MOTIVES | | | | | | | | | | | | |
| | | | | | | | | | | | | |
| | | | | | | | | | | | | |
| | | | | | | | | | | | | |

_____  **WHO?**

_____  **WHAT?**

_____  **WHERE?**

_____  **WHY?**

# 78. PLENTY OF KILLS IN THE SEA 🔍🔍🔍🔍

Logico's next meeting took place at a beachfront sushi restaurant built atop a pier. Something smelled fishy, and in addition to that, something was suspicious. Soon, he discovered what it was: the sushi chef had been killed.

## SUSPECTS

**BOSS CHARCOAL**

A mob boss from the good ol' days when being a mob boss from the good ol' days meant something.

**5'11" • RIGHT-HANDED • DARK BROWN EYES • BLACK HAIR • TAURUS**

**SECRETARY CELADON**

The secretary of defense, and someone who is personally responsible for a number of climate disasters, some of which are now named after her.

**5'6" • LEFT-HANDED • GREEN EYES • LIGHT BROWN HAIR • LEO**

**GRANDMASTER ROSE**

A chess grand master who is always plotting his next move. Like how to cheat in his next game. (3. Qxe5#)

**5'7" • LEFT-HANDED • DARK BROWN EYES • DARK BROWN HAIR • SCORPIO**

**SILVERTON THE LEGEND**

An acclaimed actor of the Golden Age, now in his golden years.

**6'4" • RIGHT-HANDED • BLUE EYES • SILVER HAIR • LEO**

## LOCATIONS

### THE BAR
INDOORS

The cheapest cocktail costs $150 and is served in a thimble.

### THE VALET STAND
OUTDOORS

Leave your classic car with a guy you won't even tip.

### THE CORNER BOOTH
INDOORS

Always reserved for a celebrity who came one time three years ago.

### A TABLE BY THE DUMPSTER
OUTDOORS

Where they put the has-beens and the walk-ins.

## WEAPONS

### AN AWARD
MEDIUM-WEIGHT • MADE OF METAL

The same prestigious award again.

### A RED HERRING
MEDIUM-WEIGHT • MADE OF FISH

If you hold it by the tail, you can get some real momentum behind it.

### A FANCY PLATE
MEDIUM-WEIGHT • MADE OF CERAMIC

This plate is worth more than your head.

### CHOPSTICKS
LIGHT-WEIGHT • MADE OF WOOD

Two weapons for the price of one.

## MOTIVES

TO CREATE A
DIVERSION

OUT OF FRUSTRATION

TO INHERIT A FORTUNE

TO PROVE THEY'RE
TOUGH

## CLUES & EVIDENCE

- The bartender gave Logico a scrambled note: EHT UPCSSTE AT TEH ARB HDA IRVESL AHRI.

- An award was found where they put the has-beens.

- As an old-school mob boss, Boss Charcoal always wanted to prove he was tough.

- The suspect at the valet stand had dark brown hair.

- A scrambled government report was handed to Logico: REESCRYTA ENDOLAC DDI OTN WANT TO LILK OUT FO TTOSUNRFIAR.

- The Taurus brought a red herring. So typical of a Taurus.

- The person with a weapon worth more than your head wanted to inherit a fortune.

## STATEMENTS

(Remember: The murderer is lying. The others are telling the truth.)

**Boss Charcoal:** Look here: chopsticks were at the valet stand.

**Secretary Celadon:** I was not in the corner booth.

**Grandmaster Rose:** Don't neglect your theory: Secretary Celadon brought an award.

**Silverton the Legend:** Boss Charcoal did not bring a fancy plate.

SUSPECTS     MOTIVES     LOCATIONS

WEAPONS

LOCATIONS

MOTIVES

WHO?

WHAT?

WHERE?

WHY?

# 79. MURDER AT THE MOVIES

Deductive Logico hadn't heard from the producers of *Murdle: The Movie* in a couple of days, so he went to watch a mystery at a movie theater near his hotel. When he couldn't find his seat, he went to find the usher. And when he couldn't find the usher, he found that he was dead.

## SUSPECTS

**PEARL, AMERICAN GUILD OF EDITORS**

The editor of some of the best and highest-grossing movies ever made, though never both at once.

**5'5" • RIGHT-HANDED • BLUE EYES • BLOND HAIR • AQUARIUS**

**HACK BLAXTON**

He's one of the best paid writers in Hollywood, and one of the worst.

**6'0" • RIGHT-HANDED • LIGHT BROWN EYES • BALD • SAGITTARIUS**

**SUPERFAN SMOKY**

He knows the shooting locations of every Midnight mystery, but not how to make friends.

**5'10" • LEFT-HANDED • BLACK EYES • DARK BROWN HAIR • VIRGO**

**DIRECTOR DUSTY**

A true filmmaker. He cares about the art of cinema, even (or especially) above human life.

**5'10" • LEFT-HANDED • HAZEL EYES • BALD • PISCES**

## LOCATIONS

### THE PROJECTION BOOTH
INDOORS

This is a classic place to murder someone, for obvious reasons, especially if you've already seen the movie and know when the loud parts are.

### THE BOX OFFICE
INDOORS

Tickets are expensive, but not as expensive as popcorn, which is not as expensive as drinks.

### THE LOBBY
INDOORS

Back in the day, there was a giant chandelier. But it kept falling and crushing people in mysterious ways. Now there are just framed posters.

### THE THEATER
INDOORS

For legal reasons, we can't say that it's an IMAX. But also, we can't say that it's not an IMAX.

## WEAPONS

### A RITUAL DAGGER
MEDIUM-WEIGHT • MADE OF BONE

It's made out of bone. Hopefully not human!

### AN AWARD
MEDIUM-WEIGHT • MADE OF METAL

Does everybody have one of these things?

### A STALE CANDY BAR
LIGHT-WEIGHT • MADE OF CHOCOLATE

Hard as a crowbar, it's been here since *Lawrence of Arabia*.

### POISONED POPCORN
MEDIUM-WEIGHT • MADE OF CORN & OIL

Freshly popped and freshly poisoned, too. Almond flavored and scented!

## MOTIVES

 TO SEE IF THEY COULD

 TO GET THEIR MOVIE MADE

TO GET A BETTER SEAT

TO STEAL AN IDEA

## CLUES & EVIDENCE

- Whoever was carrying the stale candy bar was left-handed.

- The projectionist gave Logico a scrambled clue: AHKC XBATNOL IDD NTO WNAT OT ETG A TBTERE TSAE.

- The smell of almonds was overwhelming in the box office.

- The person with an award wanted to steal an idea.

- Pearl, AGE, was seen slipping a ritual dagger into her purse.

- Deep down, Superfan Smoky wanted to see if he could kill.

- A piece of chocolate was found on the floor of the theater.

## STATEMENTS

**(Remember: The murderer is lying. The others are telling the truth.)**

**Pearl, AGE:** I seem to have noticed that Hack Blaxton brought poisoned popcorn.

**Hack Blaxton:** Imagine this: Director Dusty brought an award.

**Superfan Smoky:** Director Dusty did not bring poisoned popcorn.

**Director Dusty:** I'm very busy, but a ritual dagger was in the projection booth.

|  | SUSPECTS | | | | MOTIVES | | | | LOCATIONS | | | |
|---|---|---|---|---|---|---|---|---|---|---|---|---|
| WEAPONS | | | | | | | | | | | | |
| | | | | | | | | | | | | |
| | | | | | | | | | | | | |
| | | | | | | | | | | | | |
| LOCATIONS | | | | | | | | | | | | |
| | | | | | | | | | | | | |
| | | | | | | | | | | | | |
| | | | | | | | | | | | | |
| MOTIVES | | | | | | | | | | | | |
| | | | | | | | | | | | | |
| | | | | | | | | | | | | |
| | | | | | | | | | | | | |

_____

**WHO?**

_____

**WHAT?**

_____

**WHERE?**

_____

**WHY?**

# 80. THE COST OF THE RENT IS THE REAL KILLER 🔍🔍🔍🔍

Once it was clear Logico would be in Tinseltown for a while, he got himself a room in a nice Hollywood apartment building. He quickly learned that he had only gotten a good deal because the former tenant had been murdered.

## SUSPECTS

**UNCLE MIDNIGHT**

When his dad died, he bought a desert mansion with a pool and retired. He was seventeen.

**5'8" • LEFT-HANDED • BLUE EYES • DARK BROWN HAIR • SAGITTARIUS**

**BOSS CHARCOAL**

A mob boss from the good ol' days when being a mob boss from the good ol' days meant something.

**5'11" • RIGHT-HANDED • DARK BROWN EYES • BLACK HAIR • TAURUS**

**DR. CRIMSON**

She's the smartest doctor she's ever met, according to her, and she's probably right. Yeah, she smokes, but if she gets cancer, she'll find a cure.

**5'9" • LEFT-HANDED • GREEN EYES • RED HAIR • AQUARIUS**

**EXECUTIVE PRODUCER STEEL**

The richest, smartest, and meanest producer in Hollywood. For now.

**5'6" • RIGHT-HANDED • GRAY EYES • WHITE HAIR • ARIES**

## LOCATIONS

### THE ROOFTOP GARDENS
OUTDOORS

Beautiful rooftop gardens
tended by workers who could
never afford to live here.

### THE BOILER ROOM
INDOORS

Many famous celebrities have
been weirded out by the ominous vibes in here.

### THE TINIEST ROOM
INDOORS

Once a closet, now it costs
more every month than your
dad saw in his entire life.

### THE PENTHOUSE
INDOORS

The highest floor if you don't
count the rooftop gardens, so
the penthouse owners don't.

## WEAPONS

### A STRANGLIN' SCARF
LIGHT-WEIGHT • MADE OF COTTON

In sunny Hollywood, the only
use for a scarf is stranglin'.

### AN ANTIQUE TYPEWRITER
HEAVY-WEIGHT • MADE OF METAL

From the 1950s, which, in Hollywood, is the late classical
era.

### A GOLDEN BIRD
HEAVY-WEIGHT • MADE OF GOLD

This flamingo statue is worth
a fortune.

### A GHOST DETECTOR
MEDIUM-WEIGHT • MADE OF METAL & TECH

It's not great at detecting
ghosts, but it's pretty good at
electrocuting people.

## MOTIVES

 TO SEE IF THEY COULD

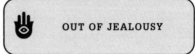 AS PRACTICE

TO JOIN A CULT

OUT OF JEALOUSY

## CLUES & EVIDENCE

- The person with an antique typewriter wanted to kill to see if they could.

- A scrambled message was scrawled on the bathroom wall: XEEUE-VICT RCORPDUE ELEST ADH A LDOGNE BDRI.

- Whoever would kill out of jealousy was left-handed.

- On a doctor's salary, Dr. Crimson could only afford the tiniest room, which is where she was.

- The person who wanted to kill as practice was not in the boiler room.

- Forensics found traces of a cotton weapon in the penthouse.

- A witness saw Boss Charcoal enjoying the flowers in the beautiful garden.

## STATEMENTS

(Remember: The murderer is lying. The others are telling the truth.)

**Uncle Midnight:** Hey now, my only motivation to kill would be as practice.

**Boss Charcoal:** Executive Producer Steel did not bring an antique typewriter.

**Dr. Crimson:** An antique typewriter was not in the tiniest room.

**Executive Producer Steel:** Boss Charcoal was not in the tiniest room.

|  | SUSPECTS | MOTIVES | LOCATIONS |
|---|---|---|---|

WEAPONS

LOCATIONS

MOTIVES

_____

**WHO?**

_____

**WHAT?**

_____

**WHERE?**

_____

**WHY?**

"LO-GI-CO! LO-GI-CO!" the crowd chanted. But the actor playing Deductive Logico wouldn't come out. Finally, the real Logico came out, and announced that the actor had been murdered. The crowd went wild.

## SUSPECTS

**SILVERTON THE LEGEND**

An acclaimed actor of the Golden Age, now in his golden years.

**6'4" • RIGHT-HANDED • BLUE EYES • SILVER HAIR • LEO**

**PRESIDENT MIDNIGHT**

The CEO of Midnight Movies. He cares about art and business, but definitely not in that order.

**6'2" • RIGHT-HANDED • BLACK EYES • BLACK HAIR • CAPRICORN**

**DIRECTOR DUSTY**

A true filmmaker. He wants to make a masterpiece. To do that, he might have to make a murder.

**5'10" • LEFT-HANDED • HAZEL EYES • BALD • PISCES**

**JUDGE PINE**

(Former) master of the courtroom and possessed of a firm belief in justice, as decided by her and her alone.

**5'6" • RIGHT-HANDED • DARK BROWN EYES • BLACK HAIR • TAURUS**

## LOCATIONS

### THE PARKING LOT
OUTDOORS

One unfortunate attendee is trying to solve a locked car mystery: his keys are inside, but he's not.

### THE CONVENTION FLOOR
INDOORS

Where all the indie mystery writers are selling their wares to people in detective cosplay.

### THE EXHIBIT HALL
INDOORS

Where *Murdle: The Movie* is being announced by Midnight Movies, much to the chagrin of the indies.

### THE FOOD COURT
INDOORS

Where you can order the best in mystery-themed food, like a clueberry muffin.

## WEAPONS

### A MAGNIFYING GLASS
MEDIUM-WEIGHT • MADE OF METAL & GLASS

You could use this to find a clue or as part of a costume.

### A CROWBAR
MEDIUM-WEIGHT • MADE OF METAL

Honestly, they're used more often for crime than anything else.

### AN EXPLODING PIPE
LIGHT-WEIGHT • MADE OF A PIPE & A BOMB

Smoking kills, especially when you use a pipe bomb.

### A MOVIE-EDITION HARDBACK
MEDIUM-WEIGHT • MADE OF PAPER

They reissued *Murdle* in hardback with a movie-related tie-in cover. It's awful.

## MOTIVES

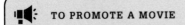 TO PROMOTE A MOVIE

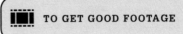 TO GET GOOD FOOTAGE

 FOR COLD HARD CASH

 TO STEAL A PART

## CLUES & EVIDENCE

- The person who wanted to steal a part was by a locked car.
- The Crude Order of Light do not admit people with blue eyes.
- Whoever was in the exhibit hall was left-handed.
- Director Dusty had a motive to kill for cold hard cash.
- All of the suspects were members of either the Crude Order of Light or the Ancient Song of Pitch.
- Magnifying glasses were banned from the convention floor for being too cliché.
- The only present member of the Ancient Song of Pitch brought a crowbar.
- Judge Pine just wanted to promote a movie.
- Whoever wanted to get good footage had a medium-weight weapon.

## STATEMENTS

(Remember: The murderer is lying. The others are telling the truth.)

**Silverton the Legend:** Let me tell you how it is: a magnifying glass was in the exhibit hall.

**President Midnight:** As president, I can tell you Silverton the Legend was in the parking lot.

**Director Dusty:** I'm very busy, but Judge Pine brought an exploding pipe.

**Judge Pine:** The facts are clear: a crowbar was in the parking lot.

SUSPECTS    MOTIVES    LOCATIONS

WEAPONS

LOCATIONS

MOTIVES

WHO?

WHAT?

WHERE?

WHY?

# 82. MURDER IN THE PARK 🔍🔍🔍🔍

To decompress after the murder at MysteryCon, Deductive Logico decided to have a fun day in the Great Park, but it was hard to enjoy the beautiful hills, panoramic views, and grand historic significance when you had a murder to solve: a tourist had been killed.

## SUSPECTS

**MX. TANGERINE**

Proving that non-binary people can be murderers, too: they are a hiker, birdwatcher, and suspect.

5'5" • LEFT-HANDED • HAZEL EYES • BLOND HAIR • PISCES

**PEARL, AGE**

The editor of some of the best and highest-grossing movies ever made, though never both at once.

5'5" • RIGHT-HANDED • BLUE EYES • BLOND HAIR • AQUARIUS

**LORD LAVENDER**

A politically conservative MP in the House of Lords, as well as the musical theater composer behind such hits as *Humming Down the Hill* and *The Man in Beige*.

5'9" • RIGHT-HANDED • GREEN EYES • GRAY HAIR • VIRGO

**CHANCELLOR TUSCANY**

As the head of Deduction College, she has deduced that sometimes the weather is so perfect you just have to go to the park.

5'5" • LEFT-HANDED • GREEN EYES • GRAY HAIR • LIBRA

## LOCATIONS

### THE GREEK THEATER
OUTDOORS

A huge outdoor theater, perfect for watching the orchestra or a touring Scandinavian Viking band.

### THE OLD ZOO
OUTDOORS

Where animals used to be kept in cramped, squalid spaces, no better than a struggling actor's apartment today.

### THE FAMOUS CAVES
OUTDOORS

A famous actor was named after a street that was named after these caves.

### THE HOLLYWOOD SIGN
OUTDOORS

Like all pieces of true Hollywood history, it had its start as a real estate scam.

## WEAPONS

### A FIRE EXTINGUISHER
HEAVY-WEIGHT • MADE OF METAL & CHEMICALS

You can put out a fire or somebody's lights.

### A LOG
HEAVY-WEIGHT • MADE OF WOOD

A big, heavy oak log. Somebody killed the tree so that the tree could kill somebody.

### AN ANTIQUE HELMET
HEAVY-WEIGHT • MADE OF METAL

It's rusty and it looks awesome.

### A ROCK
MEDIUM-WEIGHT • MADE OF ROCK

When you can't find another weapon, a rock is always nearby. It has a distinctive chip in it.

## MOTIVES

 BECAUSE THEY COULD

 TO DESTROY A RIVAL'S CAREER

 TO ESCAPE BLACKMAIL

 TO STEAL A RUBY

## CLUES & EVIDENCE

- Whoever wanted to escape blackmail had gray hair—maybe from the blackmail.

- An interestingly distinctive chip was discovered next to a giant *H*.

- The Path of the Ancient Dead only admitted Libras.

- In a rare public appearance, Pearl, AGE, was seen on stage at a theater.

- Logico was given a scrambled note by a park ranger: XM ERTNE-AGIN WAS NESE TWHI A FRIE IGSITEUENXRH.

- A member of the Path of the Ancient Dead was at a place the size of a struggling actor's apartment.

- The person with an antique helmet wanted to destroy a rival's career.

## STATEMENTS

(Remember: The murderer is lying. The others are telling the truth.)

**Mx. Tangerine:** Whoever had the log wanted to escape blackmail.

**Pearl, AGE:** A Pisces was not in the old zoo.

**Lord Lavender:** Whoever would kill because they could was at the Hollywood sign.

**Chancellor Tuscany:** As an academic, I can assert Mx. Tangerine was at the Hollywood sign.

|  | SUSPECTS | MOTIVES | LOCATIONS |
|---|---|---|---|

WEAPONS

LOCATIONS

MOTIVES

_____ WHO?

_____ WHAT?

_____ WHERE?

_____ WHY?

# 83. PARKING IS MURDER 🔍🔍🔍🔍

Finally, Deductive Logico was invited to Midnight Movie Studios, where he could tour the lot and witness the filming of his movie. But first, he had to solve a problem more horrifying than any he had previously faced: parking. (Also, a valet had been murdered.)

## SUSPECTS

**LORD LAVENDER**

A politically conservative MP in the House of Lords, as well as the musical theater composer behind such hits as *College of Jazz* and *Pieces of Fear*.

5'9" • RIGHT-HANDED • GREEN EYES • GRAY HAIR • VIRGO

**SIGNOR EMERALD**

An Italian jeweler of great renown, Signor Emerald has traveled the world in search of rare, precious stones, which are always falling out of his pockets.

5'8" • LEFT-HANDED • LIGHT BROWN EYES • BLACK HAIR • SAGITTARIUS

**OFFICER COPPER**

The best part of being a policewoman criminal is that you can cut out the middleman and fail to investigate your own crimes.

5'5" • RIGHT-HANDED • BLUE EYES • BLOND HAIR • ARIES

**PEARL, AGE**

The editor of some of the best and highest-grossing movies ever made, though never both at once.

5'5" • RIGHT-HANDED • BLUE EYES • BLOND HAIR • AQUARIUS

## LOCATIONS

**PARKING LOT A**
OUTDOORS

The good parking lot. Close to the entrance. Where the executives and stars park.

**THE SECURITY BUILDING**
INDOORS

A more sophisticated security system than most military bases.

**PARKING LOT B**
OUTDOORS

The bad parking lot. Far away from the entrance. It costs money to park here.

**THE FOUNTAIN**
OUTDOORS

A fountain, filled by the water tower, dedicated to the memory of all the extras injured on set.

## WEAPONS

**A GIANT SCREENPLAY**
HEAVY-WEIGHT • MADE OF PAPER

It sets up a franchise, so it's got an extra fifty pages that are incredibly boring.

**AN AWARD**
MEDIUM-WEIGHT • MADE OF METAL

The more Logico sees these, the less he thinks they're worth.

**A GOLF CART**
HEAVY-WEIGHT • MADE OF METAL, PLASTIC, & RUBBER

Good for peeling out on tiny tires or running somebody over.

**A BATON**
MEDIUM-WEIGHT • MADE OF METAL

A great tool for brutalizing innocent people.

## MOTIVES

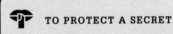 TO PROTECT A SECRET

 BECAUSE THEY WERE IN A HURRY

 TO GET A BETTER SPOT

 TO ROB A GRAVE

## CLUES & EVIDENCE

- Officer Copper was a member of the Order.

- The person who wanted to protect a secret was not in the building directly to the west of the studio tour check-in stand. (See Exhibit D.)

- Deductive Logico deduced that, based on the time of his next meeting, Signor Emerald was definitely in a hurry.

- Only members of the Order were allowed to carry batons on the lot.

- A script page setting up a sequel was discovered next to a commemorative fountain.

- Pearl, AGE, was seen hanging around in the eastern parking lot. (See Exhibit D.)

- Whoever wanted to get a better spot had a medium-weight weapon.

## STATEMENTS

(Remember: The murderer is lying. The others are telling the truth.)

**Lord Lavender:** Officer Copper was in the security building.

**Signor Emerald:** Lord Lavender was driving a golf cart.

**Officer Copper:** Whoever wanted to get a better spot was in parking lot B.

**Pearl, AGE:** I seem to have noticed that Officer Copper wanted to rob a grave.

| | SUSPECTS | | | | MOTIVES | | | | LOCATIONS | | | |
|---|---|---|---|---|---|---|---|---|---|---|---|---|
| **WEAPONS** | | | | | | | | | | | | |
| | | | | | | | | | | | | |
| | | | | | | | | | | | | |
| | | | | | | | | | | | | |
| **LOCATIONS** | | | | | | | | | | | | |
| | | | | | | | | | | | | |
| | | | | | | | | | | | | |
| **MOTIVES** | | | | | | | | | | | | |
| | | | | | | | | | | | | |
| | | | | | | | | | | | | |

_____

**WHO?**

_____

**WHAT?**

_____

**WHERE?**

_____

**WHY?**

# 84. THE TOUR OF DEATH 🔍🔍🔍🔍

Once Logico had found parking, he realized he was hours early, so he decided to take the studio tour to kill time. Unfortunately, time wasn't all that was killed: the tour guide had been murdered. And Logico was on the case.

## SUSPECTS

**SUPERFAN SMOKY**

He knows the shooting locations of every Midnight mystery, but not how to make friends.

5'10" • LEFT-HANDED • BLACK EYES • DARK BROWN HAIR • VIRGO

**SISTER LAPIS**

A nun who travels the world, doing God's work on His dime. Her habit is cashmere, but her habit is spending.

5'2" • RIGHT-HANDED • LIGHT BROWN EYES • LIGHT BROWN HAIR • CANCER

**OFFICER COPPER**

Being a studio guard might not technically make you an officer, but you still get to yell at people.

5'5" • RIGHT-HANDED • BLUE EYES • BLOND HAIR • ARIES

**COACH RASPBERRY**

One of the best coaches this side of the Mississippi, regardless of which side you're on.

6'0" • LEFT-HANDED • BLUE EYES • BLOND HAIR • ARIES

## LOCATIONS

**THE WATER TOWER BAR & GRILL**
INDOORS

A themed restaurant that serves drinks in glasses in the shape of the tower.

**THE STATUE OF MIDNIGHT I**
OUTDOORS

A statue to the founder of Midnight Movies, the great Midnight I.

**THE CITY BACKLOT**
OUTDOORS

Where they shoot outdoor city scenes. Cleaner than any actual city ever was.

**THE STUDIO TOUR CHECK-IN STAND**
OUTDOORS

Where the tourists check in for the studio tour.

## WEAPONS

**A FIRE EXTINGUISHER**
HEAVY-WEIGHT • MADE OF METAL & CHEMICALS

You can put out a fire or somebody's lights.

**A FLAG**
LIGHT-WEIGHT • MADE OF POLYESTER

Flags can be very dangerous in many ways. Like, for example, strangulation.

**A GOLF CART**
HEAVY-WEIGHT • MADE OF METAL, PLASTIC, & RUBBER

For getting around a studio or running somebody over.

**A FAKE AWARD**
MEDIUM-WEIGHT • MADE OF METAL

Why would you bring a fake one when the real ones are everywhere?

## MOTIVES

**TO RENEGOTIATE THEIR CONTRACT**

**TO BREAK INTO THE INDUSTRY**

**TO HIDE AN AFFAIR**

**TO MEET A CELEBRITY**

## CLUES & EVIDENCE

- Sister Lapis had always wanted to meet a celebrity.

- The person driving a golf cart did not want to break into the Industry.

- Officer Copper desperately wanted to hide an affair.

- A fake award was leaning against a monument to the founder of the studio.

- The person who wanted to renegotiate their contract was at the studio tour check-in stand.

- One of the underpaid PAs handed Logico a scrambled note that read: REHVWOE DAH A LFGA WSA EYNLETDIIF IGRTH DDHENA.

- Zoomed-in surveillance footage showed that whoever was in the city backlot had black eyes.

## STATEMENTS

(Remember: The murderer is lying. The others are telling the truth.)

**Superfan Smoky:** Oh, wow! Officer Copper brought a fake award.

**Sister Lapis:** A Virgo did not bring a fake award.

**Officer Copper:** I was not at the studio tour check-in stand.

**Coach Raspberry:** I did not bring a fake award.

|  | SUSPECTS | | | | MOTIVES | | | | LOCATIONS | | | |
|---|---|---|---|---|---|---|---|---|---|---|---|---|
| WEAPONS | | | | | | | | | | | | |
| | | | | | | | | | | | | |
| | | | | | | | | | | | | |
| | | | | | | | | | | | | |
| LOCATIONS | | | | | | | | | | | | |
| | | | | | | | | | | | | |
| | | | | | | | | | | | | |
| | | | | | | | | | | | | |
| MOTIVES | | | | | | | | | | | | |
| | | | | | | | | | | | | |
| | | | | | | | | | | | | |
| | | | | | | | | | | | | |

WHO? _____

WHAT? _____

WHERE? _____

WHY? _____

# 85. QUIET ON SET . . . TOO QUIET! 🔍🔍🔍🔍

Filming on *Murdle: The Movie* had begun, and though the studio was buying up land to use as shooting locations, they were actually filming all of the movie on sound stages on the lot. Unfortunately, they had to stop production when the effects supervisor was killed.

## SUSPECTS

**BOSS CHARCOAL**

A mob boss from the good ol' days when being a mob boss from the good ol' days meant something.

5'11" • RIGHT-HANDED • DARK BROWN EYES • BLACK HAIR • TAURUS

**PRESIDENT MIDNIGHT**

The CEO of Midnight Movies. He cares about making movies and money, but definitely not in that order.

6'2" • RIGHT-HANDED • BLACK EYES • BLACK HAIR • CAPRICORN

**A-LIST ABALONE**

The most talented and in-demand actress of all time this month.

5'6" • RIGHT-HANDED • HAZEL EYES • RED HAIR • LIBRA

**MIDNIGHT III**

He argues that detectives are the next superheroes, and mysteries the next tentpole.

5'8" • LEFT-HANDED • DARK BROWN EYES • DARK BROWN HAIR • LIBRA

## LOCATIONS

# A
### SOUND STAGE A
INDOORS

Inside is a set of the mysterious caves where Logico caught Irratino.

# B
### SOUND STAGE B
INDOORS

Inside is a set of Logico's office. Although less orderly than he kept it.

# C
### SOUND STAGE C
INDOORS

Inside is a set of Irratino's childhood home. Although less messy than he kept it.

# D
### SOUND STAGE D
INDOORS

Filled entirely with green screens.

## WEAPONS

### A "PROP" KNIFE
LIGHT-WEIGHT • MADE OF METAL & RUBBER

Weirdly it's as sharp as a real knife.

### A SANDBAG
HEAVY-WEIGHT • MADE OF SAND & CANVAS

You could swing it or drop it. Either way, its job is to be heavy.

### A C-STAND
HEAVY-WEIGHT • MADE OF METAL

For holding up lights. Or swinging at skulls.

### AN ELECTRICAL CABLE
MEDIUM-WEIGHT • MADE OF METAL & RUBBER

Shock, strangle, or even beat! A multipurpose tool.

## MOTIVES

 TO TAKE OVER A STUDIO

 TO WIN AN AWARD

 TO STEAL A PART

 TO GET OUT OF A BAD MOVIE

## CLUES & EVIDENCE

- Whoever wanted to get out of a bad movie had a heavy-weight weapon.

- The Cult of the Dark Gleam only admits people with dark brown eyes.

- The second shortest suspect did not bring a C-stand.

- A member of the Cult of the Dark Gleam was in the northeast sound stage. (See Exhibit D.)

- A-List Abalone was surrounded by green walls.

- Boss Charcoal had a "prop" knife.

- A member of the Cult of the Dark Gleam wanted to steal a part.

- President Midnight wanted to win an award.

- The person who wanted to take over a studio was in the northwest sound stage. (See Exhibit D.)

## STATEMENTS

(Remember: The murderer is lying. The others are telling the truth.)

**Boss Charcoal:** Look here: a sandbag was in sound stage D.

**President Midnight:** I was not in sound stage B.

**A-List Abalone:** Talk to my agent, but privately, Boss Charcoal was in sound stage A.

**Midnight III:** Let me jump in: whoever had the C-stand wanted to win an award.

**WHO?**

**WHAT?**

**WHERE?**

**WHY?**

# 86. MURDER ON SOUND STAGE B 🔍🔍🔍🔍

Logico was stunned when he stepped onto the set of his own office and found everything recreated perfectly, including the method actors who seemed to get so into playing their characters that one of them murdered the actor playing the landlord.

## SUSPECTS

**COSMONAUT BLUSKI**

Not actually Cosmonaut Bluski, but a method actor who insists on you addressing him as such.

6'2" • LEFT-HANDED • DARK BROWN EYES • BLACK HAIR • ARIES

**GENERAL COFFEE**

Again, this is an actor, playing a part, but he demands you call him "General" or he'll quit.

6'0" • RIGHT-HANDED • DARK BROWN EYES • BALD • SAGITTARIUS

**THE AMAZING AUREOLIN**

She has been added to a bunch of the scenes from the movie as sort of Logico's sidekick.

5'6" • LEFT-HANDED • GREEN EYES • BLOND HAIR • ARIES

**DR. CRIMSON**

Yeah, she's an actor playing a doctor, but she's also an actual doctor who quit to go into acting.

5'9" • LEFT-HANDED • GREEN EYES • RED HAIR • AQUARIUS

## LOCATIONS

### THE CLOSET
INDOORS

All of Logico's prop clothes are sorted by color, instead of alphabetically!

### THE WAITING ROOM
INDOORS

There's an almost identical bell to Logico's, and a sign that says WAIT, PLEASE.

### THE MAIN OFFICE
INDOORS

A desk, bookshelves filled with prop books, and a view of the . . . sky? It's supposed to be bricks!

### THE BALCONY
FAKE OUTDOORS

Logico's fire escape, but it's in front of a matte painting of the sky, and it is not an exit.

## WEAPONS

### A FIRE EXTINGUISHER
HEAVY-WEIGHT • MADE OF METAL & CHEMICALS

You can put out a fire or some-body's lights.

### A RED HERRING
MEDIUM-WEIGHT • MADE OF FISH

If you hold it by the tail, you can get some real momentum behind it.

### A BOOBY-TRAPPED FEDORA
MEDIUM-WEIGHT • MADE OF ▓▓▓▓▓

Whatever you do, don't try it on.

### A VIAL OF POISON
LIGHT-WEIGHT • MADE OF GLASS & TOXINS

Your typical vial of poison. Don't underestimate the classics.

## MOTIVES

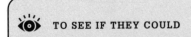 TO SEE IF THEY COULD

 OUT OF JEALOUSY

 TO WIN AN AWARD

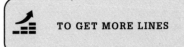 TO GET MORE LINES

## CLUES & EVIDENCE

- The person who wanted to win an award was waiting in the waiting room.

- The bald person wanted to see if they could kill.

- The suspect who wanted to see if they could was not a member of the Way of Unholy Light.

- Every suspect with green eyes was in the Way of Unholy Light.

- Logico was handed a scrambled note by a security guard: SCAUOOTMN ISLBUK DHA A IEFR HSGIERTIXNUE.

- The clothes in the closet had been handled by a right-handed suspect.

- The actor playing Logico's sidekick wanted to get more lines.

- Anybody with a booby-trapped fedora would kill out of jealousy.

## STATEMENTS

**(Remember: The murderer is lying. The others are telling the truth.)**

**Cosmonaut Bluski:** The second shortest suspect was not in the closet.

**General Coffee:** Ugh . . . whoever wanted to get more lines was in the main office.

**The Amazing Aureolin:** A red-haired suspect was on the balcony.

**Dr. Crimson:** As a doctor, trust me: a red herring was in the closet.

SUSPECTS    MOTIVES    LOCATIONS

WEAPONS

LOCATIONS

MOTIVES

WHO?

WHAT?

WHERE?

WHY?

# 87. THE WATER TOWER BAR & KILL 🔍🔍🔍🔍

Deductive Logico had worked up an appetite, so he went to grab a bite at the Water Tower Bar & Grill. The food was bad. But there was a murder while he was there, so at least he had something to occupy his time. You see, a bartender had been killed.

## SUSPECTS

**BACKGROUND MARENGO**

You'll never remember her, which is why she's a good extra, and a great murderer.

**5'5" • LEFT-HANDED • LIGHT BROWN EYES • DARK BROWN HAIR • GEMINI**

**MIDNIGHT III**

Obsessed with scouting locations for *Murdle: The Movie,* he thinks that is how he'll put Midnight Movies back on top.

**5'8" • LEFT-HANDED • DARK BROWN EYES • DARK BROWN HAIR • LIBRA**

**DIRECTOR DUSTY**

A true filmmaker. The only thing he cares about is getting his movie made. No matter what.

**5'10" • LEFT-HANDED • HAZEL EYES • BALD • PISCES**

**AGENT ARGYLE**

Unlike Agent Ink, Argyle does not have a heart of gold, or a heart at all.

**6'4" • RIGHT-HANDED • LIGHT BROWN EYES • DARK BROWN HAIR • VIRGO**

## LOCATIONS

### THE BAR
INDOORS

The drinks are watered down with authentic water-tower water.

### THE BACK PORCH
OUTDOORS

Featuring a great view of the water tower and any celebrities that might go by.

### THE GRILL
INDOORS

The steaks are grilled at room temperature to save money.

### THE BATHROOMS
INDOORS

Featuring the actual water from the water tower.

## WEAPONS

### A FORK
LIGHT-WEIGHT • MADE OF METAL

A lot more gruesome than a knife, if you think about it.

### A BOTTLE OF WINE
MEDIUM-WEIGHT • MADE OF GLASS & ALCOHOL

Watch out for stains, because the red doesn't come out.

### A DVD BOX SET
MEDIUM-WEIGHT • MADE OF WOOD

This is a luxurious box set meant to be an heirloom.

### A FAKE ROSE
LIGHT-WEIGHT • MADE OF PLASTIC

The plastic stem is strong enough to strangle somebody.

## MOTIVES

TO GET OUT OF A BAD MOVIE

TO WIN AN AWARD

TO TAKE OVER HOLLYWOOD

TO BREAK INTO THE INDUSTRY

## CLUES & EVIDENCE

- The metal weapon reflected the light brown eyes of the person who had it.

- The person who wanted to get out of a bad movie was fretting about it in view of the water tower.

- The person with a bottle of wine did not want to break into the Industry. They had wine instead!

- Whoever wanted to win an award was right-handed.

- Director Dusty was seen hanging around the bathrooms.

- A fake rose petal was next to a watered-down cocktail. It had a cinematic look to it.

- Midnight III brought a DVD box set. (Was it for research? Or murder?)

## STATEMENTS

(Remember: The murderer is lying. The others are telling the truth.)

**Background Marengo:** Ooh! I brought a fork.

**Midnight III:** Well, a bottle of wine wasn't on the back porch.

**Director Dusty:** Agent Argyle wasn't on the back porch, either.

**Agent Argyle:** Midnight III was not in the bar.

|  | SUSPECTS | | | | MOTIVES | | | | LOCATIONS | | | |
|---|---|---|---|---|---|---|---|---|---|---|---|---|
| **WEAPONS** | | | | | | | | | | | | |
| | | | | | | | | | | | | |
| | | | | | | | | | | | | |
| | | | | | | | | | | | | |
| | | | | | | | | | | | | |
| **LOCATIONS** | | | | | | | | | | | | |
| | | | | | | | | | | | | |
| | | | | | | | | | | | | |
| | | | | | | | | | | | | |
| **MOTIVES** | | | | | | | | | | | | |
| | | | | | | | | | | | | |
| | | | | | | | | | | | | |
| | | | | | | | | | | | | |

_____  **WHO?**

_____  **WHAT?**

_____  **WHERE?**

_____  **WHY?**

# 88. THE REAL MURDER AT THE FAKE ESTATE 🔍🔍🔍🔍

When Logico stepped onto the set of Irratino's childhood home, he felt an overwhelming wave of sadness and grief. Losing Irratino to death had been hard, but losing him to betrayal was worse. And the feelings got even more complex when the actor playing Irratino was killed.

## SUSPECTS

**THE DUKE OF VERMILLION**

Honestly, Silverton the Legend would've been better suited physically to play the duke.

5'9" • LEFT-HANDED • GRAY EYES • WHITE HAIR • PISCES

**DAME OBSIDIAN**

An actress playing Dame Obsidian who looks—unbelievably—identical to Dame Obsidian.

5'4" • LEFT-HANDED • GREEN EYES • BLACK HAIR • LEO

**BROTHER BROWNSTONE**

They cut most of the Brother Brownstone arc from the film, so now he's just a wise monk mentor.

5'4" • LEFT-HANDED • DARK BROWN EYES • DARK BROWN HAIR • CAPRICORN

**ASTROLOGER AZURE**

Astrologer Azure was sort of a composite character for all of the Investigation Institute people.

5'6" • RIGHT-HANDED • HAZEL EYES • LIGHT BROWN HAIR • CANCER

## LOCATIONS

### THE FIFTY-CAR GARAGE
INDOORS

The classic cars are all props manufactured by the Midnight prop shop.

### THE SERVANTS' QUARTERS
INDOORS

Ironically, this is also what they call their wages. Both are small.

### THE BALCONY
FAKE OUTDOORS

You can look out over the grounds, but it's actually just a matte painting of the grounds.

### THE GROUNDS
FAKE OUTDOORS

The grass is long, thick, well-kept, and fake, like the hair of the guy who's playing Irratino.

## WEAPONS

### A HYPNOTIC POCKET WATCH
LIGHT-WEIGHT • MADE OF METAL

If you look deeply into this watch, you can tell the time.

### A DOWSING ROD
MEDIUM-WEIGHT • MADE OF WOOD

You can find water, oil, and suckers with this.

### A CRYSTAL DAGGER
MEDIUM-WEIGHT • MADE OF METAL & JEWELS

It might have some kind of ritual purpose, but it might just look great on your mantle.

### A POISONED TINCTURE
LIGHT-WEIGHT • MADE OF OIL & POISON

According to the label, one drop of this will cure all your ails. Two will kill you.

## MOTIVES

 TO ROB A GRAVE

 TO PROMOTE THE OCCULT

 TO STEAL THE ESTATE

 TO TEST OUT A PLOT

## CLUES & EVIDENCE

- The Duke of Vermillion wanted to rob a grave. It was a long-standing dream.

- On the call sheet, someone had written a scrambled observation: EORLGARTOS UZARE DAH A OHYCTNPI OETCKP WCAHT.

- A member of the Order of the Sacred Oil was in the fifty-car garage.

- Everyone with a medium-weight weapon was a member of the Order of the Sacred Oil.

- A member of the Order of the Sacred Oil wanted to test out a plot.

- A dowsing rod was discovered next to a beautiful matte painting.

- Brother Brownstone was seen cramming himself into a spot that was so cramped it reminded him of his room at the monastery.

## STATEMENTS

(Remember: The murderer is lying. The others are telling the truth.)

**The Duke of Vermillion:** A Leo brought a dowsing rod.

**Dame Obsidian:** A thought: I brought a hypnotic pocket watch.

**Brother Brownstone:** In the name of God, whoever wanted to steal the estate was in the servants' quarters.

**Astrologer Azure:** Dame Obsidian did not bring a poisoned tincture.

SUSPECTS        MOTIVES         LOCATIONS

WEAPONS

LOCATIONS

MOTIVES

_____
WHO?

_____
WHAT?

_____
WHERE?

_____
WHY?

# 89. THE POST-PRODUCTION PROCESS 🔍🔍🔍🔍

Logico was shocked to find that after they had filmed the entire movie, the work was just beginning. They still had to edit, score, sound mix, color correct, and solve the murder of the assistant editor.

## SUSPECTS

**A-LIST ABALONE**

When you're on the A-list, committing an occasional murder won't keep you from finishing a film.

5'6" • RIGHT-HANDED • HAZEL EYES • RED HAIR • LIBRA

**LORD LAVENDER**

A politically conservative MP in the House of Lords, as well as a musical theater composer who clearly has a lot of hits, although nothing compares to *Dogs*.

5'9" • RIGHT-HANDED • GREEN EYES • GRAY HAIR • VIRGO

**DIRECTOR DUSTY**

A true filmmaker. He wants to make a masterpiece. To do that, he might have to make a murder.

5'10" • LEFT-HANDED • HAZEL EYES • BALD • PISCES

**PEARL, AGE**

The editor of some of the best and highest-grossing movies ever made, though never both at once.

5'5" • RIGHT-HANDED • BLUE EYES • BLOND HAIR • AQUARIUS

## LOCATIONS

### THE WATER TOWER
OUTDOORS

Famous and empty, like the heads of their stars.

### THE SCORING STAGE
INDOORS

Where they score the movies. There's usually an orchestra or a DJ here.

### THE POST-PRODUCTION LAB
INDOORS

Where the movies are saved from their incompetent directors.

### THE WATER TOWER BAR & GRILL
INDOORS

A themed restaurant that serves drinks in glasses in the shape of the tower.

## WEAPONS

### A FILM STRIP
LIGHT-WEIGHT • MADE OF PLASTIC

Ironically, this film strip depicts a man being strangled.

### A TOXIC BLOWFISH
MEDIUM-WEIGHT • MADE OF FISH

Prepared carefully, it's safe to eat. Prepared even more carefully, it can kill.

### A GOLF CART
HEAVY-WEIGHT
MADE OF METAL, PLASTIC, & RUBBER

For getting around a studio or running somebody over.

### AN ADR MICROPHONE
MEDIUM-WEIGHT • MADE OF METAL

For dubbing. Also, for hitting people over the head.

## MOTIVES

 **TO SAVE FACE**

 **FOR POLITICAL PURPOSES**

 **TO AVENGE THEIR FATHER**

 **TO GET OUT OF A BAD MOVIE**

## CLUES & EVIDENCE

- The person who wanted to get out of a bad movie was not at the Water Tower Bar & Grill.

- The person with a film strip wanted to avenge their father.

- The tallest suspect was seen in the post-production lab.

- The person with a toxic blowfish wanted to save face.

- Lord Lavender brought a golf cart.

## STATEMENTS

**(Remember: The murderer is lying. The others are telling the truth.)**

**A-List Abalone:** Talk to my agent, but privately, a film strip was in the water tower.

**Lord Lavender:** Whoever wanted to save face was in the water tower.

**Director Dusty:** I'm very busy, but Pearl, AGE, had a motive to kill for political purposes.

**Pearl, AGE:** I seem to have noticed that A-List Abalone brought a film strip.

|  | SUSPECTS | MOTIVES | LOCATIONS |
|---|---|---|---|

WEAPONS

LOCATIONS

MOTIVES

WHO?

WHAT?

WHERE?

WHY?

# 90. DEATH AT THE AGENCY 🔍🔍🔍🔍

A little rocked by all the murders at the studio, Deductive Logico went to a talent agency in a building known as the Black Tower to see if he could get out of his contract. There, he discovered a client had been killed, which nobody else seemed to mind, because he hadn't made a profitable picture in years.

## SUSPECTS

**AGENT ARGYLE**

Unlike Agent Ink, Argyle does not have a heart of gold, or a heart at all.

6'4" • RIGHT-HANDED • LIGHT BROWN EYES • DARK BROWN HAIR • VIRGO

**SECRETARY CELADON**

The secretary of defense, and someone who is personally responsible for a number of failed states, some of which are now named after her.

5'6" • LEFT-HANDED • GREEN EYES • LIGHT BROWN HAIR • LEO

**PRESIDENT MIDNIGHT**

The CEO of Midnight Movies. He cares about his sons and his legacy, but not in that order.

6'2" • RIGHT-HANDED • BLACK EYES • BLACK HAIR • CAPRICORN

**HACK BLAXTON**

He's one of the best paid writers in Hollywood, and one of the worst.

6'0" • RIGHT-HANDED • LIGHT BROWN EYES • BALD • SAGITTARIUS

## LOCATIONS

### THE MAIL ROOM
INDOORS

This is the starting job. And if you're smart, you'll start opening your rival's letters.

### THE BALCONY
INDOORS

Here you can look down on the city you control.

### THE LOBBY
INDOORS

They have a lobby twice the size of any literary agency. Your voice echoes like a cave.

### THE BEST OFFICE
INDOORS

The best-earning agent of the month gets this office. The worst is killed.

## WEAPONS

### A STEEL KNIFE
MEDIUM-WEIGHT • MADE OF METAL

For stabbing people in the back and stealing their clients.

### AN AWARD
MEDIUM-WEIGHT • MADE OF METAL

A clearly not-so-prestigious Hollywood award.

### LEATHER GLOVES
LIGHT-WEIGHT • MADE OF LEATHER

Beware those who wear leather gloves. They've already killed a cow: who's next?!

### A THOUSAND-PAGE CONTRACT
HEAVY-WEIGHT • MADE OF PAPER

Sign your rights, life, and future away.

## MOTIVES

 TO PROVE A POINT

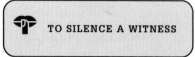 TO SILENCE A WITNESS

TO TAKE OVER A STUDIO

FOR RELIGIOUS REASONS

## CLUES & EVIDENCE

- The person with a steel knife did not want to prove a point.

- Secretary Celadon was in the Order of the Black Death.

- A cowhide glove was found in a cavernous space.

- The person who wanted to silence a witness was in the balcony.

- All members of the Order of the Black Death had a motive to kill for religious reasons.

- Someone with no hair brought a document to sign their life away.

- A comprehensive report on one of the suspects was compiled, then hastily scribbled onto a note and passed to Logico: NGEAT YLRGEA ASW NESE IN EHT LAIM ROOM WHTI AN RAADW BUEESAC HE AENDWT TO TKAE OVRE A TDOSUI.

## STATEMENTS

(Remember: The murderer is lying. The others are telling the truth.)

**Agent Argyle:** A thousand-page contract was not in the lobby.

**Secretary Celadon:** Hack Blaxton did not bring leather gloves.

**President Midnight:** As president, Secretary Celadon was in the best office.

**Hack Blaxton:** President Midnight was not in the mail room.

SUSPECTS     MOTIVES     LOCATIONS

WEAPONS

LOCATIONS

MOTIVES

_____ **WHO?**

_____ **WHAT?**

_____ **WHERE?**

_____ **WHY?**

# 91. THEY BILL YOU DOUBLE FOR DYING 🔍🔍🔍🔍

Logico drove to an entertainment law firm he was recommended, but when he got there, he saw the size of their lobby and knew immediately that it was too expensive for him. Fortunately, a lawyer had just been murdered, so he offered to solve it in return for a discount.

## SUSPECTS

**AGENT ARGYLE**

Unlike Agent Ink, Argyle does not have a heart of gold, or a heart at all.

**6'4" • RIGHT-HANDED • LIGHT BROWN EYES • DARK BROWN HAIR • VIRGO**

**HACK BLAXTON**

He was a little embarrassed to run into his brother here, since he'd changed his last name.

**6'0" • RIGHT-HANDED • LIGHT BROWN EYES • BALD • SAGITTARIUS**

**JUDGE PINE**

Master of the courtroom and possessed of a firm belief in justice, as decided by her and her alone.

**5'6" • RIGHT-HANDED • DARK BROWN EYES • BLACK HAIR • TAURUS**

**BLACKSTONE, ESQ.**

Incredibly talented at the most important skill for an attorney: finding employment at another firm when you're fired from your first for murder.

**6'0" • RIGHT-HANDED • BLACK EYES • BLACK HAIR • SCORPIO**

## LOCATIONS

### A PARTNER'S OFFICE
INDOORS

Pictures of the partner with every world leader, especially the bad ones.

### THE ARCHIVES
INDOORS

Ancient legal books going back to the Code of Hammurabi. They belong in a museum.

### THE BREAK ROOM
INDOORS

A full-time coffee barista, a walk-in fridge, and a fountain filled with priceless wine.

### THE LOBBY
INDOORS

This lobby makes that other law firm's lobby look like the bathroom at a used car lot.

## WEAPONS

### A HUGE PILE OF PAPERWORK
HEAVY-WEIGHT • MADE OF PAPER

Mostly contracts acquiring the land for shooting locations for *Murdle: The Movie*.

### A BAG OF CASH
HEAVY-WEIGHT • MADE OF CLOTH & PAPER

Great for bribery or just general corruption.

### A GOLDEN PEN
LIGHT-WEIGHT • MADE OF METAL & INK

This pen was used to sign the Magna Carta.

### AN ANTIQUE CLOCK
HEAVY-WEIGHT • MADE OF WOOD & METAL

Tick, tock, tick, tock. Technically, time is killing us all slowly.

## MOTIVES

 TO GET REVENGE

 AS PART OF A REAL ESTATE SCAM

 OUT OF FRUSTRATION

 TO GET A HIGHER PERCENTAGE

## CLUES & EVIDENCE

- Whoever wanted to kill as part of a real estate scam had black hair.

- Whoever wanted to get a higher percentage had light brown eyes.

- A secretary had written a quick, scrambled note and given it to Logico: TEH SORENP OHW DOLWU LILK UTO FO UFRTOSRANTI AWS NI ETH HAVCIERS.

- The person with a golden pen wanted to get revenge.

- A Sagittarius was seen chatting up a coffee barista.

- A faint ticking sound was heard next to a picture of a dictator.

## STATEMENTS

(Remember: The murderer is lying. The others are telling the truth.)

**Agent Argyle:** Here is the deal: Hack Blaxton brought a bag of cash.

**Hack Blaxton:** Picture it: a huge pile of paperwork was in the lobby.

**Judge Pine:** Judicially, whoever had the antique clock wanted to get a higher percentage.

**Blackstone, Esq.:** I'll give you my statement now and my bill later: Judge Pine brought a huge pile of paperwork.

SUSPECTS     MOTIVES     LOCATIONS

WEAPONS

LOCATIONS

MOTIVES

_____ **WHO?**

_____ **WHAT?**

_____ **WHERE?**

_____ **WHY?**

# 92. MURDER AT THE MYSTERY SHOW 🔍🔍🔍🔍

Deductive Logico called the one person he knew could help, Inspector Irratino, and asked how he could escape Hollywood. And Irratino told him, "Calm down, and go to this address." When Logico got there, he found a small theater staging a Hollywood Mystery Show.

Being a professional, he was able to solve the whodunit well before the final act.

## SUSPECTS

**ASSISTANT APPLEGREEN**

Her father was proud that she has finally left that commune, but then she moved to Hollywood . . .

5'3" • LEFT-HANDED • BLUE EYES • BLOND HAIR • VIRGO

**BACKGROUND MARENGO**

You'll never remember her, which is why she's a good extra, and a great murderer.

5'5" • LEFT-HANDED • LIGHT BROWN EYES • DARK BROWN HAIR • GEMINI

**SUPERFAN SMOKY**

He knows the shooting locations of every Midnight mystery, but not how to make friends.

5'10" • LEFT-HANDED • BLACK EYES • DARK BROWN HAIR • VIRGO

**MISS SAFFRON**

Gorgeous and stunning, but maybe not all there in the brains department. Or maybe that's what she wants you to think. Or maybe she wants you to think that's what she wants you to think.

5'2" • LEFT-HANDED • HAZEL EYES • BLOND HAIR • LIBRA

## LOCATIONS

### THE AUDIENCE
INDOORS

This is a loud audience. They keep yelling and heckling and that seems to be the point.

### THE LIGHTING BOOTH
INDOORS

A single person controls all the lights from a tiny, cramped booth full of knobs and switches.

### THE STAGE
INDOORS

On one side, the maestro plays the keyboard. On the other, the hostess serves drinks and gossips with the Scryptkeeper.

### THE GREEN ROOM
INDOORS

Where the actors do their makeup and drugs. A single blue bulb lights the room. So, it's more of a blue room.

## WEAPONS

### A JUG OF WHISKEY
MEDIUM-WEIGHT • MADE OF METAL & TOXINS

This is probably the most dangerous weapon in the book, if you count long-term effects.

### A FAKE ROSE
LIGHT-WEIGHT • MADE OF PLASTIC

The plastic stem is strong enough to strangle somebody.

### A "PROP" KNIFE
LIGHT-WEIGHT • MADE OF METAL & RUBBER

Weirdly it's as sharp as a real knife. Wait a second—

### A GHOST LIGHT
HEAVY-WEIGHT • MADE OF METAL & GLASS

A theater superstition says you should always leave a light on. This is that light.

## MOTIVES

 **ON BEHALF OF THE INDUSTRY**

 **FOR THEMATIC REASONS**

 **TO CREATE A DIVERSION**

 **TO PROMOTE THE OCCULT**

## CLUES & EVIDENCE

- A ghost light was found under a blue light.

- A "prop" knife was never taken on stage, which really hurt the case that it was a prop.

- Miss Saffron had a light-weight weapon.

- The second tallest suspect was the only one who wasn't a member of the Hollywood Mystery Society.

- The person with a jug of whiskey wanted to create a diversion.

- Whoever wanted to promote the occult had dark brown hair.

- Members of the Hollywood Mystery Society are not allowed to be near knobs.

- The person who wanted to kill on behalf of the Industry was in the audience.

## STATEMENTS

**(Remember: The murderer is lying. The others are telling the truth.)**

**Assistant Applegreen:** I took notes on this: the tallest suspect was on the stage.

**Background Marengo:** Ooh! I brought a jug of whiskey.

**Superfan Smoky:** I did not bring a ghost light.

**Miss Saffron:** What do I know? Well, Assistant Applegreen was in the audience.

|  | SUSPECTS | | | | MOTIVES | | | | LOCATIONS | | | |
|---|---|---|---|---|---|---|---|---|---|---|---|---|
| **WEAPONS** | | | | | | | | | | | | |
| | | | | | | | | | | | | |
| | | | | | | | | | | | | |
| | | | | | | | | | | | | |
| **LOCATIONS** | | | | | | | | | | | | |
| | | | | | | | | | | | | |
| | | | | | | | | | | | | |
| | | | | | | | | | | | | |
| **MOTIVES** | | | | | | | | | | | | |
| | | | | | | | | | | | | |
| | | | | | | | | | | | | |
| | | | | | | | | | | | | |

_____

**WHO?**

_____

**WHAT?**

_____

**WHERE?**

_____

**WHY?**

# 93. DEATH IN THE MAGICK SHOPPE 🔍🔍🔍🔍

Tucked into a corner, Logico found the Hollywood Mystery Shoppe, a movie-magick emporium. It has everything you need to make it in the movies: spell books, magick powders, lighting equipment, and a dead clerk. Again, why had Irratino sent him to these people?

## SUSPECTS

**BISHOP AZURE**

A bishop in a local church, Azure has been known to pray for both her friends and her enemies. Of course, she asks for different things . . .

**5'4" • RIGHT-HANDED • LIGHT BROWN EYES • DARK BROWN HAIR • GEMINI**

**DIRECTOR DUSTY**

A true filmmaker. He wants to make a masterpiece. To do that, he might have to make a murder.

**5'10" • LEFT-HANDED • HAZEL EYES • BALD • PISCES**

**COMRADE CHAMPAGNE**

A communist and a rich one. Comrade Champagne likes nothing more than to travel the world, sharing the message of communism while sipping on the finest sparkling wines.

**5'11" • LEFT-HANDED • HAZEL EYES • BLOND HAIR • CAPRICORN**

**UNCLE MIDNIGHT**

When his dad died, he bought a desert mansion with a pool and retired. He was seventeen.

**5'8" • LEFT-HANDED • BLUE EYES • DARK BROWN HAIR • SAGITTARIUS**

# LOCATIONS

### THE SECRET ROOM
INDOORS

A secret room used for conducting magick rituals and photo shoots.

### THE BACK OFFICE
INDOORS

Where the proprietor—a Hollywood mystery writer—does most of his writing.

### THE FRONT PORCH
OUTDOORS

There's an inviting sign offering supplies for "all your magickal mystery needs."

### THE MAIN ROOM
INDOORS

You can buy all sorts of magick supplies, mystery books, and more.

# WEAPONS

### A CRYSTAL BALL
HEAVY-WEIGHT • MADE OF CRYSTAL

If you look into it, it will tell you your future, so long as your future is a crystal ball.

### AN AWARD
MEDIUM-WEIGHT • MADE OF METAL

One of the most commonplace items in all of Hollywood, it seems.

### A SWORD CANE
MEDIUM-WEIGHT • MADE OF METAL

Sharp and hidden. Looks like an ordinary cane.

### A CURSED DAGGER
MEDIUM-WEIGHT • MADE OF METAL & JEWELS

A dying duchess cursed this dagger when she used it to end her own life.

## MOTIVES

 TO STEAL A CRYSTAL

 TO PROMOTE THE OCCULT

 ON BEHALF OF THE INDUSTRY

 TO HELP SELL A SCRIPT

## CLUES & EVIDENCE

- The suspect with the crystal ball had blond hair.

- The second shortest suspect was in the Cult of the Black Cow.

- Whoever was in the main room was right-handed.

- The person who wanted to steal a crystal was in the back office.

- A member of the High Order of the Dark Rain brought a cursed dagger.

- The dead clerk had written a note in a scrambled hand before they died: EWVEORH AHD NA RAADW WSA ITHRG-EDDAHN.

- Director Dusty was in a room he had previously used for photo shoots.

- The person with a sword cane wanted to kill on behalf of the Industry.

- Nobody in the Cult of the Black Cow was also in the High Order of the Dark Rain: they were rivals.

## STATEMENTS

(Remember: The murderer is lying. The others are telling the truth.)

**Bishop Azure:** Whoever had the cursed dagger wanted to help sell a script.

**Director Dusty:** I was not in the back office.

**Comrade Champagne:** I was not in the main room.

**Uncle Midnight:** Hey now, Director Dusty was in the secret room.

SUSPECTS     MOTIVES     LOCATIONS

WEAPONS

LOCATIONS

MOTIVES

WHO?

WHAT?

WHERE?

WHY?

# 94. A RITUAL KILLING 🔍🔍🔍🔍

But then, five members of the Hollywood Mystery Society took Logico into the secret back room. They blew out all the lights, and then they began to sing and dance, performing some kind of magick ritual, when suddenly—a scream! When the lights came on, one of them was dead.

## SUSPECTS

**BACKGROUND MARENGO**

You'll never remember her, which is why she's a good extra, and a great murderer.

**5'5" • LEFT-HANDED • LIGHT BROWN EYES • DARK BROWN HAIR • GEMINI**

**SUPERFAN SMOKY**

He knows the shooting locations of every Midnight mystery, but not how to make friends.

**5'10" • LEFT-HANDED • BLACK EYES • DARK BROWN HAIR • VIRGO**

**ASSISTANT APPLEGREEN**

Maybe one day she'll make her father proud again. Or maybe she'll murder someone.

**5'3" • LEFT-HANDED • BLUE EYES • BLOND HAIR • VIRGO**

**MX. TANGERINE**

Proving that non-binary people can be murderers, too, they are an artist, poet, and suspect.

**5'5" • LEFT-HANDED • HAZEL EYES • BLOND HAIR • PISCES**

## LOCATIONS

### THE BATHROOM
INDOORS

Even a secret ritual room needs a bathroom (that's part of the building code).

### THE SECRET ENTRANCE
INDOORS

It's behind a bookshelf in the Hollywood Mystery Shoppe. Just grab the right book.

### THE FLOOR SIGIL
INDOORS

A bunch of wild lines and circles on the floor that have occult significance.

### THE ALTAR
INDOORS

Where the leader of the ritual stands and conducts the proceedings.

## WEAPONS

### A BOTTLE OF WINE
MEDIUM-WEIGHT • MADE OF GLASS & ALCOHOL

Watch out for stains, because the red doesn't come out.

### A ROSE FLAG
LIGHT-WEIGHT • MADE OF CANVAS

There's a red rose on a black background on the flag.

### AN AWARD
MEDIUM-WEIGHT • MADE OF METAL

They use this in their rituals. It does have some kind of power.

### A HEAVY CANDLE
HEAVY-WEIGHT • MADE OF WAX

It's heavy, yet it lightens the room.

## MOTIVES

 BECAUSE THE VIBES WERE OFF

 ON BEHALF OF THE INDUSTRY

 TO MAKE GOOD ART

 TO TAKE OVER HOLLYWOOD

## CLUES & EVIDENCE

- Either someone who wanted to kill on behalf of the Industry was in the secret entrance, or an award was.

- The suspect with the rose flag wanted to take over Hollywood.

- A red stain was discovered in the bathroom.

- Only members of the Order of the Rose & Key wanted to make good art.

- A member wrote a hastily scribbled message: VERHEOW OWULD IKLL CEEBAUS HET ESIBV WERE FFO SWA A GIRVO.

- Background Marengo never set foot on the floor sigil.

- A drop of wax was discovered on the altar.

- Assistant Applegreen was not in the Order of the Rose & Key.

## STATEMENTS

(Remember: The murderer is lying. The others are telling the truth.)

**Background Marengo:** Ooh! Superfan Smoky brought a bottle of wine.

**Superfan Smoky:** Oh, wow! A bottle of wine was in the bathroom.

**Assistant Applegreen:** Simply put, I brought a flag.

**Mx. Tangerine:** The person with the bottle of wine could kill because the vibes were off.

SUSPECTS    MOTIVES    LOCATIONS

WEAPONS

LOCATIONS

MOTIVES

WHO?

WHAT?

WHERE?

WHY?

# 95. A FREE PRESS CAN COST A KILLING 🔍🔍🔍🔍

Deductive Logico smuggled Inspector Irratino out of house arrest and into Hollywood, where they celebrated at Logico's apartment before heading to a local Hollywood trade, a newspaper for the Industry. "Midnight Movies is involved in a global conspiracy!" The first thing the editor said was that they needed proof. The second was that their assistant editor had just been killed.

## SUSPECTS

**EDITOR IVORY**

It turns out, being a murderer hurts your romance-genre employment prospects. It does not hurt your Hollywood trade employment prospects.

**5'6" • LEFT-HANDED • LIGHT BROWN EYES • GRAY HAIR • SCORPIO**

**BOOKIE-WINNER GAINSBORO**

Gainsboro's six-thousand-page dirt novel does not pay the bills. So he's a journalist, too. That, also, doesn't pay the bills.

**6'0" • LEFT-HANDED • HAZEL EYES • LIGHT BROWN HAIR • GEMINI**

**HACK BLAXTON**

Hack Blaxton would never work as a journalist. He's here for a feature interview.

**6'0" • RIGHT-HANDED • LIGHT BROWN EYES • BALD • SAGITTARIUS**

**COMRADE CHAMPAGNE**

Comrade Champagne is here to see if he could unionize the workforce, and put them on the path to seizing the presses.

**5'11" • LEFT-HANDED • HAZEL EYES • BLOND HAIR • CAPRICORN**

## LOCATIONS

### THE BULLPEN
INDOORS

Where all the writers pitch stories and new slang terms. Filled with crumpled-up ideas.

### THE PRINTING PRESS
INDOORS

An enormous machine of gears and belts and rollers.

### THE BALCONY
OUTDOORS

Don't look down! Not only is it scary, but also, someone might push you.

### THE ROOFTOP
OUTDOORS

Back in the seventies, there was a helipad up here. Now there's a billboard for arthritis medicine.

## WEAPONS

### A LETTER OPENER
LIGHT-WEIGHT • MADE OF METAL

A sharp knife used by people who won't just rip their letters open.

### A LAPTOP
MEDIUM-WEIGHT • MADE OF METAL & TECH

The machine you work on. It's connected to every distraction ever made.

### A MARBLE BUST
HEAVY-WEIGHT • MADE OF MARBLE

It's a bust of a famous journalist, but don't look him up—you won't like what you find.

### A PRINTER
HEAVY-WEIGHT • MADE OF PLASTIC & TECH

If you're over the age of fifty, you probably use one of these.

## MOTIVES

 TO SEIZE POWER

 OUT OF FRUSTRATION

 TO STOP THE REVOLUTION

 TO ESCAPE BLACKMAIL

## CLUES & EVIDENCE

- Whoever wanted to seize power was left-handed.

- The author of a book about dirt is not a member of the Anointed Ones.

- A letter opener was wedged in between a belt and a gear, making a grinding sound.

- The suspect with the same height as Bookie-Winner Gainsboro was seen with a laptop.

- A member of the Anointed Ones was on the rooftop.

- An intern handed Logico a scrambled note: HTE TCUSPES THIW A TRNRPEI TENWDA OT POST EHT TOROUENVLI.

- The person who would kill out of frustration was thinking about it on the balcony.

- The suspect who wanted to escape blackmail was seen indoors.

## STATEMENTS

(Remember: The murderer is lying. The others are telling the truth.)

**Editor Ivory:** Well, I was at the printing press.

**Bookie-Winner Gainsboro:** I have a Bookie, so take it from me: a marble bust was on the balcony.

**Hack Blaxton:** Bookie-Winner Gainsboro brought a letter opener.

**Comrade Champagne:** Take it from me, a working man: I brought a marble bust.

|  | SUSPECTS | | | | MOTIVES | | | | LOCATIONS | | | |
|---|---|---|---|---|---|---|---|---|---|---|---|---|
| WEAPONS | | | | | | | | | | | | |
| | | | | | | | | | | | | |
| | | | | | | | | | | | | |
| | | | | | | | | | | | | |
| LOCATIONS | | | | | | | | | | | | |
| | | | | | | | | | | | | |
| | | | | | | | | | | | | |
| | | | | | | | | | | | | |
| MOTIVES | | | | | | | | | | | | |
| | | | | | | | | | | | | |
| | | | | | | | | | | | | |
| | | | | | | | | | | | | |

WHO?

WHAT?

WHERE?

WHY?

# 96. BREAKING AND INVESTIGATING 🔍🔍🔍🔍

Deductive Logico and Inspector Irratino snuck onto the lot by using an old trick: lying. They dressed up as mechanics and wore fake mustaches and walked right in. Eventually, they realized why it had been so easy: the security guard had been killed.

## SUSPECTS

**MIDNIGHT III**

He thinks the fact that his father splits his focus between making movies and making money is ruining the studio.

5'8" • LEFT-HANDED • DARK BROWN EYES • DARK BROWN HAIR • LIBRA

**SECRETARY CELADON**

The secretary of defense, and someone who is personally responsible for a number of war crimes, some of which are now named after her.

5'6" • LEFT-HANDED • GREEN EYES • LIGHT BROWN HAIR • LEO

**PRESIDENT MIDNIGHT**

The CEO of Midnight Movies. He cares about art and business, but definitely not in that order.

6'2" • RIGHT-HANDED • BLACK EYES • BLACK HAIR • CAPRICORN

**EXECUTIVE PRODUCER STEEL**

The richest, smartest, and meanest producer in Hollywood. For now.

5'6" • RIGHT-HANDED • GRAY EYES • WHITE HAIR • ARIES

## LOCATIONS

### THE LUXURY THEATER
INDOORS

Where footage is screened for executives who can't direct, but can somehow give notes.

### THE BUNGALOWS
INDOORS

Where the talent lives while they're working on a movie, so the studio doesn't have to pay for hotel rooms.

### THE PROP SHOP
INDOORS

Where they make all the fake knives, fake cars, and fake tears.

### THE LOCKED STAGE
INDOORS

Nobody knows what's in here. It's been locked for years.

## WEAPONS

### A DECK OF MAROT CARDS
LIGHT-WEIGHT • MADE OF PAPER

You can use these murder-themed tarot cards to read your future.

### AN AWARD
MEDIUM-WEIGHT • MADE OF METAL

By this point, Logico was convinced they could be used for paperweights.

### A C-STAND
HEAVY-WEIGHT • MADE OF METAL

For holding up lights. Or swinging at skulls.

### A MAGNIFYING GLASS
MEDIUM-WEIGHT • MADE OF METAL & GLASS

You could use this to find a clue or to bonk somebody.

## MOTIVES

 TO GET THE RECOGNITION THEY DESERVE

 TO PROMOTE A MOVIE

 TO GET REVENGE

 TO TAKE OVER HOLLYWOOD

## CLUES & EVIDENCE

- The person who wanted to promote a movie was in the bungalows.

- A fortune-telling card was discovered in the building directly north of the Luxury Theatre. (See Exhibit D.)

- Everybody in the Order of Buried Talents wanted to get the recognition they deserved.

- Analysts discovered traces of a weapon made of metal on the clothing of Midnight III.

- A scrambled message was found in the security guard's papers: EHT SORNPE HWTI A FIAINGNYMG SAGSL DNTEWA TO TEKA EORV DOLLOWOHY.

- A Capricorn had the C-stand. (The *C* stood for Capricorn.)

- Everybody with an award joined the Order of Buried Talents.

- Whoever was in the building directly east of the studio tour check-in was right-handed. (See Exhibit D.)

## STATEMENTS

**(Remember: The murderer is lying. The others are telling the truth.)**

**Midnight III:** I was not in the luxury theater.

**Secretary Celadon:** A magnifying glass was in the locked stage.

**President Midnight:** Midnight III did not bring a magnifying glass.

**Executive Producer Steel:** Look: I wanted to take over Hollywood.

WEAPONS

LOCATIONS

MOTIVES

WHO?

WHAT?

WHERE?

WHY?

# 97. BUNGALOW MORAL CHARACTER 🔍🔍🔍🔍

So Deductive Logico and Inspector Irratino, after solving one murder on the lot, went over to the bungalows to interview the temporary residents about the ruins. They couldn't come up with a pretext for the intrusion, but fortunately, when they arrived, an extra had been killed.

## SUSPECTS

**HACK BLAXTON**

He's one of the best paid writers in Hollywood, and one of the worst.

**6'0" • RIGHT-HANDED • LIGHT BROWN EYES • BALD • SAGITTARIUS**

**SILVERTON THE LEGEND**

An acclaimed actor of the Golden Age, now in his golden years.

**6'4" • RIGHT-HANDED • BLUE EYES • SILVER HAIR • LEO**

**A-LIST ABALONE**

The most talented and in-demand actress of all time this month.

**5'6" • RIGHT-HANDED • HAZEL EYES • RED HAIR • LIBRA**

**UNCLE MIDNIGHT**

When his dad died, he bought a desert mansion with a pool and retired. He was seventeen.

**5'8" • LEFT-HANDED • BLUE EYES • DARK BROWN HAIR • SAGITTARIUS**

## LOCATIONS

### 1
**BUNGALOW 1**
INDOORS

For beginning writers. It has a bedroom, a kitchen, and a bathroom, but they're all the same room.

### 2
**BUNGALOW 2**
INDOORS

When they upgrade you to Bungalow 2, you know you've made it. A full-sized refrigerator? Wow.

### 3
**BUNGALOW 3**
INDOORS

A bungalow for the stars. You have your own balcony, and your shower has two showerheads.

### 4
**BUNGALOW 4**
INDOORS

A luxury bungalow that is absolutely never occupied, as a way of making sure even the stars know their place.

## WEAPONS

**AN ANTIQUE TYPEWRITER**
HEAVY-WEIGHT • MADE OF METAL

From the 1920s, which, in Hollywood, makes it neolithic.

**AN AWARD**
MEDIUM-WEIGHT • MADE OF METAL

This one is for Best Movie Adapted from a Puzzle Book. Very prestigious.

**A GIANT SCREENPLAY**
HEAVY-WEIGHT • MADE OF PAPER

It sets up a franchise, so it's got an extra fifty pages that are incredibly boring.

**A FOUNTAIN PEN**
LIGHT-WEIGHT • MADE OF METAL & INK

With this, you can sign checks or stab necks. Unfortunately, it leaks ink.

## MOTIVES

 FOR MONEY

 TO GET REVENGE

TO STEAL A PRIZED BOOK

 TO WIN AN AWARD

## CLUES & EVIDENCE

- The person with a giant screenplay did not want to kill for money.

- An ink stain was discovered in a one-roomed bungalow.

- Logico received a tip from a journalist, written in the Next Letter Code: VGNDUDQ VZMSDC SN VHM ZM ZVZQC VZR KDES-GZMCDC.

- Uncle Midnight was seen next to a full-sized refrigerator.

- Either A-List Abalone was under two showerheads, or A-List Abalone brought an antique typewriter.

- The person who wanted to get revenge was in Bungalow 4.

## STATEMENTS

(Remember: The murderer is lying. The others are telling the truth.)

**Hack Blaxton:** Picture it: I was in Bungalow 4.

**Silverton the Legend:** Let me tell you how it is: an antique typewriter was in Bungalow 2.

**A-List Abalone:** Talk to my agent, but privately, Silverton the Legend brought an antique typewriter.

**Uncle Midnight:** Hey now, a giant screenplay was in Bungalow 3.

|  | SUSPECTS | | | | MOTIVES | | | | LOCATIONS | | | |
|---|---|---|---|---|---|---|---|---|---|---|---|---|
| **WEAPONS** | | | | | | | | | | | | |
| 🖊️(typewriter) | | | | | | | | | | | | |
| 🏆(statue) | | | | | | | | | | | | |
| 📄 | | | | | | | | | | | | |
| ✏️ | | | | | | | | | | | | |
| **LOCATIONS** | | | | | | | | | | | | |
| 1 | | | | | | | | | | | | |
| 2 | | | | | | | | | | | | |
| 3 | | | | | | | | | | | | |
| 4 | | | | | | | | | | | | |
| **MOTIVES** | | | | | | | | | | | | |
| 💰 | | | | | | | | | | | | |
| ⚔️ | | | | | | | | | | | | |
| 📖 | | | | | | | | | | | | |
| 🏆 | | | | | | | | | | | | |

_____

**WHO?**

_____

**WHAT?**

_____

**WHERE?**

_____

**WHY?**

# 98. STAGE FRIGHT 🔍🔍🔍🔍

Dame Obsidian led them over to the mysterious sound stage on the western edge of the studio. Outside its locked door, Pearl, AGE, and Midnight III were arguing over the ending of *Murdle: The Movie*. But when Dame Obsidian held up the key, they both seemed shocked.

"Nobody has been in the locked sound stage in years," Pearl said.

"Maybe it's time they did," replied Midnight III. "Let's see what Dad's been up to."

Dame Obsidian unlocked the door, and they all crept inside. But when they were surrounded by darkness, they all heard a scream. Somebody had killed Irratino! Again!

## SUSPECTS

**PEARL, AGE**

The editor of some of the best and highest-grossing movies ever made, though never both at once.

**5'5" • RIGHT-HANDED • BLUE EYES • BLOND HAIR • AQUARIUS**

**OFFICER COPPER**

The only non-murdered security guard on the Midnight Movies lot.

**5'5" • RIGHT-HANDED • BLUE EYES • BLOND HAIR • ARIES**

**DAME OBSIDIAN**

Sure, she's murdered a ton of people, but nobody else seems to get punished for killing, so why should she?

**5'4" • LEFT-HANDED • GREEN EYES • BLACK HAIR • LEO**

**MIDNIGHT III**

Believes that *Murdle: The Movie* will help restore the studio to its original glory.

**5'8" • LEFT-HANDED • DARK BROWN EYES • DARK BROWN HAIR • LIBRA**

## LOCATIONS

**A TARP**
INDOORS

It's covering something huge in the middle of the warehouse.

**A LARGE TANK**
INDOORS

Where the oil is stored as it awaits refinement.

**A GREAT MACHINE**
INDOORS

Some kind of refining equipment or separation tank, or maybe something else?

**A PUMPJACK**
INDOORS

It's working overtime to pump oil out from under the studio.

## WEAPONS

**AN OIL DRUM**
HEAVY-WEIGHT • MADE OF METAL & OIL

Really more of a can than a drum: you've never seen a band feature an oil drum solo.

**A KNIFE**
MEDIUM-WEIGHT • MADE OF METAL

You can use this for lots of things, like chopping vegetables, or murder.

**A PIECE OF REBAR**
MEDIUM-WEIGHT • MADE OF METAL

A long piece of metal. If this isn't a weapon, then nothing is. Often found with cement.

**A SHOVEL**
MEDIUM-WEIGHT • MADE OF METAL & WOOD

The great thing about using a shovel to kill is it can also dig a hole to help hide the body.

## MOTIVES

 TO GET A PROMOTION

 TO TAKE OVER A STUDIO

 TO PROTECT A SECRET

 TO WIN AN AWARD

## CLUES & EVIDENCE

- Officer Copper brought an oil drum.

- A member of the Ancient Blood of Beasts had the knife.

- Irratino was clutching a scribbled note in his hand that read: HET OPNSER IHWT A CEEPI FO ERABR IDD TNO NTWA TO NIW AN WRAAD.

- Midnight III was seen examining a mysterious tarp.

- A member of the Ancient Blood of Beasts wanted to get a promotion.

- Whoever had the shovel was next to the pumpjack.

- Only people with blue eyes are allowed to join the Ancient Blood of Beasts.

- Pearl, AGE, wanted to protect a secret.

## STATEMENTS

(Remember: The murderer is lying. The others are telling the truth.)

**Pearl, AGE:** I seem to have noticed that Officer Copper was by a great machine.

**Officer Copper:** I was not near the tarp.

**Dame Obsidian:** Midnight III was not by a great machine.

**Midnight III:** A piece of rebar was not by a great machine.

SUSPECTS    MOTIVES    LOCATIONS

WEAPONS

LOCATIONS

MOTIVES

WHO?

WHAT?

WHERE?

WHY?

# 99. THE FOUNDING OF MIDNIGHT MOVIES 🔍🔍🔍🔍

Suddenly, it all made sense to Deductive Logico. And with the help of Inspector Irratino's visualization techniques, he could travel back in time (in his mind) and see the founding of the studio as clear as sepia-tinted day. It had been born, not out of a love of cinema, but out of greed. You see, the original owner of the land had been murdered.

## SUSPECTS

**MIDNIGHT I**

The original founder of Midnight Movies. A genius in getting people to work harder for less. And one of the meanest men to ever live.

5'11" • RIGHT-HANDED • BLUE EYES • DARK BROWN HAIR • GEMINI

**TEENAGE MIDNIGHT**

He was a teenager back then, and his father had just given him this ridiculous tophat.

6'2" • RIGHT-HANDED • BLACK EYES • BLACK HAIR • CAPRICORN

**PRÉSIDENT AMARANTH**

The literal French *président*, Amaranth loves spending time with his constituents, especially a certain one percent of them.

5'10" • RIGHT-HANDED • GRAY EYES • RED HAIR • GEMINI

**CHAIRMAN CHALK**

He figured out the publishing business years ago and never looked back. He called ebooks a "fad" and still owns a rotary phone. He is worth a billion dollars.

5'9" • RIGHT-HANDED • BLUE EYES • WHITE HAIR • SAGITTARIUS

## LOCATIONS

### AN OIL DERRICK
OUTDOORS

They're digging another well right now with this massive derrick.

### A PUMPJACK
OUTDOORS

It's working hard, bobbing up and down, bringing oil up from the ground.

### THE ANCIENT RUINS
OUTDOORS

You can see them from the edge of the fields, silhouetted in the light of the setting sun.

### THE OFFICES
INDOORS

Air-conditioned to such a low temperature that it uses most of the energy they produce.

## WEAPONS

### A CROWBAR
MEDIUM-WEIGHT • MADE OF METAL

Honestly, they're used more often for crime than anything else.

### A PIECE OF REBAR
MEDIUM-WEIGHT • MADE OF METAL

A long piece of metal. If this isn't a weapon, then nothing is. Often found with cement.

### AN OIL DRUM
HEAVY-WEIGHT • MADE OF METAL & OIL

Really more of a can than a drum: you've never seen a band feature an oil drum solo.

### A SHOVEL
MEDIUM-WEIGHT • MADE OF METAL & WOOD

The great thing about using a shovel for murder is it can also dig a hole to help hide the body.

## MOTIVES

 TO FOUND A STUDIO

 TO BREAK A UNION

 TO GAIN AN INHERITANCE

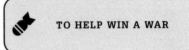 TO HELP WIN A WAR

## CLUES & EVIDENCE

- Either Teenage Midnight was at the pumpjack, or Midnight I brought a shovel.

- The shortest suspect had a rivalry with the person who brought an oil drum.

- The person who wanted to help win a war was at the pumpjack.

- Président Amaranth was relaxing in an air-conditioned room.

- The suspect in the ancient ruins had dark brown hair.

- The person who wanted to found a studio was standing beside the ancient ruins.

- The person with the oil drum wanted to gain an inheritance.

## STATEMENTS

(Remember: The murderer is lying. The others are telling the truth.)

**Midnight I:** As clear as day, Chairman Chalk brought a piece of rebar.

**Teenage Midnight:** I did not bring a piece of rebar.

**Président Amaranth:** The shovel was at the ruins.

**Chairman Chalk:** Hmm . . . Midnight I brought a shovel.

SUSPECTS          MOTIVES          LOCATIONS

WEAPONS

LOCATIONS

MOTIVES

WHO?

WHAT?

WHERE?

WHY?

# 100. MURDER AT THE *MURDLE* PREMIERE ९९९९

The night before *Murdle: The Movie* premiered at the luxury theatre at Midnight Movie Studios, Deductive Logico got a call. "I know who framed Irratino!" said a mysterious voice, but when Logico asked who, the line went dead.

The next night, at the premiere, Logico and Irratino arrived in their tuxedos and found that the vice president of Midnight Movies had been killed. In his pocket, Logico found a slip of paper with his phone number on it. If Logico could solve this murder, he could solve the whole mystery at once.

## SUSPECTS

**MIDNIGHT III**

The grandson of the founder. Will he succeed in his plan to restore Midnight Movies to its Golden Age?

5'8" • LEFT-HANDED • DARK BROWN EYES • DARK BROWN HAIR • LIBRA

**PRESIDENT MIDNIGHT**

The CEO of Midnight Movies. Would he murder dozens just to keep himself in power?

6'2" • RIGHT-HANDED • BLACK EYES • BLACK HAIR • CAPRICORN

**DAME OBSIDIAN**

Has the world's greatest mystery writer simply been adding more murders to her portfolio?

5'4" • LEFT-HANDED • GREEN EYES • BLACK HAIR • LEO

**INSPECTOR IRRATINO**

The esoteric detective. But has everything he's ever said been a lie?

6'2" • LEFT-HANDED • GREEN EYES • DARK BROWN HAIR • AQUARIUS

## LOCATIONS

### THE STAGE
INDOORS

If you get invited to a movie here, you pay by being forced to listen to the on-stage Q&A afterward.

### THE PLUSH SEATING
INDOORS

Red velvet seats, just like in the old days. There's gum on them from the old days, too.

### THE EMERGENCY EXIT
INDOORS

It's hard to find, because the studio has taped over the emergency lights in order to make the theater perfectly dark.

### THE CONCESSIONS STAND
INDOORS

All of the concessions are free and, as a result, ridiculously tiny. Grab a handful of popcorn and a capful of soda.

## WEAPONS

### AN AWARD
MEDIUM-WEIGHT • MADE OF METAL

The most important thing in all of Hollywood. And also, it's meaningless.

### A RED HERRING
MEDIUM-WEIGHT • MADE OF FISH

If you hold it by the tail, you can get some real momentum behind it.

### A SELENITE WAND
MEDIUM-WEIGHT • MADE OF CRYSTAL

For casting spells and bashing skulls.

### A BOTTLE OF WINE
MEDIUM-WEIGHT • MADE OF GLASS & ALCOHOL

Watch out for stains, because the red doesn't come out.

## MOTIVES

 TO HOLD ON TO POWER

 TO TAKE OVER A STUDIO

 TO GET REVENGE

 TO DRILL FOR OIL

## CLUES & EVIDENCE

- The letter connected to the *O* in the labyrinth engraved on the side of the ancient ruins is not the first letter of the last name of the suspect who wants to take over a studio. (See Exhibit C.)

- The suspect at the concessions stand was a member of the Academy of Moving Images.

- The Investigation Institute issued their report (See Exhibit B):

⚛ ✂ ♐ ♂ ♈ ♂ ♒ ☉ W ♒ ☽

♉ ♇ ♈ ☢ ♇ ♍ ♇ ☽ ♊ ♇

- A selenite wand was next to old gum, and nobody would have let a red herring on the stage.

- Either the person with an award wanted to drill for oil, or Dame Obsidian brought a bottle of wine.

- The Academy of Moving Images only admits people with black hair.

- A filmgoer scribbled their thoughts on a piece of paper and handed it to Logico: PESNERTID IGTMDHNI TENDWA TO OLDH TNOO REWPO.

- The Detective Club finally got in touch with Logico, and they sent him a message in their traditional code: GSV HVXLMW HSLIGVHG HFHKVXG DZH HVVM DRGS ZM ZDZIW. (See Exhibit A.)

## STATEMENTS

(Remember: The murderer is lying. The others are telling the truth.)

**Midnight III:** Let me jump in: my father brought a selenite wand.

**President Midnight:** My son wanted to take over the studio.

**Dame Obsidian:** Whoever wanted to get revenge was at the concessions stand.

**Inspector Irratino:** President Midnight was not at the concessions stand.

SUSPECTS     MOTIVES     LOCATIONS

WEAPONS

LOCATIONS

MOTIVES

**WHO?**

**WHAT?**

**WHERE?**

**WHY?**

# 101. ONE MORE THING

After the trial was over, and the crimes of ███████████ had been exposed, and *Murdle: The Movie* had become the greatest film success of all time, Deductive Logico upgraded to a slightly bigger office—with room for a partner.

But one day, as he was closing up, he found a message nailed to his door. On it was a terrible coded message, terrible because Logico could not crack it. Can you?

```
01010348051360530560351537141548294537
05482121074579214879317931140801143101
37293714081553054529031401070308370703
31075308371460371335603708026021313760
07154829074515143702130848153714487902
48294548533507456037211421601315141305
79130503131435480713481437136001140201
08010115081414370879011408370837213137
08020802292108601401140301031431483745
35314503294545150329310335290337013703
02356001601448214531605315310121031305
```

If you (like Logico) cannot solve it alone, then perhaps one of your fellow detectives can help. Join the Detective Club at Murdle.com, and together, you will surely be able to solve this mystery, and many more.

# HINTS

1. While Deductive Logico was investigating the case, the phone in the mansion rang. When he answered it, a confident voice said, "I just cast some runes, Logico, and they said that Dame Obsidian ate with a fork." Before Logico could ask who they were, they hung up.

2. Logico found a message in a bottle. He opened it and found a letter addressed to him! It read, "Logico, the stars are clear: a torn-out clump of bear fur was in the ancient ruins."

3. One piece was just a page of computer paper taped to the wall, and it read, "Logico! Our mediums say an abstract statue was next to a pigeon." At least he understood what this one was saying.

4. Logico received a strange message via telegraph. Once he had cracked the morse code, he saw that it said, "Ley lines reveal. Stop. VP Mauve. Stop. Beside steam engine. Stop."

5. On a lark, Deductive Logico checked his own chart, and he found a weird message that read, "Logico! I had a vision of Dr. Crimson standing on the roof!" Who were these from?

6. Logico didn't need to rely on a spooky occult message this time—he saw with his own two eyes that Cosmonaut Bluski was standing right next to the awesome dragon mural.

7. A delivery boy arrived and handed Logico a note that simply read, "I

stared into a flame and scryed for the truth, and here it is: the deacon had the shears!"

8. The backup butler handed Logico a note which read: "Based on a card I drew from the marot (the murder tarot), Sir Rulean had an antique clock."

9. When Logico was lost in the maze, he looked up and saw that some-one had sky-written a message in the clouds: "Lavender swam in the fountain!" Whoever was leaving these messages had real resources behind them.

10. Written in fog on the bathroom mirror was a message that read, "According to my political dowsing rod, the corner booth had a communist in it."

11. The phone rang, and the assistant barista called him over. A spooky voice on the other end whispered, "According to Nostradamus, the guy with the Bookie had a brick, too."

12. Logico went for a walk to clear his head, and he saw graffiti on the street that said, "The signs are clear: Captain Slate was in the rare books room."

13. Somebody had scribbled a note in the margins near the end: "Corporal Coffee had a stabbin' knife." Logico was upset that someone was writing in the book, but the hint was helpful.

14. Scribbled on the copyright page was a note: "Baron Maroon was the first member of the Investigation Institute."

15. Logico flipped to the back of the book and found that someone had written a hint: "Chapter 5 says that the pirate cove had a cannon for

self-defense!"

16. Logico heard an agent in the other room screaming into a phone, "Stop calling! Nobody knows a Deductive Logico! Nobody cares that Editor Ivory was on the balcony!"

17. Another boat cruised by with a banner hanging from the flagpole, and the banner read: "Like the cards of the marot, those letters are shuffled around. The first word is 'whoever.'"

18. A representative made an announcement: "I've just received this message: we've been asked to tell you that the letters in the words of that note are rearranged, and that Silverton the Legend brought a fountain pen. That's a strange message, but that's what it says."

19. Deductive Logico got a mysterious phone call, and the person whispered, "The town that will have food disruptions fortunately has a sextant." That's a bizarre prank call.

20. Logico displayed his Deduction College diploma prominently in the waiting room. He didn't need a mysterious note to tell him that.

21. In all of the legal filings about this place, there was—bizarrely—a scribbled note addressed to Deductive Logico. It read, "According to a psychic vision, the confidant's message can be read if you replace each letter with the next one in the alphabet."

22. Logico got a text from an unknown number: "Our crystal guy says that the marble bust was in the partner's office—I'd bet you ten million dollars!" It was. Fortunately, Logico didn't bet.

23. A mysterious figure dropped off a mysterious package. Once security had properly inspected it, they gave it over to Deductive Logico. In-

side was a single page of paperwork and a note that read, "I found this page in the parking lot."

24. "All right," said Officer Copper, "what wise guy put this sticky note on my back saying that according to the zodiac I had the gavel?!"

25. Deductive Logico received a text that simply said, "You're on your own here."

26. Logico finally checked his mail and found a mysterious red envelope. On the outside, someone had scrawled, "You can trust Mayor Honey."

27. Carved into an oak (that was already dead) was a note that read: "Grandmaster on road!"

28. They had a person at the Institute whose job was to solve mysteries psychically, and that person confidently declared that Herbalist Onyx was at the observatory.

29. Written in the fog on the bathroom mirror was a helpful hint: "Trust the sociologist!"

30. Deductive Logico found a slip of paper in his pocket that read, "Trust the High Raven!"

31. Deductive Logico radioed Inspector Irratino and asked him for help: "Ah, I just had a dream about this!" he said. "Mauve had a log!"

32. Deductive Logico called Inspector Irratino in. He had fasted for forty-eight hours and then revealed the results of a hunger vision he had had to a very impatient Deductive Logico: "A drop of disgusting ooze was on a leather strap."

33. Irratino secretly showed Deductive Logico the crystal skull he had brought. "Does this help?"

34. Inspector Irratino consulted a sign he had seen in the stars and then pronounced his declaration: "Brother Brownstone is telling the truth."

35. Inspector Irratino consulted a riddle he had heard whispered on the winds, and then pronounced his declaration: "Philologist Flint brought a selenite wand."

36. Irratino flipped through his dream journal and pointed, picking out individual letters at random. Ultimately, they spelled, "The crime was in the cargo hold."

37. Inspector Irratino cast some runes, looked up their meaning in a book, decided he liked his own interpretation more, and then declared, "Mayor Honey brought an old sword."

38. Inspector Irratino consulted a vision he had experienced and then pronounced his declaration: "A crystal dagger was found under an enormous bed."

39. Irratino went into a seance in his room. When he came out of it, he said, "The murder happened in the ballroom."

40. Inspector Irratino went into a trance and intoned, "Viscount Eminence wore the gloves to hide his pale and bony hands."

41. The inspector used his mental powers to perceive a new fact in this case: "The Amazing Aureolin had a quasi-perpetual motion machine!" He had less success bending spoons.

42. Irratino studied the leftover coffee grounds in the bottom of a mug and deduced two things: 1) General Coffee had a boiling pot, and 2) this place needed better coffee filters.

43. Inspector Irratino shouted out, "Why, God?!" and he heard nothing, so he shouted, "How, God?!" and he heard, "The penguin was poisoned!"

44. Irratino got everyone to study his program and then, using handwriting analysis, proclaimed that Judge Pine was in the backstage woods.

45. Inspector Irratino consulted a tarot card he had drawn and then pronounced his declaration: Editor Ivory was seen hanging around next to a totally not-disgusting raw egg.

46. Inspector Irratino studied the code carefully and said, "This is a typical Investigation Institute code: each symbol stands for the first letter of the symbol's meaning."

47. Inspector Irratino consulted a sign he had seen in the stars and then pronounced his declaration: "Astrologer Azure was beside a collapsed roof."

48. Inspector Irratino consulted a dream he had dreamt and then pronounced his declaration: "Sister Lapis brought a holy relic."

49. Inspector Irratino was acting weird, but when Logico asked, he said that, actually, he was just remote viewing a drop of wax on a twisted tree.

50. Deductive Logico recognized the coded message from the Investigation Institute from Case 46: A Cruise to Die For 2.

51. Logico thought about what Irratino would do. So, he thought about what Irratino would say, and the first thing he thought was, "The person who wanted to steal a body had a broom."

52. That's strange: a hint was still written in the fog on the mirror. It said, "The second shortest suspect had the hypnotic pocket watch."

53. Logico drew a marot card from Irratino's old deck and guessed that it meant that Baron Maroon was seen on a nice little hill.

54. Logico looked up at the stars and tried to imagine what they might mean? Perhaps that Mauve had a bear trap? Irratino would know.

55. Logico remembered another part of his dream: "A climbing axe was under the gate." He wished he had dreamed about Irratino instead.

56. Logico knew, intuitively, from his time with Irratino that the cop was the one with yarn.

57. Logico tried to follow Irratino's instructions for astral projection, but he forgot some crucial step, so instead of traveling through the astral realm as he pleased, he was stuck in the vestibule of the church. He did notice a powder burn there!

58. Logico imagined where Irratino would have hidden a message, and then he imagined what that message would have been. Perhaps, "The Duchess of Vermillion was in the fountain."

59. Inspector Irratino consulted a tarot card he had drawn and then pronounced his declaration: "Editor Ivory was seen hanging around next to a nuclear reactor."

60. Logico imagined Irratino reading his palm, and telling him that Comrade Champagne had an aluminum pipe.

61. Logico dowsed the island, like Irratino had taught him, and he found a broom bristle on a collapsed roof.

62. The daily newspaper had been replaced by a weekly newspaper, then a monthly newspaper, then a website, then a blog. And the blog just posted an unsourced comment that said, "A neighbor saw Mr. Ordinary Blue Sky carrying an aluminum pipe."

63. One day, one of the hooded monks sang, "A holy red stain was on forbidden books." Did Logico recognize the voice?

64. Logico heard some students shouting about a shadowy figure in Old Main.

65. Logico remembered where he'd seen the reference book: on the front steps. He also remembered how much he missed Irratino.

66. Logico pored over the texts in great detail, until he found a strange reference to the slender fingers of Viscount Eminence clutching a ballot box.

67. Logico closed the book and then opened it at random, a technique Irratino called "bibliomancy," and he learned that Sir Rulean had been in the ancient ruins.

68. With some basic numerology he learned from Irratino, Deductive Logico was able to calculate that Captain Slate was beside some space jets.

69. Deductive Logico used a deck of marot cards to discover a pile of sawdust under somebody's car (then, he discovered that magicians do not like marot cards: it's a totally different kind of magic).

70. Deductive Logico didn't have to tap into the mysteries of the occult to see that the two kids on top of each other were leaning on the fence.

71. Inspector Irratino once told Logico that this was a complete sentence: "Ruin runes ruin ruin runes." He also said that if he ever had a case in New Aegis, look for metal in the dry well.

72. Deductive Logico had a glimpse of a vision in one of the crystals, and it told him that Supreme Master Cobalt was seen hanging around beside a delicious cocktail.

73. Deductive Logico used one of the oldest esoteric methods of all—going by your gut—to determine that the second shortest suspect had hyperallergenic oil.

74. Deductive Logico examined the clouds above them, and by making out the shapes, he was able to determine that Dr. Seashell, DDS, bought a selenite wand after all.

75. Logico got a second look, and he could tell that the suspect who was the same height as Blackstone, Esq., had a giant bone.

76. Deductive Logico placed an awkward phone call. "Is it okay for you to call me while I'm under house arrest? Nevertheless, my tea leaves say that Steel was in the Great Park."

77. Logico dialed Irratino's house and Irratino answered on the first ring: "Steel had the piano wire!"

78. "I've been looking at the stars above us, Logico. And they tell me that the chess player was near a classic car." Maybe, Logico thought, I shouldn't keep calling, but it was hard to resist.

79. "Logico, it's good to hear from you. I think, if you look, you'll find a chip of actual bone was discovered in the lobby. Or, at least, I did when I was remote viewing from house arrest."

80. Irratino returned Logico's voicemail in seconds. "According to the numbers I've been running, the person who wanted to join a cult was in the boiler room."

81. Logico got a text from Irratino under house arrest: "I just scryed into a candle flame, and President Midnight was eating some food with a funny name. Well, it wasn't that funny. But it was trying to be."

82. During an awkward video call, Inspector Irratino consulted a tarot reading he had performed and then pronounced his declaration: "Chancellor Tuscany was seen with a log."

83. Irratino sent another text: "This isn't esoteric knowledge, Logico. I just saw on a studio webcam that Lord Lavender was hanging around next to a fountain. I hope you're doing well out there."

84. After talking about the weather, Irratino talked about the case: "Sister Lapis and Coach Raspberry must both be telling the truth, or else Superfan Smoky is lying, too. See, now you've got me using logic!"

85. Deductive Logico got a marot card in the mail, and by now, he knew the marot well enough to know it meant that Boss Charcoal wanted to steal a part. And that Irratino was thinking of him.

86. Logico called Irratino again, and Irratino told him he had a dream

he would call, and that in the dream, Irratino told him that General Coffee "wanted to see if he could." Did Logico understand what that meant? Logico did.

87. Inspector Irratino consulted a sign he had seen in the stars and then DMed his declaration to Deductive Logico: Background Marengo was next to a watered-down cocktail.

88. Inspector Irratino loved hearing the latest updates from the field. "The guy playing me died? Was he handsome? Did he also know that Dame Obsidian was on the balcony?"

89. Logico's hands shook as he dialed Irratino, but he reached his voice-mail. "I'm sorry. I'm currently away from the phone right now, but if this is Deductive Logico, then the marot says that a film strip was in the water tower."

90. Irratino left Logico a voicemail that said, cryptically, "The tallest suspect was next to a bunch of letters. I know because I had a vision of them looking down on the letters. I've had visions of you, too, Logico…"

91. Inspector Irratino consulted a dream he had dreamt and then emailed his declaration to Logico: "Judge Pine had a huge pile of paperwork.—II"

92. Later, Deductive Logico would listen to this voicemail: "Logico, are you okay? Did you check the knobs for whiskey? One of our psychics just said they had a vision of that. I believe in you."

93. This time, Irratino answered on the third ring. "I'm sorry. I was on the opposite side of the mansion when I heard the phone. Importantly, Director Dusty had the cursed dagger. Even more important than that, you're about to understand everything."

94. "Logico! I got your call!" said the text Irratino sent. "Stay safe! And remember: the person with a heavy candle wanted to kill on behalf of the Industry!"

95. Logico knew that Inspector Irratino was telepathically sending him information because Irratino also texted to make sure he received it: "Did you get my message? Comrade Champagne had the marble bust!"

96. Inspector Irratino used a dowsing rod to determine that an award was in the locked stage. "Hmm, we should really investigate that stage, Logico."

97. Inspector Irratino consulted the daily horoscope for everyone involved and then pronounced his declaration: "Uncle Midnight was next to a full-sized refrigerator."

98. Inspector Irratino winked at Logico and handed him another note. Then he went back to pretending to be dead. The note read: "The killer stabbed me!"

99. Based on the historical readings Logico had done, he knew Chairman Chalk wanted to win a war.

100. Inspector Irratino knew that the Investigation Institute was using the first letter of what each of the symbols represented, and Deductive Logico knew that the Detective Club was using their typical Detective Code. And they both knew that this was the case of their lives.

# SOLUTIONS

### 1. "It was The Amazing Aureolin with a heavy candle in the enormous bathroom!"

The Amazing Aureolin kept proclaiming her innocence, but she couldn't resist Deductive Logico's arguments. He was demonstrably correct.

She all but confessed when she declared, "No cell can hold me!"

> **The Amazing Aureolin | a heavy candle | the enormous bathroom**
> Midnight III | an aluminum pipe | the bedroom
> Dame Obsidian | a fork | the screening room

### 2. "It was Father Mango with a harpoon in the docks!"

At first, Father Mango argued. Then he swore. Then he cursed. Finally he admitted defeat, saying, "How could you do this to such a holy man of God?"

> Miss Saffron | a bear trap | the ancient ruins
> Signor Emerald | an ordinary brick | the cliffs
> **Father Mango | a harpoon | the docks**

### 3. "It was Captain Slate with a glass of poisoned wine in the entry hall!"

Logico really enjoyed explaining the precise details of the murder, because it was clear what they meant.

As Captain Slate realized she was going down, she muttered, "I should have stayed in space . . ."

Captain Slate | a glass of poisoned wine | the entry hall
Bishop Azure | an abstract statue | the rooftop garden
Blackstone, Esq. | a rare vase | an art studio

## 4. "It was Chef Aubergine with an imported Italian knife in the caboose!"

Chef Aubergine stood up angrily, and she was just about to say, "I should have cooked you, Deductive Logico!" when the train—having had no conductor this entire time—flew off the tracks and into a gorge.

Vice President Mauve | a rolled-up newspaper (with a crowbar inside) | the locomotive
**Chef Aubergine | an imported Italian knife | the caboose**
Philosopher Bone | leather luggage | on the roof

## 5. "It was Officer Copper with a vial of acid in the parking lot!"

Officer Copper did not enjoy being accused of the murder she had just committed, so she immediately leapt to her feet and declared, "I am a police officer! I am above the law!"

**Officer Copper | a vial of acid | the parking lot**
Dr. Crimson | a heavy microscope | on the roof
Sister Lapis | a surgical scalpel | the gift shop

## 6. "It was General Coffee with piano wire in the dumpster!"

General Coffee didn't bother protesting his innocence. He simply flashed his government papers and excused himself. He had been told to do a job, and he did it. "End of story."

But Logico had found a note in the dead man's pocket. It read, "She moved the body in the Hollywood mansion." And if that were true, if the murder actually took place in the screening room, it would mean that The Amazing Aureolin had been framed by the mysterious Dame Obsidian. Logico had to investigate.

General Coffee | piano wire | **the dumpster**
Cosmonaut Bluski | a poisonous dart | the distracting graffiti
Midnight III | a crowbar | the metal fence

## 7. "It was Earl Grey with yarn in the manor house!"

While the constable took Earl Grey away, he bellowed, "I curse you with the heat of a thousand kettles!" But Logico still couldn't believe that he'd traveled all this way to investigate Dame Obsidian, and a man had been murdered in her house, and once again, she seemed innocent.

Dame Obsidian | a bottle of cyanide | the chapel
Deacon Verdigris | a pair of gardening shears | the ancient ruins
**Earl Grey | yarn | the manor house**

## 8. "It was Sir Rulean with an antique clock in the spooky attic!"

So it seemed like Sir Rulean was the kind of person who kills somebody else's butler.

He tried to argue, "It's just a butler!" But he was Dame Obsidian's butler, and not only did she care, but she had a higher rank than he even pretended to have, and so he was hauled off by the constable.

Dame Obsidian | an axe | the master bedroom
**Sir Rulean | an antique clock | the spooky attic**
Miss Saffron | a magnifying glass | the grounds

## 9. "It was Miss Saffron with poisoned tea in the lookout tower!"

As Deductive Logico walked everyone through Saffron's maze of contradictions, she surrendered with a simple, "Well, I guess I'm going to jail then." So, Logico wandered back into the hedge maze, where he discovered something suspicious about Dame Obsidian's body: it was missing!

Lord Lavender | a flowerpot | the fountain
**Miss Saffron | poisoned tea | the lookout tower**
Constable Copper | a pair of gardening shears | the ancient ruins

**10. "It was Grandmaster Rose with a crystal ball in the center bar!"**
The moment Logico said that, the bar erupted into cheers. And as the rest of the bar hauled him outside (to give him a parade), he shouted, "I'm the king of the board and the bar!"

> Brother Brownstone | a bottle of wine | the cramped bathroom
> Comrade Champagne | a corkscrew | the corner booth
> **Grandmaster Rose | a crystal ball | the center bar**

**11. "It was Coach Raspberry with a metal straw in the courtyard!"**
Coach Raspberry was hooting and hollering while the other patrons dragged him away. Logico wasn't sure if this ruined his coffee spot, or made it even better. Sure, there was a murder, but he also got to do some great deductive work. Like his coffee, it was bittersweet.

> General Coffee | a poisoned cup of coffee | the counter
> **Coach Raspberry | a metal straw | the courtyard**
> Bookie-Winner Gainsboro | an ordinary brick | the bean room

**12. "It was Comrade Champagne with a bone folder in the discount rack!"**
Comrade Champagne protested that he was only being arrested because of "the bourgeoisie reactionaries who will never stop the revolution," but Logico wasn't paying attention: he was grabbing every Dame Obsidian novel he could find.

> Captain Slate | a tote bag | the rare books room
> **Comrade Champagne | a bone folder | the discount rack**
> Director Dusty | a paperback | the front counter

**13. "It was Justice Pine with tainted moonshine in the 'hotel'!"**
Logico declared this almost five pages into the book, and then felt so proud of himself that he knew the answer. You see, Obsidian had figured out that people like it more when they can guess the ending. The reviews are worse, but the sales are better.

Cowboy Raspberry | a cactus | the watering hole
**Justice Pine | tainted moonshine | the "hotel"**
Corporal Coffee | a stabbin' knife | the saloon

### 14. "It was Viscount Eminence with a jeweled scepter in a coffee house!"

Logico declared this out loud about two sentences after it was revealed in the book. The dame had finally bested him! At first, he was frustrated, but as her fictional detective explained all the clues, Logico found himself in awe.

Baron Maroon | a knife | The Investigation Institute
**Viscount Eminence | a jeweled scepter | a coffee house**
Earl Grey | the plague | a potentially haunted mansion

### 15. "It was Blackbeard with a cannon in the pirate cove!"

The final scene was devastating. Blackbeard, it turned out, had blacked out, and when he learned what he had done, he was broken, shouting, "My beloved parrot! Why! Why?!"

Honestly, Logico thought it was a pretty emotional ending. And the book was so well researched: there were maps of the pirate cove showing where it was in the real world, even. But when Logico turned the final page, he got to the acknowledgments, and he read something he thought was pretty strange: "If my body ever disappears, contact my agent!"

**Blackbeard | a cannon | the pirate cove**
Bluebeard | a scimitar | the pirate ship
Nobeard | a fake treasure map | the great whirlpool

### 16. "It was Assistant Applegreen with a giant stack of books in the best office!"

Assistant Applegreen denied it at first, but Logico kept saying that only the person who actually ran everything around here could have done this, and finally, she admitted it: "Fine! I was fed up with doing all the work and getting none of the recognition!"

Fortunately for her, the agency thought that showed initiative, and they promoted her (to head assistant). Meanwhile, Agent Ink approached Deductive Logico and told him, "Obsidian trusted me to handle her work. Have you considered publishing your case files?"

Editor Ivory | an antique typewriter | the balcony
**Assistant Applegreen | a giant stack of books | the best office**
Agent Ink | a ream of paper | the unsolicited submissions room

**17. "It was Bookie-Winner Gainsboro with a baby shark on the deck!**
As Bookie-Winner Gainsboro was led away in handcuffs, he shouted, "Curse you, Logico! Whatever your accomplishments, I promise you this: you'll never win a Bookie! Mark my words, Logico! You'll never win a Bookie!"

**Bookie-Winner Gainsboro | a baby shark | the deck**
Chairman Chalk | a golden pen | the dining hall
Agent Ink | an antique anchor | the engine room

**18. "It was Philosopher Bone with a heavy book back stage!"**
But that's not important: what's important is that Deductive Logico won the Bookie! In fact, he was so proud he could barely hear Philosopher Bone loudly declaiming about how he could prove (philosophically) that he should be let go "regardless of whom I did or did not kill!"

**Philosopher Bone | a heavy book | back stage**
Deductive Logico | a Bookie | a nominee table
Silverton the Legend | a fountain pen | the stage

**19. "It was Secretary Celadon with a poisoned candle in The Republic of Drakonia!"**
Secretary Celadon cited geopolitical necessities, precedent, and, finally, diplomatic immunity as reasons her book should still be published, even though she was a murderer. (It was.)

Everyone on the book tour told Logico that what they liked most about his book was how Dame Obsidian's body disappeared, and unlike in her novels, the solution was open-ended. Logico didn't like that feedback at all.

## 20. "It was Cosmonaut Bluski with a Deduction College diploma in the waiting room!

Cosmonaut Bluski expressed regret for what he had done: he had meant to kill Deductive Logico, and he mistook this person for him. "Nevertheless, communism shall prevail!"

Logico admired his optimism. And when he logged on to his old computer, he found a message: "Meet me here. There's something I want to show you." Then there was a printout of an old pirate map with an *X* that marked the spot. It was signed, "D.O."

## 21. "It was Dame Obsidian with a piece of rebar in an oil derrick!"

Dame Obsidian chuckled. But Chairman Chalk called the authorities, and they had her taken away. "I'll see you at trial!" she shouted. Logico asked what had happened.

Midnight III explained that they'd all been invited here in the same way Logico had. When Chairman Chalk and he arrived, Dame Obsidian said she wanted to show them something, and then she showed them a dead body.

"What was her point?" Logico asked.

"It was a royalty negotiation strategy," Chairman Chalk replied. "She wanted more. And to be honest, it worked. I'm gonna pay her more."

"You're safe now," Logico said, but Chairman Chalk just chuckled.

Meanwhile, Midnight III was staring off at the ancient ruins with a furrowed brow.

> Chairman Chalk | an oil drum | the offices
> Midnight III | a crowbar | the ancient ruins
> **Dame Obsidian | a piece of rebar | an oil derrick**

## 22. "It was Blackstone, Esq., with a marble bust in a partner's office!"

Blackstone, Esq., disputed each of Logico's claims, relying on intricate and subtle arguments that even Logico had difficulty following. But the long and short of it was, he was probably not going to see any jail time for it, as, after all, this was the service he provided to his clients.

> Dame Obsidian | confusing contracts | an associate's office
> Vice President Mauve | poisoned ink well | the lobby
> **Blackstone, Esq. | a marble bust | a partner's office**

## 23. "It was Coach Raspberry with the scales of justice in the judge's chambers!"

"Well, dang, ya got me!" Coach Raspberry said.

Logico was reassured to learn that it had nothing to do with Dame Obsidian, but he wondered if it was logical to be reassured of that. After all, weren't two murderers worse than one?

> **Coach Raspberry | the scales of justice | the judge's chambers**
> Officer Copper | a notary stamp | the actual courtroom
> Father Mango | a huge pile of paperwork | the parking lot

## 24. "It was Judge Pine with a flag in the judge's bench!"

And Logico explained his theory that the judge had suspected the jury was going to find Dame Obsidian not guilty, when to the judge, she was obviously guilty.

"I decide what is justice!" Judge Pine roared in response.

Dame Obsidian got another trial and sold more books and—unfortunately for her—was found guilty of multiple murders and sentenced to life behind bars.

> **Judge Pine** | **a flag** | **the judge's bench**
> Officer Copper | a gavel | the jury box
> Dame Obsidian | a baton | the gallery

### 25. "It was The Amazing Aureolin with a rope of designer clothes in the parking lot!"

"Haha, yes it was! I did it! Finally! She put me in jail, but I had my revenge!"

Logico walked home that night, and he couldn't help but feel bad for Dame Obsidian. After all, she had a certain charm to her, even if she was a serial murderer.

But when he got back to his office, he found a message waiting for him. It was written in one of the codes he had encountered before, but which one?

SGZS ONNQ ZTQDNKHM, H'UD EQZLDC GDQ SVHBD MNV! XNT LTRS TMCDQRSZMC SGZS H GZC SN CN DUDQXSGHMF H CHC (ADBZTRD H VZMSDC SN, ZMC H GZUD SN CN DUDQXSGHMF H VZMS). ATS KTBJX ENQ XNT, H'UD NASZHMDC DMNTFG LZSDQHZK ENQ ZMNSGDQ RDUDQZK ANNJR, VGHBG H'KK OTAKHRG "ONRSG TLNTRKX," RN H VNM'S MDDC SN JHKK ENQ ZVGHKD. TMSHK MDWS SHLD! SNNCZKNN!

> Secretary Celadon | a pair of literal golden handcuffs | a private suite
> **The Amazing Aureolin** | **a rope of designer clothes tied together** | **the parking lot**
> Miss Saffron | a quarter-million-dollar lawyer | the spa

### 26. "It was General Coffee with a heavy package in the mail truck!"

"A good soldier admits when he's defeated," General Coffee admitted, but Logico wasn't listening. He was reading a letter he'd received.

It still wasn't his royalty check. It was an invitation, asking him to travel across the world to a mysterious place called the Investigation Institute and meet with their president.

And it made a great argument: money.

> Dr. Crimson | a stamp stamp | the sorting room
> Mayor Honey | a letter opener | the long line
> **General Coffee | a heavy package | a mail truck**

## 27. "It was Coach Raspberry with the ritual dagger in the ancient ruins!"

Members of the Detective Club were called in to escort him away. They towed Logico's car away, too, and they drove him the rest of the way to the Investigation Institute.

Coach Raspberry's final statement was recorded as this: "Well, dang, ya got me!"

> **Coach Raspberry | a ritual dagger | the ancient ruins**
> Officer Copper | a poisonous spider | the skull rock
> Grandmaster Rose | a shovel | the only road

## 28. "It was Chef Aubergine with hyperallergenic oil in the miniature golf course!"

"I should have cooked you, you strange man!" she replied. Which was basically a confession.

Once Logico had solved that, he went up to the chateau and knocked on the door. Nobody answered. The door just creaked open by itself . . .

> Cryptozoologist Cloud | a quasi-perpetual motion machine | an impossible hedge maze
> Herbalist Onyx | a dowsing rod | the observatory
> **Chef Aubergine | hyperallergenic oil | the miniature golf course**

## 29. "It was Philologist Flint with a selenite wand in the ballroom!"

While Philologist Flint protested his innocence, Logico wore him down until he said, "I have known the etymology of regret. Now, I know its meaning."

Now, Logico was led to the highest office in the chateau, and he knocked on that door, as well. And once again, it opened by itself.

> Sociologist Umber | a cursed dagger | the front driveway
> **Philologist Flint | a selenite wand | the ballroom**
> Numerologist Night | an exclusive pin | the arcane attic

### 30. "It was Herbalist Onyx with a pseudo-scientific apparatus on the book ladder!"

Immediately, the dead president sat up and declared, "Do you see, private eyes?! I told you this man is exactly who we need!"

Then, he turned to Deductive Logico and explained, "I am Inspector Irratino, the president of the Investigation Institute. We investigate the mysteries of the world through any means necessary, whether empirically supported or not. We believe in everything until proven otherwise, and that's just what we want you to do: prove otherwise. We'll send you to investigate mysterious cases, and you report back what you've found. And in return, we're willing to pay you a whole lot of money."

Logico replied, "You had me at 'a whole lot of money.'"

> Numerologist Night | a deck of marot cards | on the couch
> **Herbalist Onyx | a pseudo-scientific apparatus | on the book ladder**
> High Alchemist Raven | a hypnotic pocket watch | behind his desk

### 31. "It was Lady Violet with a broom in the thick forest!"

First, Lady Violet said she was innocent. Then, she said she would hex Logico. The second declaration sort of undermined the first, and when Logico pointed that out, she started yelling about a conspiracy against her.

"This is just a plot to undermine my position in the coven!" But the witches weren't having it.

> Lady Violet | a broom | the thick forest
> Vice President Mauve | a log | the central fire
> The Duchess of Vermillion | a cauldron | the ancient ruins

**32. "It was Vice President Mauve with a giant magnet in the rooftop!"**
Logico revealed that Mauve had been funding the mad scientist to work on her metaverse schemes, and the assistant had gotten in the way.

Logico proved it, and the private eyes came and took her away. She cried, "This is why we need a metaverse! No one could arrest me in the metaverse!"

> **Vice President Mauve | a giant magnet | the rooftop**
> Principal Applegreen | a brain in a jar | the operating table
> Captain Slate | a soup ladle | the giant lever

**33. "It was Bishop Azure with a skeleton arm in the grand entrance!"**
Initially, Bishop Azure claimed that it was heresy to accuse her of murder. Then, she claimed that she had to commit murder to stop heresy. Either way, it wasn't looking good.

Logico reported back: "No ancient magick. Just murder!"

> Inspector Irratino | a crystal skull | the sacred chamber
> **Bishop Azure | a skeleton arm | the grand entrance**
> Chancellor Tuscany | a ritual dagger | the high altar

**34. "It was Viscount Eminence with a vial of a deadly poison in the huge mausoleum!"**
Viscount Eminence's poisons had been causing people to hallucinate seeing ghosts in the graveyard. But before he could be arrested, he disappeared.

All that was left was a piece of paper that read, "No jail can hold me."

> Sir Rulean | a string of prayer beads | the gift shop
> **Viscount Eminence | a vial of a deadly poison | the huge mausoleum**

## 35. "It was Numerologist Night with a soup ladle by the ancient ruins!"

Numerologist Night tried to explain how the numerological significance of the date showed that they weren't actually guilty, but Irratino pointed out that they had forgotten to carry a two.

"Oh, well, in that case, I surrender!"

Assistant Applegreen | a pseudo-scientific apparatus | the library
Philologist Flint | a selenite wand | the barracks
**Numerologist Night | a soup ladle | the ancient ruins**

## 36. "It was Captain Slate with a flare in the cargo hold!"

"It wasn't the Bermuda Triangle that killed them!" Slate roared. "It was my careful planning!"

"See!" Logico claims. "More evidence for rationality!"

"Ah," Irratino said. "But you need to win them all: I only need to win once!"

Mx. Tangerine | a sailor's rope | the captain's quarters
Admiral Navy | poisoned rum | overboard
**Captain Slate | a flare | the cargo hold**

## 37. "It was Mayor Honey with an old sword in a second-hand shop!"

"The people will hear about this! They'll hear!" he exclaimed. But then, once an advisor had whispered in his ear, he began to say, "You know what, on second thought, maybe the people don't have to hear about this."

Logico and Irratino laughed about that later that night, and then Logico asked him where he grew up. Irratino said, "Funny you should mention it . . ."

Father Mango | a magnifying glass | a chain restaurant
**Mayor Honey | an old sword | a second-hand shop**
Officer Copper | an axe | a used car lot

## 38. "It was Astrologer Azure with a crystal dagger in the enormous bedroom!"

"The stars say you'll pay for this, Logico!" she exclaimed.

Once the private eyes had taken her away, Logico told Irratino, "You know, I can't help noticing you might have grown up a little more well-to-do than I did."

Irratino shook his head. "Money isn't everything, Logico."

Brother Brownstone | a ouija board | the grounds
The Duke of Vermillion | a heavy codebook | the 50-car garage
**Astrologer Azure | a crystal dagger | the enormous bedroom**

## 39. "It was Lady Violet with the poisoned muffin in the ballroom!"

"Yes! I killed him! I loved him! He, a commoner! And he rejected me! Yes, he, a commoner! So I killed him. I would do it again. But I'd do anything to bring him back."

When Logico and Irratino returned to the Institute, they discovered the hotel had closed thirty years ago. When they went back, it was now an empty lot.

Irratino claimed that was proof of the paranormal, but Logico said they must have just gotten confused about the address. Or maybe there had been some kind of gas leak.

"You're impossible!" Irratino exclaimed.

Lord Lavender | a golden pen | the boiler room
Miss Saffron | a laundry bag filled with knives | the grand
    entrance
**Lady Violet | a poisoned muffin | the ballroom**

## 40. "It was Signor Emerald with a globe in the clock room!"

Logico theorized that Signor Emerald was not as rich as he let on, and had robbed the bank only out of necessity, and that he should not be treated harshly.

"I will admit that I murdered, but never that I am poor!" Signor Emerald declared. "Throw the book at me!"

Meanwhile, Logico realized that Irratino had withdrawn one million dollars from the bank and put it in a duffel bag. His curiosity was piqued.

> The Duke of Vermillion | a laptop | the back room
> **Signor Emerald | a globe | the clock room**
> Viscount Eminence | leather gloves | the vault

### 41. "It was Dr. Crimson with the dowsing rod on the roof!"

Dr. Crimson shouted, "Sure! I killed the psychic, only because I found out they weren't! They tried to make a fool out of me, so I made them pay!"

Needless to say, the Psychic Research Laboratory did not get the million.

> The Amazing Aureolin | a quasi-perpetual motion machine | the grounds
> **Dr. Crimson | a dowsing rod | the roof**
> The Duchess of Vermillion | a crystal ball | the isolation chamber

### 42. "It was General Coffee with the boiling pot in the courtyard!"

And finally, the coffee shop banned him, which was the worst punishment he'd ever received for a murder. When he'd been led away, Irratino asked Logico what was so occult about this place. Logico replied, "Their drip coffee is divine and their lattes are magical."

Irratino tried a latte and agreed. "But I don't know if it qualifies for the million."

"Oh, now that it'll cost you, you're a skeptic!"

> Sister Lapis | a butter knife | the parking lot
> Grandmaster Rose | a metal straw | the bathroom
> **General Coffee | a boiling pot | the courtyard**

**43. "It was The Duchess of Vermillion with poisoned hot chocolate in the frozen wastelands!"**

"But why?!" cried Irratino.

The duchess replied, "Because it was greater and more dignified than I. And I could not stand something to be greater than I." Even convicted, she was impenitent.

Logico could do more to ease Irratino's suffering. "Would a hug help?" No. "Would a movie help?" No. "Would it help if I revealed that my expertise in poison caused us to identify an antidote, thereby saving the penguin from what was thought to be certain death?"

That helped a lot, and they celebrated all night.

> Chancellor Tuscany | an icicle dagger | the ping pong room
> **The Duchess of Vermillion | poisoned hot chocolate | the frozen wastelands**
> Mx. Tangerine | an ice axe | the barracks

**44. "It was Judge Pine with a stage sword in the backstage woods!"**

"This is not justice!" Judge Pine declared. "I decide what justice is!" She swung at Inspector Irratino with her gavel, but he accidentally dodged it when he bent down to pick a flower to give to Logico.

> Earl Grey | a toxic program | the stage
> Sister Lapis | medium | the front tree
> **Judge Pine | a stage sword | the backstage woods**

**45. "It was Editor Ivory with a shovel in the concession stand!"**

As she was led away, she yelled, "You won't DNF me! I'll be back! Oh, I'll be back!"

And when she was gone, Logico said, "Okay, so there was nothing haunted here."

"Oh right," Irratino said, "I just made that up so we could go see a movie."

Logico didn't mind.

## 46. "It was Principal Applegreen with a toxic blowfish on the deck!"

Logico started going through the whole thing, and he was just getting to the part that proved that Principle Applegreen was guilty all along, when suddenly, there was a loud crash!

The cruise liner had run aground.

"I'd grade this whole trip an F-plus!" Principal Applegreen lamented.

Admiral Navy | the steering wheel | the dining hall
Vice President Mauve | a fishing spear | the captain's quarters
**Principal Applegreen | a toxic blowfish | on the deck**

## 47. "It was Baron Maroon with an old sword in the dead woods!"

But when Logico explained how he understood the Baron's frustration with the captain for crashing the boat, the Baron interrupted, "You think that's why I killed him?! That proves you're a bad detective. That's not why I killed him! I killed him because he slept with my wife!"

Legally speaking, that was not a good defense. So they tied him up and threw him in the lighthouse. But they had other things to worry about: nobody had reception on their phones, and someone had smashed the radio on the ship.

Mx. Tangerine | a toxic blowfish | the cliffside lighthouse
**Baron Maroon | an old sword | the dead woods**
Astrologer Azure | a shovel | the ruined church

## 48. "It was Sister Lapis with a holy relic in the flooded pews!"

Sister Lapis laughed a strange, uncanny laugh when she was accused. "Don't you get it? Don't you see? It wasn't the captain that brought us to this island. It wasn't the ship! It was the devil!"

Irratino conceded that was a possibility, but Logico reminded her that she hadn't killed the devil. She had killed the first mate.

"The first mate of the devil!" she roared. They tied her up and threw her in the lighthouse, and Logico and Irratino spent that night trying to keep each other warm.

> Philosopher Bone | a string of prayer beads | the overgrown organ
> Brother Brownstone | a rock | the cracked altar
> **Sister Lapis | a holy relic | the flooded pews**

### 49. "It was Sir Rulean with a prayer candle in the gnarled tree!"

"I'm sorry! I don't know what came over me! There's something wrong with this island! It made me do it. Don't you see?!"

Ah, the old "the island made me do it" defense. Logico had heard that one before, and Sir Rulean was already being tied up and thrown in the lighthouse by the time he finished his monologue.

"This is pretty special, isn't it?" Logico asked Irratino. "Solving mysteries together on a mysterious island." But Irratino seemed preoccupied. What was he thinking about?

> Chancellor Tuscany | a rock | the ancient ruins
> **Sir Rulean | a prayer candle | the gnarled tree**
> Earl Grey | a trained monkey | the moving cave

### 50. "It was Sir Rulean with a rock in the light itself!"

But Logico didn't stick around to hear Sir Rulean's defense, because one of the castaways told him that Irratino was fading fast. So he ran to the cove and held him.

"Irratino, hold on!" Logico shouted.

But all Irratino could say was, "The ancient ruins . . ."

And then, he was gone.

So many mysteries go unsolved. Like, what could they have been to each other? And why did it have to be this way? And, perhaps most important of all: What did he mean by his final words?

Baron Maroon | a sailor's rope | the generator
**Sir Rulean | a rock | the light itself**
Sister Lapis | a bottle of oil | a secluded cove

## 51. "It was Earl Grey with a cauldron in the huge mausoleum to rob the victim!"

"He had my bags!" Earl Grey roared. "Antique tea bags that I let him borrow, and I suspected he was brewing them, instead of appreciating them as the art they were! So, yeah, maybe I robbed him, but I was robbing back my own bags! And he tried to stop me! So I killed him! Fine!"

Logico didn't care about these speeches. He cared about revenge.

Astrologer Azure | a ghost detector | the entrance gate | to see
    if they could
**Earl Grey | a cauldron | the huge mausoleum | to rob the victim**
Mx. Tangerine | a broom | the gift shop | to steal a body
Cryptozoologist Cloud | a skeleton arm | the weird shack | to
    hide an affair

## 52. "It was Philologist Flint with a hypnotic pocket watch in an impossible hedge maze to inherit a fortune!"

"And I would have, if not for you! Inspector Irratino willed this whole place to that guard, because he said he could be trusted! Except that guard trusted me! 'Cause of my hypnotic pocket watch! And I used it to get him to put me in the will. And then, well, you've figured out what I did then. And I would have gotten away with it if not for you!"

Logico didn't care about catching this philologist. He cared about revenge.

Numerologist Night | a crystal ball | the miniature golf course |
    to prove they're tough
High Alchemist Raven | a quasi-perpetual motion machine | the
    great tower | to fight for love
Herbalist Onyx | a dowsing rod | the grand chateau | because
    they could

## 53. "It was Sociologist Umber with an old sword in the moving cave for the revolution!"

She claimed the cultist was a reactionary, fighting for the status quo. Logico could understand wanting to overturn the world. There were things that were good, and things that were true, and he wished they were the same. But they often weren't.

"What do you know about the ancient ruins?" he asked. She gave him a lot of words but no hints. He didn't care about theory. He cared about revenge.

Cryptozoologist Cloud | an axe | the gnarled tree | to get revenge
Baron Maroon | a log | the little hill | to scare a bear away
Judge Pine | a heavy candle | the ancient ruins | to steal a prized book
**Sociologist Umber | an old sword | the moving cave | for the revolution**

## 54. "It was Admiral Navy with an axe in the cliffs to impress a lady!"

"What kind of lady would be impressed by you killing someone?"

"The kind of lady I'm looking for."

Deductive Logico didn't want a lady. He wanted revenge.

Vice President Mauve | a bear trap | the ancient ruins | to avenge their father
**Admiral Navy | an axe | the cliffs | to impress a lady**
Agent Ink | an oar | the docks | to steal a treasure map
Grandmaster Rose | an ordinary brick | the haunted grove | out of madness

## 55. "It was Mayor Honey with a poisonous spider in the ancient ruins as part of a real estate scam!"

"Curse you, Logico! I could have turned this whole resort into luxury apartments! And then I could have formed a town, and then I could have run for mayor of that town!"

"So you don't know anything about the ancient ruins?" He didn't. So Logico didn't care about Mayor Honey. As the Detective Club would say, ZOO SV XZIVW ZYLFG DZH IVEVMTV.

> **Mayor Honey** | **a poisonous spider** | **the ancient ruins** | **as part of a real estate scam**
>
> Principal Applegreen | a pair of gardening shears | the hot springs spa | to rob the victim
>
> Coach Raspberry | a bow and arrow | the party lake | to see if they could
>
> Chancellor Tuscany | a climbing axe | the entrance gate | to escape blackmail

## 56. "It was Father Mango with a knitting needle in the chapel to scare a bear away!"

"The bear cornered me and the shopkeep in the chapel! He was hungry and ferocious and he meant to eat us. So I knew I had to scare that bear or else. So I screamed and stabbed the shopkeep right in front of the bear, which terrified the bear and caused him to flee."

"So you don't know anything about the ancient ruins?"

Father Mango kept talking about the bear. But Logico didn't care about the bear. Like you'd say in a mirror: EGNEVER TUOBA DERAC EH.

> Mister Shadow | a bottle of cyanide | the quaint garden | as part of a real estate scam
>
> **Father Mango** | **a knitting needle** | **the chapel** | **to scare a bear away**
>
> Lord Lavender | an antique flintlock | the new development | to steal an idea
>
> Officer Copper | yarn | the ancient ruins | to steal a body

## 57. "It was Brother Brownstone with yarn in the choir loft for religious reasons!"

The parishioner had committed horrible crimes, Brother Brownstone explained, and the order to which he belonged compelled him to take matters into his own hands.

But Logico didn't care about religious orders. He cared about revenge.

> Father Mango | a bottle of wine | the graveyard | a ghost made them
> Bishop Azure | a holy relic | on the front steps | as practice
> Deacon Verdigris | an antique flintlock | the vestibule | because they were becoming their parents
> **Brother Brownstone | yarn | the choir loft | for religious reasons**

## 58. "It was Baron Maroon with a flowerpot in the secret garden to protect a secret!"

"If everybody knew about the secret garden, it would just be a garden! The gardener discovered it, ergo, he must be killed."

"But now, we all know about it."

The Baron had to be restrained. But Logico didn't care about being attacked.

What did he care about?

> Viscount Eminence | poisoned tea | the lookout tower | to see what it felt like to kill
> Lord Lavender | a pair of gardening shears | the ancient ruins | as a scientific experiment
> The Duchess of Vermillion | a brick | the fountain | to steal a prized book
> **Baron Maroon | a flowerpot | the secret garden | to protect a secret**

## 59. "It was Chairman Chalk with a commemorative pen in the dining hall to improve book sales!"

But Logico, as he clearly explained, didn't care about book sales. He cared about revenge.

"Oh, that would be great for sales. If you got bloody revenge on the guy who killed your friend."

"He was more than a friend," Logico replied.

"For sales, it's better if he's just a friend."

> Bookie-Winner Gainsboro | confusing contracts | the deck | by
>    the order of a cult
> **Chairman Chalk | a commemorative pen | the dining hall | to**
>    **improve book sales**
> Editor Ivory | an antique anchor | the engine room | to steal a
>    prized book
> Agent Ink | a tote bag | overboard | to comfort Logico

### 60. "It was Mx. Tangerine with an old sword by the ancient ruins by the order of a cult!"

This was his first lead, and he followed it. "What does the cult have to do with the ruins?"

"What?" said Mx. Tangerine. "I was told to kill the old-timer to keep him from leaving. The ruins had nothing to do with it. Those are just some rocks that we use for killing."

Turns out it wasn't a lead. It was a dead end.

Logico didn't care for dead ends. (He cared about revenge.)

> Comrade Champagne | an aluminum pipe | the old mill | to
>    motivate Logico
> **Mx. Tangerine | an old sword | the ancient ruins | by the order**
>    **of a cult**
> Assistant Applegreen | a magnifying glass | the meeting house
>    | to teach them a lesson
> Principal Applegreen | an antique clock | the library | to prevent
>    a change in the will

### 61. "It was Président Amaranth with a broom in the ruined church to rob a grave!"

"Fine!" the *président* replied. "An ancient sacred scepter is buried on this island along with my namesake, the great French *président* Amaranth! I was going to recover the scepter and use it to cement my leadership! Now look what you've done! You've destabilized Europe!"

But Logico didn't care about the stability of Europe. He cared about revenge.

> Mister Shadow | an "alien" artifact | the cliffside lighthouse | to help win a war
>
> **Président Amaranth | a broom | the ruined church | to rob a grave**
>
> Captain Slate | a crystal skull | the mysterious woods | to save face
>
> Midnight III | an axe | the wrecked cruise ship | to close a business deal

## 62. "It was Mr. Ordinary Blue Sky with an aluminum pipe in a second-hand shop to protect a secret!"

"Zis is ridiculous!" Mr. Ordinary Blue Sky replied. "What secret could I have?"

"You are obviously," Logico replied, "none other than Cosmonaut Bluski himself." And he proved his point by ripping off Mr. Ordinary Blue Sky's fake mustache. Everyone gasped.

"I wanted to live as regular American," he said. Everyone awwed. "So that I could crush you from within!" They all booed.

But Logico didn't care about the awws or the boos, nor did he ultimately care about that insurance adjuster job. He cared about revenge.

> Mayor Honey | a fork | the run-down mall | for money
>
> Officer Copper | an ordinary brick | the old factory | while blacked out
>
> **Mr. Ordinary Blue Sky | an aluminum pipe | a second-hand shop | to protect a secret**
>
> Dr. Crimson | an antique anchor | a used car lot | to return an insult

**63. "It was Deacon Verdigris with a bottle of sacred oil in the court-
yard to avenge their father!"**

"The parishioner that Brother Brownstone killed was my father," the Deacon cried, "and I was bound, by blood, to defend him!"

Brother Brownstone's brother Brownstone was listening when she
said that, and Logico didn't know if Deacon Verdigris was long for this
world.

But Logico didn't care about Deacon Verdigris. He cared about revenge. But just then, Brother Brownstone's brother Brownstone gave him
a note from his brother Brother Brownstone that read, "The answer to
your questions is not found in the future, but the past."

> Father Mango | sacramental wine | the forbidden library | to
>   prove they're tough
> **Deacon Verdigris | a bottle of sacred oil | the courtyard | to
>   avenge their father**
> Sister Lapis | a prayer candle | the cliffs | out of madness
> Brother Brownstone | a string of prayer beads | the chapel | for
>   religious reasons

**64. "It was Chancellor Tuscany with a heavy backpack in the book-
store for the greater good!"**

"That librarian was awful and should've been fired years ago," Chancellor Tuscany said. "I did a good deed, but I should have known better than
to kill when our smartest graduate was visiting."

"Flattery will get you nowhere," Logico replied.

"What about bribery?"

It was tempting, but Logico kept his mind on revenge. "Give me ac-
cess to the Old Main archives and we can talk."

> Dean Glaucous | a graduation cord | the arboretum | to prove
>   a point
> Mister Shadow | a crystal skull | Old Main | to stop Logico
> **Chancellor Tuscany | a heavy backpack | the bookstore | for
>   the greater good**

## 65. "It was Dean Glaucous with an old computer in the chancellor's office as a scientific experiment!"

"My thesis was simple! A library could function without a chief librarian, but not without an assistant, too! Now you have ruined my experiment by removing the double-blind."

"But what's the purpose of that experiment?" Logico asked.

"Science needs no purpose but knowledge!" bellowed the dean.

But Logico didn't care about science . . .

**Dean Glaucous | an old computer | the chancellor's office | as a scientific experiment**

Philosopher Bone | a laptop | the teacher's lounge | because they could

Editor Ivory | a marble bust | the roof | for political purposes

Cryptozoologist Cloud | a heavy book | the front steps | to impress a lady

## 66. "It was Président Amaranth with a sacred scepter in the Seine to become king!"

The histories were clear—Président Amaranth ascended to power with this scepter, and no one ever suspected he had used it as a murder weapon, having killed a rival in the waters of the Seine.

This was the way the world was, Logico knew. The bad guys got away with it.

But Logico didn't care about ancient history. He cared about future revenge.

**Président Amaranth | a sacred scepter | the Seine | to become king**

Amiral Marine | a political treatise | the ancient ruins | to stop the revolution

Viscount Eminence | a ballot box | the barricades | for the revolution

## 67. "It was The Duke of Vermillion with Excalibur in Camelot on a dare!"

That's right, based on Deductive Logico's research, the whole war began when the Duke of Vermillion stole Excalibur on a dare. Once he had it, he started swinging it around just as a jester was doing cartwheels, and—well, long story short—it caused decades of bloodshed.

Examining Exhibit C, Logico rearranged the letters, and found that it spelled "I RULE ANON," meaning that someone would rule soon. Was this a reference to Président Amaranth? Or to King Arthur? Or to someone else, who planned to rule somehow with the ancient ruins?

Ultimately, though, Logico didn't care who ruled. He cared about revenge.

Lord Lavender | the grail | the enchanted lake | for religious reasons
Lady Violet | an antique helmet | Avalon | because it was logical
**The Duke of Vermillion | Excalibur | Camelot | on a dare**
Sir Rulean | a bottle of wine | the ancient ruins | to steal a body

## 68. "It was Captain Slate with an air tank in the lunar lander out of space madness!"

Of course, the government had hushed up the whole thing. They couldn't have people thinking that anybody who visited the moon might come down with space madness.

But the question Logico had was—what else were they covering up?

Logico didn't care about space madness, as you know. He cared about—wait a second! Logico quickly rearranged the letters on the ruins one more time and spelled the name of a person who must be deeply connected to the mystery of the ancient ruins. Perhaps even the one behind it all!

Coach Raspberry | a human skull | the lunar rover | as a scientific experiment

## 69. "It was High Alchemist Raven with a saw in the parking lot because a ghost made them!"

None of the magicians believed in the spooky kind of magic, so they all thought that was a bad reason to murder (unlike protecting the secrets of card tricks). But High Alchemist Raven confessed ("You have uncovered my greatest alchemical secret: murder!") and was carted away.

And then, Logico turned to the Amazing Aureolin and showed her the evidence, and he confronted her about her obviously fake name. "You maroon!" Aureolin replied. "It doesn't anagram to Aureolin—there's an extra *N* on the labyrinth rune! If anything, that stands for 'Not Aureolin.' You should learn how to spell!"

Logico didn't care about spelling. But that was pretty embarrassing.

> Mister Shadow | a bottle of cheap liquor | the piano room | to steal an idea
>
> **High Alchemist Raven | a saw | the parking lot | a ghost made them**
>
> The Amazing Aureolin | the ace of spades | the main stage | to protect a magical secret
>
> Superfan Smoky | a trained vicious rabbit | the close-up table | because they broke the code

## 70. "It was Mister Shadow with a shovel in the dumpster to silence a witness!"

Mister Shadow laughed—and although it was modified by some kind of voice-altering technology, the laugh still sounded familiar to Logico. "Who are you?" Logico asked.

"I'm the person who is going to tell you where to find the secret of the ancient ruins: in the desert community of New Aegis."

And then, before Logico could ask any follow-ups, Mister Shadow vanished. Not, like, magically. He just ran away really quickly. Instead of following him, Logico followed his lead.

> Babyface Blue | a scimitar | the metal fence | to steal an idea
> Blackstone, Esq. | a red herring | the distracting graffiti | to teach them a lesson
> **Mister Shadow | a shovel | the dumpster | to silence a witness**
> Silverton the Legend | a vial of poison | a burnt-out car husk | for bloodlust

## 71. "It was Mayor Honey with a dowsing rod in a UFO crash site to protect a secret!"

"What?!" Mayor Honey declared. "What secret could I possibly have?"

Logico replied, "You're obviously the same Mayor Honey from my hometown, and you clearly got the idea of claiming to be a different person from Cosmonaut Bluski."

"What?! I've never heard of either of these people!"

But Logico didn't have time to argue. He gave the other townspeople his notes and his deduction grid and let them take care of it, while he moved on. He didn't care about Mayor Honey, you see . . .

> Uncle Midnight | a prayer candle | a kitschy restaurant | while trippin' out, man
> Bookie-Winner Gainsboro | a selenite wand | a crystal shop | out of jealousy
> **Mayor Honey | a dowsing rod | a UFO crash site | to protect a secret**
> The Crystal Goddess | a bent spoon | the town square | as a scientific experiment

## 72. "It was Blackstone, Esq. with a crystal ball in the outdoor meditation space for money!"

Blackstone, Esq., had a secret plan to sell the crystal shop to a corporate hedge fund that was going to establish it as a global franchise. Blackstone didn't believe in crystals, but he did believe in money. And he ran away with it before Logico stopped him.

But Logico did not care about stopping him.

> Supreme Master Cobalt | a deck of marot cards | the rooftop bar | because the vibes were off
> Numerologist Night | a crystal dagger | the giant safe | to prove their love
> **Blackstone, Esq. | a crystal ball | the outdoor meditation space | for money**
> Dr. Seashell, DDS, | a channeled text | the sage section | to steal a crystal

## 73. "It was Chef Aubergine with a spoon in the kitchen to prove a point!"

The sandwich chef had been arguing with Chef Aubergine about the proper way to prepare a toxic blowfish. He thought he knew better, you see? But Chef Aubergine showed him, by killing him with a spoon. "And I'd do it again!" she shouted. "Nobody questions my expertise!"

Logico did not try to stop her when she ran away. He could feel there was something strange about this town. He was getting close to what he cared about.

> Coach Raspberry | a wall knick-knack | the booths | to liven up a party
> General Coffee | a vial of poison | the front patio | out of jealousy
> **Chef Aubergine | a spoon | the kitchen | to prove a point**
> Earl Grey | hyperallergenic oil | the bathroom | to get a better seat

## 74. "It was Dr. Seashell, DDS, with a selenite wand in the government van as a scientific experiment!"

Dr. Seashell, DDS, explained, "My theories show that aliens can be contacted by these selenite wands, but only if the wands are properly charged. And how are they charged? By murder! Or, at least, that could be the case. Now, we wait. That's why it's an experiment."

For the second part of the experiment, Dr. Seashell, DDS, fled into the mouth of the cave. Logico followed him.

He was going to have his revenge.

> Secretary Celadon | a hypnotic pocket watch | the crater | to steal the UFO
>
> Sociologist Umber | a cauldron | the mouth of the cave | because the vibes were off
>
> Herbalist Onyx | a pseudo-scientific apparatus | the gift shop | by the order of a cult
>
> **Dr. Seashell, DDS | a selenite wand | the government van | as a scientific experiment**

### 75. "It was Mister Shadow with a giant magnet in a dead end to promote the occult!"

The mysterious Mister Shadow was waving his giant magnet around, so Logico knocked it out of his hand and held a flashlight to his face. He was stunned by what he saw.

It was Inspector Irratino.

Heartbreak, betrayal, and confusion swirled together in Logico's usually orderly mind. The esoteric detective stared at Logico, and then he said, "Would you believe it's not what it looks like?"

"It looks like you faked your death and have been building fake ruins and placing them everywhere as some kind of publicity stunt. Is this what you spent the million dollars on?"

"No, no, Logico, please. I found these here! I would never fake the occult!"

Logico grew cold. "Did you fake your death on the island?"

Irratino tensed up, and then he let his head fall. "It was the only way."

Logico slugged him and knocked him out cold.

Revenge didn't taste quite as sweet as he'd hoped.

> **Mister Shadow** | **a giant magnet** | **a dead end** | **to promote the occult**
> Mayor Honey | a giant bone | the new ruins | to promote the town
> Blackstone, Esq. | a globe | a big machine | for money
> Dr. Seashell, DDS | a rock | a table | to help win a war

## 76. "It was Hack Blaxton with an award in The Magic Palace to help sell a script!"

Deductive Logico didn't understand why Hack needed to murder to sell a script: Didn't he have a great career?

Hack laughed. "I had a great career yesterday. Nobody has a great career tomorrow."

(Especially when they're murderers.)

> Executive Producer Steel | a golf club | The Great Park | to prove they're tough
> **Hack Blaxton** | **an award** | **The Magic Palace** | **to help sell a script**
> Superfan Smoky | a Botox needle | The Argyle Talent Agency | to break into the Industry
> Background Marengo | a film strip | Midnight Studios | to get their movie made

## 77. "It was Executive Producer Steel with piano wire in the great hall to close a business deal!"

"Oh, you caught me!" she said, "but do you have any idea how many people are going to lose their jobs because you interfered with this deal? Thousands! So, who's the bad guy now?!"

Logico thought that the lady who murdered someone was worse than the person who figured it out, but perhaps he was biased.

> Midnight III | a rare vase | the courtyard pool | to finish their movie
> Agent Argyle | an antique typewriter | the rooftop balcony | for cold hard cash

## 78. "It was Boss Charcoal with a red herring in the corner booth to prove he's tough!"

As a mob boss, you have to prove you're tough every now and then, or else somebody gets in your face about it. Still, Logico thought maybe he could show that with push-ups or by taking boxing lessons, rather than by murdering a poor chef.

(Although, he had to concede that this particular poor chef had actually been rather rich.)

Boss Charcoal | a red herring | the corner booth | to prove he's
tough
Secretary Celadon | an award | a table by the dumpster | to
create a diversion
Grandmaster Rose | a fancy plate | the valet stand | to inherit
a fortune
Silverton the Legend | chopsticks | the bar | out of frustration

## 79. "It was Director Dusty with an award in the projection booth to steal an idea!"

"We were watching the movie," Dusty explained, "and he told me about his idea for a mystery film, and it was so good, I had to have it! So I killed him, yeah! But now I have his idea, and if they don't let me make the movie, then I won't share it with everyone, and only I will enjoy it!"

So, clearly Director Dusty would not consider himself a populist.

Pearl, AGE | a ritual dagger | the lobby | to get a better seat
Hack Blaxton | poisoned popcorn | the box office | to get their
movie made
Superfan Smoky | a stale candy bar | the theater | to see if they
could

80. "It was Uncle Midnight with a stranglin' scarf in the penthouse
out of jealousy!"

"He had a great room, man," Uncle Midnight replied. "And my nephew's
always saying if I want something I need to go and get it. So I did, man.
Is that so wrong?"

Logico thought that it was, and he was about to say as much when
he got a call from the studio that they were going to debut *Murdle: The
Movie* at that year's MysteryCon.

> Uncle Midnight | a stranglin' scarf | the penthouse | out of
> jealousy
> Boss Charcoal | an antique typewriter | the rooftop gardens |
> to see if they could
> Dr. Crimson | a ghost detector | the tiniest room | as practice
> Executive Producer Steel | a golden bird | the boiler room | to
> join a cult

81. "It was Silverton the Legend with a crowbar in the parking lot to
steal a part!"

"Look, Logico," Silverton said. "You're the role of a lifetime. I could give
you gravitas. I could make you famous. I could make myself an A-list star
again instead of just a legend. And all I had to do was whack a guy with
a crowbar. You understand, right?"

Logico did, but if Silverton was right to play the part, he'd understand
that Logico had to deduce his guilt, too. However, nobody else seemed to
care, so long as Silverton's movies were good. The studio hired him and
started buying up land for shooting locations.

> Silverton the Legend | a crowbar | the parking lot | to steal a part
> President Midnight | a magnifying glass | the food court | to get
> good footage
> Director Dusty | a movie-edition hardback | the exhibit hall | for

## 82. "It was Chancellor Tuscany with a log in the old zoo to escape blackmail!"

"Logico, you monster! You were my prized student and now you've exposed two of my murders? That's outrageous! I wish you were still in college so I could expel you."

Logico wasn't happy, either. Your alma mater's chancellor being a double murderer really devalued your degree.

Mx. Tangerine | a fire extinguisher | the famous caves | to steal a ruby
Pearl, AGE | an antique helmet | the Greek theater | to destroy a rival's career
Lord Lavender | a rock | the Hollywood sign | because they could
**Chancellor Tuscany | a log | the old zoo | to escape blackmail**

## 83. "It was Signor Emerald with a golf cart in Parking Lot A because he was in a hurry!"

"Sure!" Signor Emerald explained. "I ran over somebody with a golf cart! But, in my defense, I was in a hurry! I was late to a meeting! And circumstances like that must be considered!"

Logico didn't think these two were comparable, but he remembered that Irratino said no two things were ever comparable. But he still couldn't forgive him for what he'd done.

Lord Lavender | a giant screenplay | the fountain | to protect a secret
**Signor Emerald | a golf cart | Parking Lot A | because they were in a hurry**
Officer Copper | a baton | the security building | to rob a grave
Pearl, AGE | an award | Parking Lot B | to get a better spot

## 84. "It was Superfan Smoky with a fire extinguisher in the city back-lot to break into the Industry!"

Superfan Smoky seemed more excited to be caught than anything. He kept saying, "This is just like a Midnight mystery!" and asking if there was a chance that he could be in the Murdle movie.

> **Superfan Smoky | a fire extinguisher | the city backlot | to break into the Industry**
> Sister Lapis | an award | the statue of Midnight I | to meet a celebrity
> Officer Copper | a flag | the Water Tower Bar & Grill | to hide an affair
> Coach Raspberry | a golf cart | the studio tour check-in stand | to renegotiate their contract

## 85. "It was A-List Abalone with a sandbag in Soundstage D to get out of a bad movie!"

"Why did my agent sign me up for a movie based on a puzzle book?! I'm not even the killer! And since all my scenes are on green screen, I thought that if I killed the effects supervisor, I could get out of it!"

Logico was shocked that someone would kill to get out of a contract, because the contract he signed clearly said he would not be exempted if he murdered someone.

> Boss Charcoal | a "prop" knife | Soundstage B | to steal a part
> Midnight I | a C-stand | Soundstage C | to win an award
> **A-List Abalone | a sandbag | Soundstage D | to get out of a bad movie**
> Midnight III | an electrical cable | Soundstage A | to take over a studio

## 86. "It was Dr. Crimson with a booby-trapped fedora in the balcony out of jealousy!"

"Dr. Crimson" admitted she was caught, but she wouldn't admit that she was not Dr. Crimson.

Even as the studio guards hauled her away, she shouted, "They tried to make a fool out of me, so I made them pay!"

> Cosmonaut Bluski | a fire extinguisher | the waiting room | to win an award
> General Coffee | a vial of poison | the closet | to see if they could
> The Amazing Aureolin | a red herring | the main office | to get more lines
> **Dr. Crimson | a booby-trapped fedora | the balcony | out of jealousy**

## 87. "It was Background Marengo with a fake rose in the bar to break into the Industry!"

Deductive Logico wondered aloud why she couldn't just work hard and develop herself as an actress in order to break into the Industry, and all of the diners (as well as the entire staff) laughed uproariously for the next half hour.

"I'll never be in the background again!" Background Marengo called from behind some people.

> **Background Marengo | a fake rose | the bar | to break into the Industry**
> Midnight III | a DVD box set | the back porch | to get out of a bad movie
> Director Dusty | a bottle of wine | the bathrooms | to take over Hollywood
> Agent Argyle | a fork | the grill | to win an award

## 88. "It was Dame Obsidian with a dowsing rod in the balcony to test out a plot!"

This, Logico thought, was simply taking method acting too far. But, looking around the stage, he was struck by the thought that just because something is faked doesn't mean it wasn't real.

"You're the real Dame Obsidian, aren't you?" he asked.

"Of course, Logico. I thought you'd figured that out already. Have you figured out the significance of this yet?" She pointed to the logo of the Midnight Prop Shop: the letters *MPS* inside a circle.

Logico stared at them. They reminded him of something, but he couldn't quite place it. While he was thinking, the Dame vanished again.

> The Duke of Vermillion | a crystal dagger | the 50-car garage | to rob a grave
>
> **Dame Obsidian | a dowsing rod | the balcony | to test out a plot**
>
> Brother Brownstone | a poisoned tincture | the servants' quarters | to steal the estate
>
> Astrologer Azure | a hypnotic pocket watch | the grounds | to promote the occult

**89. "It was Lord Lavender with a golf cart in the scoring stage to get out of a bad movie!"**

While Lord Lavender protested his innocence, he lost confidence as Deductive Logico explained the case against him, and he confessed. "You can't jail a lord! It's against the law!" he exclaimed.

> A-List Abalone | a film strip | the water tower | to revenge their father
>
> **Lord Lavender | a golf cart | the scoring stage | to get out of a bad movie**
>
> Director Dusty | a toxic blowfish | the post-production lab | to save face
>
> Pearl, AGE | an ADR microphone | the Water Tower Bar & Grill | for political purposes

**90. "It was President Midnight with a steel knife in the balcony to silence a witness!"**

He pointed out that Deductive Logico had signed an NDA, and could not share this, and also that the person he had killed had signed his literal life rights away, so it wasn't technically a crime, either.

Logico decided that one thing was clear: he needed a better lawyer.

Agent Argyle | an award | the mail room | to take over a studio
Secretary Celadon | leather gloves | the lobby | for religious reasons
**President Midnight | a steel knife | the balcony | to silence a witness**
Hack Blaxton | a thousand-page contract | the best office | to prove a point

91. **"It was Agent Argyle with an antique clock in a partner's office to get a higher percentage!"**
"I wanted another percentage point of a mutual client's revenue. He disagreed. We negotiated, and long story short, he died. Is that a crime?"

Logico realized that nobody in Hollywood was going to be able to help him escape his contract. But he knew somebody who could.

**Agent Argyle | an antique clock | a partner's office | to get a higher percentage**
Hack Blaxton | a golden pen | the break room | to get revenge
Judge Pine | a huge pile of paperwork | the lobby | as part of a real estate scam
Blackstone, Esq. | a bag of cash | the archives | out of frustration

92. **"It was Miss Saffron with a 'prop' knife in the audience on behalf of the Industry!"**
"I didn't know it was real!" she cried. "I'm just so foolish!"

But Deductive Logico found a note in her pocket that read, "Kill person with prop knife then pretend you are too dumb to know."

Deductive Logico wasn't sure if this meant Miss Saffron was smart or not. Nor did he understand why Irratino had sent him here. Nor what one of the actors meant when they invited him to their "magick shoppe."

Assistant Applegreen | a ghost light | the green room | for thematic reasons
Background Marengo | a jug of whiskey | the lighting booth | to create a diversion
Superfan Smoky | a fake rose | the stage | to promote the occult
**Miss Saffron | a "prop" knife | the audience | on behalf of the Industry**

### 93. "It was Bishop Azure with an award in the main room to help sell a script!"

"My daughter always tells me that magick is the key I've been missing," Bishop Azure said, "and that if I gave up my 'silly superstition,' as she calls it, I'd be able to sell my screenplay! But the first time I try to, I'm called a murderer!"

Logico felt like she might have misinterpreted or misapplied that advice. And still, he didn't understand why Irratino had sent him here.

**Bishop Azure | an award | the main room | to help sell a script**
Director Dusty | a cursed dagger | the secret room | to promote the occult
Comrade Champagne | a crystal ball | the back office | to steal a crystal
Uncle Midnight | a sword cane | the front porch | on behalf of the Industry

### 94. "It was Assistant Applegreen with a heavy candle in the altar on behalf of the Industry!"

"Haha! That's right! I'm a traitor! I've sold you out for my boss! I've grown to identify his interests as my own! But now that I've paid my dues, I'm going to be promoted! Enough being Assistant Applegreen! Now, I'm Agent Applegreen!"

Before Logico could stop her, she left to go call her father. He looked around the ritual room, and he saw three giant letters on the floor: *SWH*.

And he asked, "What does *SWH* stand for?"

"You're looking at it upside down. That's *HMS*. And it stands for Hollywood Mystery Society."

And suddenly, Logico understood what Dame Obsidian had hinted at, and he knew Irratino had been framed: he hadn't faked the ancient ruins (see Case 75: Revenge in Cave). He had been innocent all along! Can you see what he saw?

Background Marengo | an award | the secret entrance | to make great art
Superfan Smoky | a bottle of wine | the bathroom | because the vibes were off
**Assistant Applegreen | a heavy candle | the altar | on behalf of the Industry**
Mx. Tangerine | a flag | the floor sigil | to take over Hollywood

95. **"It was Editor Ivory with a printer in the rooftop to stop the revolution!"**

"Our Comrade Champagne had radicalized our assistant editor, and it was only a matter of time before the union swept the premises. Therefore, I had to do what I had to do."

Logico and Irratino made a call to the labor board, and as they left, they talked. "How did you know that I would read the letters on the floor of the magick shoppe upside down, and realize that the letters printed on the ruins in the cave, which I thought were *SdW*, were actually *MPS*—Midnight Prop Shop—upside down? And therefore, someone at Midnight Movies was responsible!"

"What? I didn't realize that at all."

"Then why did you send me there?"

"I thought you'd learn to look inside yourself, and see the truth that your logic could not."

"Why didn't you tell me you were innocent?"

"I knew that you'd never believe anything you didn't deduce yourself. And I felt horrible about faking my death without telling you, but there were cultists everywhere. And it was the only way I thought I could shake them. The marot cards told me not to tell you, and I listened."

"If you had used logic, you would have told me."

"I know. I'm sorry."

Logico thought about that, and he decided he would accept it, in part because he was going to need Inspector Irratino's help to get to the bottom of this mystery, but also because he was beginning GL UZOO RM OLEV. (See Exhibit A.)

> **Editor Ivory | a printer | the rooftop | to stop the revolution**
> Bookie-Winner Gainsboro | a letter opener | the printing press | to seize power
> Hack Blaxton | a laptop | the bullpen | to escape blackmail
> Comrade Champagne | a marble bust | the balcony | out of frustration

## 96. "It was Secretary Celadon with a deck of marot cards in the prop shop to get revenge!"

"I saw the latest anti-war film that Hollywood put out, and I decided I had to do something about it. So I came down here to peacefully and diplomatically discuss the situation, but when a security guard tried to throw me out, I thought, 'This is my red line!' and I got revenge."

Logico was disappointed that this seemed to have absolutely nothing to do with the ruins, and the prop shop was absolutely empty, with no clues whatsoever, but Irratino cheered him up by saying, "Don't worry. All things are connected. Even things that aren't connected at all."

> Midnight III | an award | the locked stage | to get the recognition they deserve
> **Secretary Celadon | a deck of marot cards | the prop shop | to get revenge**
> President Midnight | a C-stand | the bungalows | to promote a movie
> Executive Producer Steel | a magnifying glass | the luxury theater | to take over Hollywood

## 97. "It was A-List Abalone with a giant screenplay in Bungalow 3 to steal a prized book!"

"Nobody here reads," she exclaimed, "so nobody should mind that I've stolen a book!"

"Well," Logico countered, "it isn't the theft that we mind, so much as the murder."

"Oh, please!" she replied. "He was an extra! Nobody will miss him—it's right there in the name!"

And that's when Logico noticed Dame Obsidian lurking in the darkness on the studio grounds. Irratino did, too, and he asked Logico who she was. "The one that got away," Logico said.

"Oh," Irratino replied.

"No, I mean, she was a murderer who escaped."

"Oh! That's great!" And he waved at Dame Obsidian.

She came over and joined them, and when they asked what she was doing, she held up a key. When Logico asked what it was, she smiled. And when she walked off, they followed her.

> Hack Blaxton | an award | Bungalow 4 | to get revenge
> Silverton the Legend | a fountain pen | Bungalow 1 | for money
> **A-List Abalone | a giant screenplay | Bungalow 3 | to steal a prized book**
> Uncle Midnight | an antique typewriter | Bungalow 2 | to win an award

## 98. "It was Pearl, AGE, with a knife in a great machine to protect a secret!"

It wasn't Deductive Logico who shouted that: it was Inspector Irratino! He leapt up off the ground and declared, "I knew that faking my death would reveal the traitor among us!"

But Pearl, AGE, was not happy. She screamed, "I'll have the final cut!" and leapt at Logico with her knife. But Irratino jumped in the middle of it and took a knife to the chest. By this time, Logico knew better than to worry. (Irratino was wearing a knife-proof vest.)

When the murder had been solved, Logico walked over to the mysterious tarp and ripped it off. When he saw what was beneath it, he understood everything.

| | | | |
|---|---|---|---|
| **Pearl, AGE** | **a knife** | **a great machine** | **to protect a secret** |
| Officer Copper | an oil drum | a large tank | to get a promotion |
| Dame Obsidian | a shovel | a pumpjack | to win an award |
| Midnight III | a piece of rebar | a tarp | to take over a studio |

### 99. "It was Midnight I with a shovel in the ancient ruins to found a studio!"

Logico understood, then. The ruins weren't fake. But someone needed Logico to believe that they were to throw him off the trail. So someone at Midnight Movies had faked them to frame Irratino.

But just because something is faked doesn't mean it's not real.

The ancient ruins weren't from the gods or aliens. They weren't some kind of power source. They had no power in themselves at all. They were simply ancient markers. But what they marked was more important—or, rather, more valuable—than anyone had imagined.

Beneath every single one of these ancient ruins was a vast deposit of oil. Midnight I had learned that, and that's why he founded Midnight Movies. For years, the studio had used their money, and their influence, to acquire the land that these ruins were on—to drill for oil.

That's why the ground was unsteady beneath the ruins. And that's why people would sometimes feel woozy or act hypnotized around them, because the deposits of natural gas that often accompany oil were leaking into the air.

There were so many secret societies which possessed some part of the knowledge, and almost all of them were named in reference to this great secret. Some should now be obvious, like the Order of the Sacred Oil. Some were more oblique, like the Ancient Song of Pitch (referencing the resin derived from oil). Or the Order of the Holy Earth (because when you drill, you make holes in the earth). See if you can identify more!

Dame Obsidian had figured it out during her research, so someone signed her name to that letter and summoned everyone to the oil fields (see Case 21: Oil Kill You For This). They said that if she exposed this secret, they would frame her for murder.

"But I called their bluff. I took the fall, busted out, and then laid low until I could find the evidence I needed. This place is that evidence."

"How did you figure it out?" Logico asked.

Dame Obsidian answered, "Examine the labyrinth on the ancient ruins. First, look at which alchemical symbol the labyrinth resembles." (See Exhibit B.) "Then, look at the letters on the labyrinth, starting with the *A* on the right, and write down every fourth letter in a clockwise direction. What does it spell?" (See Exhibit C.)

And now that he knew what the ancient ruins were, Logico was ready to expose the person who had framed Irratino, and who was behind the great conspiracy of secret societies, murder, and intrigue. If only he knew who they were.

| | | | |
|---|---|---|---|
| **Midnight I** | **a shovel** | **the ancient ruins** | **to found a studio** |
| Teenage Midnight | an oil drum | an oil derrick | to gain an inheritance |
| Président Amaranth | a piece of rebar | the offices | to break a union |
| Chairman Chalk | a crowbar | a pumpjack | to help win a war |

## 100. "It was Midnight III with an award on the stage to take over a studio!"

"Fine! I did it! I killed the vice president, but I only did it because he got in my way!"

"Son!" President Midnight shouted. "Stop talking! Wait until Blackstone gets here!"

"Shut up, Dad! I don't care about your lawyers. I'm sick of you altogether! You inherited a company built on oil, and you tried to make it half about movies! Your pathetic attempt to make art got in the way of what we needed to make: *money*!"

And so, he began to reveal his plan, as murderers often do.

"So, I had to take matters into my own hands. I planned most of those murders by the ancient ruins, let Deductive Logico investigate them, framed Irratino, and then optioned the rights to the movie. Using the film as a cover, I bought the land rights around every set of ruins, claiming it was for shooting locations, even as we filmed it all on the lot. People would sell their land for cheap, thinking they were dealing with a poor movie studio and not a rich oil company. I had half of Hollywood on board by carefully doling out those ridiculous awards. Once I had made billions for the studio, the Board would support replacing my half-artistically minded dad with me. And it almost worked! But then, you two started snooping around!"

He whipped around to face Deductive Logico and Inspector Irratino. "I thought if I framed one of you and brought the other out to Hollywood, I could divide and conquer. One of you, I could have easily beaten: Logico believes anything that he can wrap his head around, and Irratino believes anything that he can't. It was easy to trick one of you. But to trick both was impossible! And so I hate you both equally, and I hope you both get murdered soon! Let that be my final statement! And let that be the end of *Murdle*!"

But they wouldn't let the bad guy have the final word. And as they walked back to Logico's apartment, they talked about the case.

"You see, Irratino?" Logico said, "there's a scientific explanation for everything."

"Ah," Irratino replied, "but it simply alters the question: How could the ancients have known where those oil deposits were? They must have used occult and forgotten means to discover them! And, furthermore, how do you explain Case 68, which clearly showed . . . "

They stepped inside Logico's apartment, and continued their argument, but we'll give them their privacy. They've earned some time away from murder, at least until *Murdle: More Killer Puzzles* . . .

**Midnight III | an award | the stage | to take over a studio**

President Midnight | a red herring | the emergency exit | to hold on to power

Dame Obsidian | a bottle of wine | the concessions stand | to get revenge

Inspector Irratino | a selenite wand | the plush seating | to drill for oil

# ACKNOWLEDGMENTS

First, I would like to thank the Detective Club for all of your mystery-solving genius. And I would like to give a special commendation to the members who provided rapid testing of the puzzles as they were being written, including Alexander Maughan, Danielle Esper, Megan Beck, Ossandra White, Teagan Perret, El, Sandhya Sreekumar, Libby "Heartfelt" Stump, Blue Hansen, and Al Harder-Hyde. (And thank you to Kaela, for submitting Babyface Blue, the first fan-created and fan-voted suspect. Many more to come!)

But Murdle would not exist without my friend, Daniel Donohue, Esq., for whom it was originally made. His endless feedback and constant critiques honed it into the puzzle it is. He is a magician and a lawyer, so he can make your legal problems disappear.

Bailey Norton provided astrological analysis of all the characters. She knows the mysteries of the stars because she is one: you can probably see her do comedy in LA this week!

Thank you to Amin Osman, for being my friend and my collaborator. You gave me great notes in the shortest turnaround I have ever experienced. It was invaluable. You are a genius.

This book would not exist without my wonderful agent, Melissa Edwards, who called me up and pitched it to me out of the blue. No amount of flowers will ever be enough, but I'll try!

Thank you to Courtney Littler, my editor at St. Martin's Press, who believed in Murdle so much she made this volume 1 of 3 (and hopefully many more). Thank you for your wisdom, your knowledge, and your constant reassurance. And a special thank-you to Kelly Stone, her assistant at St. Martin's. Assistants do too much work and get too little credit, so thank you, too.

Rob Grom designed the cover of this book, and Omar Chapa designed the interiors, and without both of them, it wouldn't have looked half as good as it does. I'm deeply appreciative of their efforts, as well as Sara Thwaite's copy-editing of the text itself. Eric Meyer and Merilee Croft provided essential timelines and kept everything organized like clockwork. And you might not be reading it now if it weren't for the efforts of Stephen Erickson in marketing and Hector DeJean in publicity.

David Kwong, puzzler extraordinaire, took the time to talk to me about puzzles on the phone, and his experience and insight were invaluable. Thank you again.

A lot of dear friends helped improve Murdle with their feedback, advice, and encouragement, including Julie Pearson, Eric Siegel, Micah Sher, Levin Menekse, KD Dávila, Chai Hecht, Jessie Flitter, Shannon Sanders, Lindsey Carlson, Ray Rehberg, Kristin Walker, Jessica Berón, Eric Barnard, Dexter Walcott, Eva Darocha, Caitlin Parrish, Rob Turbovsky, Doug Patterson, Andi Kohn, Rob Goldman, Megan Sousa, and Juan Rubalcava. Thank you all so much.

To all the members of the Hollywood Mystery Society, past and future, I am a big fan of your work.

My mom, Judge Sherri Karber, is the best mom that anybody has had since Jesus. Thank you always for your endless love and support. And thank you, Judge Norman Wilkinson, for always being there for my mom, and for me, too. And thank you, Jenny Wilkinson, for being there for them when I'm in LA (and for helping them with these puzzles).

And finally, and most importantly, I want to offer my greatest gratitude to Dani Messerschmidt, my partner of ten years, for all of her love and support. I could not have made this book without you, so I hope to repay you a bit every day.

And if I didn't mention you, I owe you a drink.